DATE DUE

Robert Russell Bennett

Robert Russell Bennett, 1938. Photograph courtesy of CBS, Inc.

Robert Russell Bennett

A Bio-Bibliography

George J. Ferencz

Bio-Bibliographies in Music, Number 29
DONALD L. HIXON, Series Adviser

GREENWOOD PRESS
New York • Westport, Connecticut • London

Library of Congress Cataloging-in-Publication Data

Ferencz, George Joseph.
    Robert Russell Bennett : a bio-bibliography / George J. Ferencz.
        p.   cm. — (Bio-bibliographies in music, ISSN 0742-6968 ; no.
29)
    Includes index.
    ISBN 0-313-26472-4 (alk. paper)
    1. Bennett, Robert Russell, 1894-   —Bibliography. 2. Bennett,
Robert Russell, 1894-   —Discography. 3. Bennett, Robert Russell,
1894- . 4. Composers—United States—Biography. I. Title.
II. Series.
    ML134.B4427F4   1990
    016.78'092—dc20   90-45080

British Library Cataloguing in Publication Data is available.

Library of Congress Catalog Card Number: 90-45080
ISBN: 0-313-26472-4
ISSN: 0742-6968

First published in 1990

Greenwood Press, 88 Post Road West, Westport, CT 06881
An imprint of Greenwood Publishing Group, Inc.

Printed in the United States of America

The paper used in this book complies with the
Permanent Paper Standard issued by the National
Information Standards Organization (Z39.48-1984).

10 9 8 7 6 5 4 3 2 1

To Jane
with my sincerest thanks

Contents

Preface

Robert Russell Bennett (1894-1981) led—for some seven decades—an active professional life, both as orchestrator of others' music and as composer of a long list of concert works. He is reputed to have orchestrated all or part of some 300 Broadway and London productions between 1920 and 1976, and turned out hundreds of other published arrangements during his lifetime. The emphasis of this volume, however, is on his original works.

Spending the duration of his professional career almost entirely in New York City, Bennett made his acquaintance with those on both "sides" of the music business: Kern and Gershwin on one hand, and Rachmaninoff, Stokowski, and Reiner on the other. The great majority of his pieces were given New York premieres in the hands of prominent conductors, orchestras, and soloists.

Bennett made it clear to Kern and other songwriters that his personal preferences in music lay with the classics; though he was viewed as something of a "snob" by his Broadway associates for this reason, he saw the popular music industry as merely a money-making venture, with popular songs just another commercial commodity. This did not prevent him, however, from establishing a reputation for tastefulness, creativity, and restraint in his commercial scoring; for several decades he was acknowledged as the leading practitioner in his field.

In this volume, Bennett's commercial career is considered only to the point of including material about his arranging work in the Bibliography—most of it under General References. Individual reviews of musical plays for which he provided orchestrations lie outside the scope of this study. Appendix A, however, is devoted to a necessarily incomplete list of shows he orchestrated; Appendix B covers his film scores and a portion of his work for NBC television.

Robert Russell Bennett: A Bio-Bibliography is, like other volumes in the Greenwood Press "Bio-Bibliographies in Music" series, comprised of four principal sections. The **Biography** is by no means exhaustive, but is longer than most others in this series simply because no extended biographical study of Bennett's life and work has been completed to date.

The **Works and Performances** section, organized by genre, lists individual Bennett compositions (each preceded by a boldfaced mnemonic "W"—**W1, W2,** etc.) followed by each work's date of completion, instrumentation, publication data, dedication, duration, along with the location of the manuscript. For each composition, the premiere and selected other performances are listed chronologically; these performances are indentified by a succession of lowercase letters (**W1a, W1b, W1c,** etc.). For each composition, *"See"* references are given to Bibliography and Discography entries.

The pieces included in the **Works** section are, ostensibly, *compositions* rather than *arrangements*, though the decision to include or exclude a given Bennett creation has not always been clear-cut. His many "symphonic pictures" of Richard Rodgers's and others' Broadway scores are not listed, though his *Commemoration Symphony* (a setting of Stephen Foster's melodies, commissioned by the City of Pittsburgh) is; *The Many Moods of Christmas*, an often-performed chorus-and-orchestra setting of familiar holiday melodies, has been excluded, though his *Carol Cantatas I-IV*, a companion piece of sorts (commissioned by the First Presbyterian Church of Orlando) has been included. His masterful orchestral setting of music from Gershwin's *Porgy and Bess* (commissioned by Fritz Reiner in 1942), like the other "symphonic pictures," is not listed.

The **Discography** includes all known commercial recordings of Bennett compositions, archival recordings (mostly airchecks), and one commercial piano roll that is likely Bennett's work. The commercial recordings are arranged alphabetically by label; the archival recordings are alphabetized by title (of the composition). Each entry is assigned a "D" mnemonic, cross-referenced to any record reviews, etc. that may appear in the Works and Performances section or the Bibliography.

The annotated **Bibliography** is divided into several subsections. The first three of these sub-sections—General References, Biographical References, and Writings by Robert Russell Bennett—are organized alphabetically (by author's last name or title); the last, and largest of these subsections, References to Individual Works, is organized principally by individual compositions (listed alphabetically), with concert reviews and other references to a given work listed in alphabetical order below each sub-heading. This should facilitate use of this section, as nearly all bibliographical references to a given work are grouped together. Individual Bibliography entries are assigned boldfaced "B" mnemonics in sequence (**B1, B2, B3,** etc.).

The **Appendixes**, four in number, include Bennett-orchestrated musical plays, his film and television scores, an alphabetically arranged list of works, and a chronological list of works.

The **Index** lists names of all individuals mentioned in this volume (including performers, conductors, and authors), performing organizations, and each of Bennett's compositions.

Acknowledgments

Many thanks are to be extended to individuals and institutions who have generously assisted in the preparation of this volume:

An Idaho State University Faculty Research Grant provided the means for research travel to New York, Philadelphia, and the Library of Congress.

I am grateful to the library staffs at Idaho State University (Leonard Hitchcock, especially), the Indiana University Music Library, New York Public Library, Brigham Young University Library, Washington State University Library (Lawrence R. Stark), Free Library of Philadelphia (Edwin A. Fleischer Collection), Los Angeles Public Library, Metropolitan Toronto Reference Library, and the Music and Recorded Sound Divisions at the Library of Congress. The Bennett file at the Library of Congress, assembled principally by Gayle Harris, proved to be an unmatched resource.

Individuals who provided welcome assistance with my research inquiries include Chris Alford (Knoxville Symphony), Elsie M. Bennett (American Accordionists' Association), F. Lee Bolling, Martha Cox (Theodore Presser), David Craighead, Max Culpepper (Dartmouth College), Patricia Dale (Yaddo), Ken Darby, Ingrid Dingfelder, Vince Giordano, Edward Jablonski, Tim King (Louisville Orchestra), Irwin Kostal, Maria Lucido (Kansas City Symphony), Paul Orlando (Philadelphia Orchestra), Roy Ringwald, George T. Simon, David E. Solomon (Kappa Kappa Psi and Tau Beta Sigma), Bradley Tucker (Indiana University), and Jane E. Ward (Boston Symphony).

Speaking and corresponding with a great many individuals who knew Bennett personally and professionally has provided a wealth of detail not available in published sources, and I cannot thank them enough for their time, trouble, and unflagging encouragement: Josef Alexander, Vera Appleton, "Red" Barber, Leon Barzin, Robert Biddlecome, Robert Austin Boudreau, Carmen Carrozza, Helen Grady Cole, M.D., the late Ainslee Cox, Assunta Dell'Aquila, Alfonso Dell'Isola, Agnes DeMille, Frederick Fennell

Albert Hague, Cham-ber Huang, Donald Hyatt, Milton Katims, Milton Kaye, Burton Lane, Eleanor Lawrence, June Levant, Eddy Lawrence Manson, Bernard Mayers, Lyle "Spud" Murphy, Gordon Pope, Sid Ramin, Paul Renzi, Jr., William D. Revelli, Trude Rittman, Aaron Rosand, Edith Sagul, Franklyn Stokes, Hugh Thompson, the late Virgil Thomson, J. "Billy" VerPlanck, Myron Welch, Jack Wilson (First Presbyterian Church, Orlando), and Herbert Warren Wind. It is unfortunate that the bio-bibliography format cannot, by definition, allow the inclusion of much of the anecdotal material Bennett's associates have kindly shared with me, and I once again ask for their understanding in this regard.

The generous assistance of the following individuals merits individual mention: G. Thomas Tanselle (John Simon Guggenheim Foundation), for access to the abundance of information stored in the Foundation's files and Annual Reports; Theodore Chapin (Executive Director, Rodgers & Hammerstein), for repeatedly finding time in his busy schedule to respond--most generously--to my many inquiries; Adele Combattente, for the wealth of personal detail that can be obtained only from one who worked alongside Bennett for a great many years; Louis and Annette Kaufman, ardent supporters of my research, who have unselfishly shared letters, clippings, recordings, and a profusion of cherished memories; Jean Bennett and Kean K. McDonald, Bennett's daughter and grandson, who have graciously consented to interviews and allowed me access to Bennett's scores and personal effects.

Friends and family are to be thanked for their patience and encouragement. My colleagues at Idaho State University--music faculty members Brian Cole, Wayne Eastwood, and Norma Mastrogiacomo, especially--have been enthusiastic, understanding, and supportive.

My heartfelt thanks go to Don Hixon, series editor, and Marilyn Brownstein, Mary Blair and Mark Kane at Greenwood Press for their encouragement, patience, and fine editorial judgement.

My wife, Jane, has contributed to the successful completion of this study in countless ways. She has been unfailingly supportive, kindly consenting to manage alone the day-to-day affairs of our household during my several research trips. Her skills as researcher, writer and proofreader, too, have made this a better and more inclusive work than it otherwise might have been.

Robert Russell Bennett

Biography

Robert Russell Bennett was born in Kansas City, Missouri on June 15, 1894. He grew up in a time when recorded music was in its infancy and when, as compared to the present, a much greater percentage of Americans made a full-time living as performers or teachers. His father, George Robert Bennett, played violin in the Kansas City Symphony and first trumpet in the orchestra pit at the city's Grand Opera House; his mother, May Bradford Bennett, was a prominent local pianist and teacher.

It was a musical household, with lessons begun for the children as soon as an interest was shown. Bennett began piano lessons with his mother and, soon after, trumpet and violin with his father. Though he showed a passionate interest in sports—and once played semi-professional baseball in Kansas City—he remarked that his youth was spent "farming, playing baseball, and eating, sleeping and dreaming Johann Sebastian Bach, Wolfgang Amadeus Mozart and Ludwig van Beethoven."[1]

Bennett suffered a bout with polio at age four, and his parents were counseled to remove him from urban Kansas City to speed his recovery. They purchased a farm thirty miles to the south, in Freeman, Missouri. His parents quickly became leading musical figures there, with his father's band in demand for indoor and outdoor events of all types. Bennett soon became the "utility" member of his father's ensemble, able to fill in at a moment's notice on almost any of the brass, woodwind, or percussion instruments. This intimate familiarity with each was to serve him well in his later career as a composer and orchestrator.

Because of his frail health, Bennett did not attend public school until his twelfth year; he was taught at home by his mother. Once he had finished his schooling—this was the extent of his formal education—Bennett moved back to Kansas City. He carried on an active life as a performing musician,

---

[1]Robert Russell Bennett, "From The Notes Of A Music Arranger," *Theatre Arts* 40:11 (November 1956): 88-89.

playing piano and organ for local theaters, restaurants and hotels, as well as violin and organ for two seasons with the Kansas City Symphony. Desiring to broaden his musical horizons, he began to study counterpoint and harmony with Danish composer-conductor Dr. Carl Busch, who led the Symphony. His skills developed quickly under the tutelage of Busch, who later remarked that Bennett "could solve the most difficult counterpoint problems with ease."[2] Before his teens were over two piano compositions, *June Twilight* [W126], *Echoes of Palermo* [W123] and his violin and piano *Romance* [W144] were published by Theodore Presser's *Etude* magazine. Though these early pieces are small-scaled "salon" works exhibiting no evidence of the stylistic path his own compositions would eventually take, they show impressive attention to details of voice-leading and idiomatic use of the instruments.

New York City was then very much the center of the country's music industry, and Bennett had saved enough money by 1916 to move there. He was discouraged by his first contacts with the Musicians' Union (AFM), which Bennett later referred to as a place "where one was supposed to get jobs,"[3] but eventually found his first employment with one of New York's music publishing firms—a position as music copyist at G. Schirmer—and some undistinguished work as a pianist in theaters and restaurants; published accounts differ on the exact chronology of his early years, although the work at Schirmer apparently took place in the last months of 1916. Bennett also worked in New York as a free-lance "musical secretary" of sorts for others who lacked music notation skills. One of his first engagements as orchestrator-for-hire was for the film *Joan, the Woman*, which opened in New York early in 1917; composer William Furst hired him to assist with the orchestration of the accompanying score and also gave Bennett the opportunity to play violin in the pit orchestra.

Bennett's circle of musical acquaintants continued to grow. He was introduced to flutist Georges Barrère and many of his students at the Institute of Musical Art, including William Kincaid, who would go on to a brilliant and influential career as principal flutist for the Philadelphia Orchestra for several decades. Another Barrère student who formed a lifelong friendship with Bennett was Lamar Stringfield, who later won the 1928 Pulitzer prize for composition.

Though Bennett attended as many opera, concert and recital performances as possible during his early years in New York, he evidently did little composing. One of his few original works was the *Rondo Capriccioso* [W106] for four flutes (1916), premiered by Barrère, Kincaid, George Posselt, and Stringfield; it was published by the New York Flute Club in 1922.

---

[2]"Russell Bennett Wins Victor Prize," *Kansas City Star*, 12 June 1930.
[3]Letter, Bennett to "Miss Cuneo" [*Etude* magazine staff member?], 16 October 1930.

His budding musical career was interrupted by the first World War; he volunteered for the infantry—"lied [his] way into the Army," in Bennett's own words—but was sent to Camp Funston, Kansas, where he led an Army band, for which he evidently also did some arranging. Following his 1918 discharge, he immediately returned to New York.

Winifred Edgerton Merrill, the first woman to earn a Ph.D. (her field was mathematical astronomy) from Columbia University, was one of Bennett's employers during his earliest years in New York. He taught music lessons at Oaksmere, the private finishing school for girls she headed,[4] and assisted her in exploring her theory that an individual's signature—written on a musical staff—could suggest a melodic contour that was somehow indicative of that person's character. She and Bennett coauthored a privately printed volume describing these "Musical Autograms," detailing their procedures and providing examples of the analytical process. Mrs. Merrill's relationship with Bennett broadened the year after his 1918 return to New York, when he married her daughter, Louise. A daughter, Jean, was born in 1920.

By 1919 Bennett had found his way to the offices of F. B. Harms—later Harms, Inc.—which then dominated the Broadway and Tin Pan Alley publishing. For the next few years, time for composition was practically unavailable. His days were spent turning out dance-band arrangements of new songs published by Harms, Chappell, and other firms headquartered in New York. He quickly developed a reputation both for speed and dependability and for infusing what individuality was possible into the time-honored arranging formulas then in use. He was often able to turn out two fully scored arrangements daily; at $15.00 each, he was making a comfortable living.

It is hard to determine precisely when Bennett completed his first orchestration for a new Broadway production; his work on Jerome Kern's *Hitchy Koo of 1920* (October 1920) has been documented,[5] but it is probable that there were earlier opportunities. His association with Gershwin had begun by 1919—Bennett's daughter, Jean, recalls him saying that he had lived with George and Ira Gershwin in his "bachelor days" before his 1919 marriage[6]—and it seems likely that Bennett was in some way involved in Gershwin's *La La Lucille* (May 1919) or other early shows. His introduction to this segment of the music business was as an assistant orchestrator, brought in to complete last-minute arranging against pressing deadlines. His first show as "lead" orchestrator was probably Kern's *Daffy Dill* (August 1922); from that point on, he remained Kern's first-choice orchestrator for both his Broadway

[4]Interview with Jean Bennett, New York City, 24 September 1989.
[5]Manuscript scores are held by the Music Division, Library of Congress.
[6]Interview, 24 September 1989.

shows and Hollywood films. Of the songwriters Bennett worked with, Kern was the one with whom he eventually developed the closest personal friendship.

The names of prominent Broadway orchestrators then, as now, remained unknown to most of the theater public; until the 1930s, their names were not always included in a show's credits. Bennett's rise in the field was hastened by the death of Frank Saddler in March of 1921. Saddler had established himself as the most respected and in-demand theater arranger in New York—his work included most of the early Kern and Irving Berlin shows.

Bennett's involvement with theater music broadened. In addition to his scoring—all or in part—from ten to twenty shows a season, he began composing incidental music for stage plays. Arthur Hopkins produced a series of Shakespeare plays in 1921 and 1922, *Macbeth*, *Romeo and Juliet*, and *Hamlet*; these starred Lionel, Ethel, and John Barrymore, respectively. Bennett composed incidental music for the three productions, making resourceful use of the small instrumental forces available to him. The pieces for *Hamlet* were scored for string quartet, three trumpets, timpani and a "musical saw," the last of which was used to portray Hamlet's father's ghost.

Bennett's services were soon in demand by Florenz Ziegfeld (*Follies*, 1923), Kern (*Stepping Stones*, 1923), Vincent Youmans (*Wildflower*, 1923), Gershwin (*Lady be Good*, 1924), and, later, Berlin and Richard Rodgers. As lucrative as this demanding work was, he had hardly completed a serious piece of his own since his 1916 *Rondo Capriccioso*. He realized that he didn't want to end up like so many commercial orchestrators who, though once composers with a promising future, soon found themselves abandoning their own writing, not having completed an original work in years.

Bennett, like many aspiring American composers of his generation, considered study in Europe essential and Nadia Boulanger was quickly becoming the teacher of choice. Aaron Copland was among the first wave of Americans to arrange to study with her in the early 1920s, and once remarked that he may have been among those who recommended that Bennett study with Boulanger. The record is unclear as to when Bennett first made contact with her; it may have been as early as 1922.

In mid-1926, Bennett sailed for Paris with his family. He had no connections on the continent and little or nothing in the way of compositions with which to introduce himself. In one later account, he recalls having brought the score of *Sights and Sounds* along, which he considered to be his only work of any consequence to date, but this is in conflict with the "Paris, 1929" inscription on the manuscript score[7] and his contemporary letters, which state that the piece was written during his Guggenheim fellowship.

---

[7]Ms. in Edwin A. Fleischer Collection, Free Library of Philadelphia.

Lessons with Boulanger began soon after his arrival. She thought him a more polished composer than most of the Americans she had worked with (he was 32), and he was one of the few who had established himself professionally before journeying to Europe. The first works he completed under her tutelage were his first *Symphony* [**W34**], dedicated to Carl Busch, and the *Charleston Rhapsody* [**W6**].

Though Bennett had brought a few thousand dollars in savings along with his family to Paris, he was not able to disassociate himself entirely from commercial arranging. This work took him back to the U. S. (Kern's *Criss Cross* and *Lucky*, among others) and to London, scoring Rodgers's *One Dam Thing After Another* and Albert Sirmay's *Princess Charming* (for which Bennett also composed some music) late in 1926 and in the first months of 1927. The summer of 1927, while living in Gargeville, he completed his *Sonata for Violin and Piano* [**W109**]—performed later that year in Paris—and several other pieces.

At this time, Bennett was at least as much interested in a career as a conductor and critic as in composing. He had not entered an original work in a composition contest for more than a decade, but realized that these competitions were necessary for professional recognition. *Musical America* magazine announced a contest for a new symphonic work by an American, with a $3000 prize to the winner, and Bennett entered his *Symphony*. The jury, consisting of Leopold Stokowski, Frederick Stock, Walter Damrosch, Serge Koussevitzsky, and Alfred Hertz, eventually awarded the prize (in June 1928) to Ernest Bloch for his rhapsody, *America, I Build for You*, with "honorable mentions" going to Bennett and Louis Gruenberg (*Jazz Suite*), Samuel Gardner (*Broadway*), and Wintter Watts (*The Piper*).[8] This gave Bennett encouragement, and he continued to compose while supporting himself and his family on earnings from theater work.

Returning to the U. S. in the fall of 1927, Bennett scored Gershwin's *Funny Face*, Rodgers's *A Connecticut Yankee*, and his biggest success to date, Kern's *Show Boat*. He had taken Frank Saddler's place as New York's premier orchestrator, with a reputation for taste, creativity and the very necessary ability to turn out finished orchestration at an astonishing rate of speed.

Bennett applied for a Guggenheim fellowship in November 1927, just after completing the scoring for the Washington, D.C. tryout of *Show Boat*. He had little in the way of serious works to list, and his prize from the *Musical America* competition was months away. He was, however, awarded a $2500 fellowship to make possible a year devoted solely to composing, which was to begin in May 1928. At this time he planned to continue his studies with Boulanger and then, hopefully, find a position conducting at one of Germany's smaller opera houses.

---

[8]"Ernest Bloch Wins $3000 Music Prize," *New York Times*, 8 June 1928, 29.

Bennett's commercial assignments continued. He was called to London late in 1927 to score some new shows, and spent the next few months there, assisting with Kern's *Blue Eyes*. A London production of *Show Boat* was mounted, necessitating much rescoring by Bennett, typical of most American shows exported across the Atlantic.

Early in May he left for Paris to begin his year as a Guggenheim Fellow. He was apparently able to absent himself almost entirely from the theatrical world for more than a year, resulting in an impressive number of newly composed works, including the *Abraham Lincoln* symphony, an orchestral tone poem, *Paysage*, and two theme-and-variations works for women's chorus and piano [W87 and 88]. A woodwind quintet, *Toy Symphony*, was written for the Elizabeth Sprague Coolidge contest announced by the Library of Congress. Dance rhythms and other characteristics of America's popular music figured in his *Fox Trots* for piano, which later appeared frequently on the concert programs of Jose Iturbi. Two small pieces for flute and piano, *Nocturne* [W102] and *Dance* [W95], were performed by Bennett and Quinto Maganini, another Guggenheim Fellow, in Fontainebleau that summer. Spending the year in Paris and Berlin, he became an established figure in artistic circles, making his acquaintance with such notables as Arthur Honegger, Maurice Ravel, Vladimir Dukelsky, Dmitri Tiomkin, and Samuel Dushkin.

Still uncertain about the future direction of his career, Bennett entered another composition contest. Sponsored by the American company, Victor Records, the "Victor Symphonic Contest" for "Original Works of Music by Composers of American Citizenship" promised a total of $35,000 in prize money for various types of compositions, with an astounding $25,000 to go to the winning symphonic work. He entered two recently completed orchestra pieces, his *Abraham Lincoln* symphony and *Sights and Sounds*. The jury was again a distinguished one: Koussevitzsky, Stokowski, and Stock, along with Rudolph Ganz and Olga Samaroff. Bennett felt that even a mention in this contest would be an omen to persevere as a composer; he was pleased to learn that, as the judges felt no one work to be clearly superior to all of the others, the $25,000 prize would be divided five ways. Bennett received two $5000 awards for his entries; the remainder of the prize money, $5000 apiece, went to Bloch (*Helvetia*), Copland (*Dance Symphony*), and Gruenberg (*Symphony*).[9]

Freed from commercial assignments, Bennett was able to turn out a considerable number of new works, some of them receiving performances in Paris and, perhaps, Berlin. Realizing that it would be financially impossible to live in Europe with his family for another year, even with a renewal of his fellowship, he instead requested and received a three-month extension,

---

[9]"Recorded Music: Casals As Conductor," *New York Times*, 14 September 1930, VIII:7.

beginning in May of 1929. Financial considerations aside, he realized that the longer he absented himself from New York, the more difficult his return to commercial arranging would be. He left Europe at the end of the summer, having made the decision to pursue his composing rather than his once-desired career as a conductor.

By the late 1920s Bennett had fully accepted the reality of commercial arranging as a way to support his family and make possible time to compose. Boulanger had assured him that most every composer had to teach, conduct, or arrange in order to make a living, and that he need feel no shame in this. Part of maintaining his separate musical "identities" was the use of two versions of his name—"Russell Bennett" for his popular writing (he was always "Russell" to his acquaintances) and his full name for his original compositions. Bennett's works began to appear more and more frequently on New York concert programs, although he was never able to stay away from commercial writing for long.

Hollywood, having just switched to sound films, lured songwriters, actors, and musicians away from New York, where the effects of the Depression were being felt on Broadway. Bennett traveled west with Jerome Kern in mid-1930 to score Kern's film *Men of the Sky* (Kern's songs were cut before release). Bennett and Oscar Levant were the pianists for the premiere of his *March for Two Pianos and Orchestra* [W24] with the Los Angeles Philharmonic in July, but he returned to New York shortly thereafter.

Following the awarding of the Victor competition prizes in September, Bennett's visibilty as a composer increased. His prize-winning *Abraham Lincoln* was premiered by Stokowski and the Philadelphia Orchestra, he was nominated for membership in ASCAP,[10] and he became involved with the League of Composers. Still, he remained active in the theater, scoring such notable productions as Gershwin's *Girl Crazy* and *Of Thee I Sing*, Kern's *The Cat and the Fiddle*, and Arthur Schwartz's *The Band Wagon*. Because of his growing success as a composer, his name lent considerable prestige to the shows he scored.

Bennett's reputation as both serious composer and commercial orchestrator continued to grow, and it was at about this time that Howard Hanson took an interest in his works and began to program them frequently on his "All-American" Music Festival concerts at Rochester's Eastman School. New works, such as his *Concerto Grosso for Dance Band and Orchestra* [W14], and yet-unheard pieces composed in Europe—including *Endimion* [W41] and *Paysage* [W29]—received first hearings at these concerts. Hanson also included the *Concerto Grosso* in an "All-American" program in Berlin in January 1933, where he conducted the Berlin Philharmonic.

---

[10]Kern nominated Bennett for membership in November, 1931; the nomination was seconded by Otto Harbach.

Bennett was among the many composers hoping to establish an identifiable national "school" of distinctly American works during the first decades of the century. Though several of his pieces composed overseas showed a Parisian influence, many of the others were attempts to forge a new style. Bennett never thought of himself as a composer of "symphonic jazz"—an often-used catch-phrase in the 1920s—but borrowed rhythmic and harmonic materials, as well as instrumental colors, from the popular idiom of the day. He was, at the same time, enriching the rhythmic and harmonic language of the musical theater with his increasingly sophisticated show orchestrations.

A good deal of Bennett's composition remained totally uninfluenced by the popular sphere, very much in sympathy with what other "modern" composers were doing. His *Three Chaucer Poems* were presented at the first Yaddo Festival (Saratoga Springs, NY) in 1932, and Bennett was a member of the Central Music Committee formed to plan the 1933 festival. Writers in *Modern Music* began to make increasing mention of his serious work and to express hope for his continued development.

Bennett returned to Europe in May of 1932, living in Paris and Vienna while completing his opera *Maria Malibran*. The libretto was by New York music critic Robert A. Simon. Distractions appeared in the form of orchestrations to be done for Fritz Kreisler's operetta, *Sissy*, and more Broadway assignments. He also agreed to write concertos for Kreisler and Spanish pianist José Iturbi[11] (it is not known that either was ever completed), and by year's end was hardly any closer to finishing *Malibran*.

His "dual career" continued to flourish; while scoring Kern's *Roberta*, Gershwin's *Pardon My English*, Porter's *Anything Goes*, and dozens of other shows, he found time to complete a variety of orchestral and chamber works. In 1934 he also took on his first position as music director for a weekly radio show, Rudy Vallee's "Royal Gelatin Hour."

Maria Malibran was finally finished in 1934; a suite of *Orchestral Fragments* from the opera was prepared for Alfred Wallenstein's Los Angeles Philharmonic, and a production was promised at the Juilliard School, which had been giving first performances of several American operas. The performances in April 1935 generated a great amount of coverage in the New York press, and the reviews were generally favorable. The student cast included Risë Stevens, Josephine Antoine, and others who were soon to join the roster of the Metropolitan Opera.

Most of the remainder of the decade was to be spent in Hollywood; Broadway was to do almost entirely without Bennett for nearly five years. For his 1935 film, *I Dream Too Much*, Kern insisted that Bennett be brought into do the orchestrations rather than music director Max Steiner (who had

---

[11]"Orchestrator on His Own," *Time*, 12 December 1932, 33.

previously been an orchestrator in New York).[12] Bennett worked on approximately 30 films in varying capacities as composer, music director/conductor, and orchestrator. He was under contract to RKO for much of that period, and scored most of the big-budget musical films of those years with scores by Kern and Gershwin, *Swing Time*, *Damsel in Distress*, and *Shall We Dance* among them. A lasting friendship was formed with virtuoso violinist Louis Kaufman when both were recording the score for Paramount's 1936 film version of Kern's *Show Boat*—Bennett as orchestrator and conductor, Kaufman as concertmaster for the recording sessions.[13] Bennett later wrote *Hexapoda* [W101] and *Allemande* [W91] for Kaufman.

Bennett's work in Hollywood included a fair number of dramatic films as well; he helped orchestrate Alfred Newman's music for *Gunga Din* and *The Hunchback of Notre Dame* and Franz Waxman's *Rebecca* score. Little time was available for composition on his own, but he felt so honored by the League of Composers commission awarded him in 1936—resulting in his orchestral work, *Hollywood*—that he turned down a considerable number of lucrative commercial assignments in order to fulfill his commission. The Columbia Broadcasting System similarly commissioned his *Eight Etudes for Orchestra* in 1938.

Though he was paid well, Bennett was hardly happy with his work in Hollywood. His social activities ranged from tennis with Gershwin to visits with Rachmaninoff, but the decision was made to sell their Hollywood home and return east. He had been asked to compose music for the 1939-1940 New York World's Fair, but perhaps the most attractive offer of employment was from WOR radio, broadcasting on the Mutual network. Bennett was given almost free rein in serving as musical director for his own half-hour weekly program, "Russell Bennett's Notebook."

The Music Committee for the World's Fair, headed by Olin Downes, commissioned Bennett to write a series of original works to be performed at the Lagoon of Nations beginning on opening day—April 30, 1939. These *Tone Poems for Band* [W74], each fifteen minutes in length, were written to be synchronized with elaborately lit fountain displays designed by Jean Labatut; Bennett's recent experience in writing film scores to predetermined timings must have served him well. His first band works, they were performed repeatedly (one fifteen-minute show nightly) by the World's Fair Band, an excellent free-lance group of experienced symphony wind players.

Bennett's friendship with violinist Louis Kaufman seems, in retrospect, somehow inevitable. The two were active in both commercial and more serious-minded music, and shared similar points of view on the merits

---

[12]Oscar Levant, *A Smattering of Ignorance* (New York: Garden City Publishing Co., Inc., 1940), 100.
[13]Letter from Louis and Annette Kaufman to author, 26 September 1988.

of both. Kaufman's dual career encompassed both his Hollywood concertmaster duties and touring, nationally and internationally, as a recital and concerto soloist. In addition to his early efforts to locate and return to the repertory many Baroque masterpieces, Kaufman has always been a champion of contemporary music. He premiered many new concertos in the U. S. and Europe, and his recitals almost always included recently composed works.

Bennett's *Hexapoda* for violin and piano (1940), one of his best-known works, owes its creation to Kaufman's encouragement. As Bennett wrote:

> Louis and Annette Kaufman were having dinner with my wife and me on a Friday evening in West Los Angeles when he . . . spent part of the evening trying to persuade me that the low-down music of the day was worth saving by a serious-minded composer. . . . This was on a Friday night, and on Sunday morning I rang him up and said, "The pieces are done but I have to copy the violin parts for you tonight. They'll be ready tomorrow." He said, "What pieces?" and I said, "So what was all that campaign Friday night if you don't even remember it?" Anyway, he and I played the first performance of *Hexapoda* at Town Hall in New York not long thereafter.[14]

Hexapoda, a virtuoso challenge for any violinist and an audience favorite, was soon taken up by Jascha Heifetz, Carroll Glenn, and other prominent violinists of the 1940s, and the 1941 recording by Kaufman and Bennett [D4] was the first commercial record of any Bennett composition.

Bennett had some unfinished business to attend to in Los Angeles, but was able to return to New York by late summer to begin preparations for his Mutual radio program. To be called "Russell Bennett's Notebook," it was a surprisingly eclectic half hour of "musical Americana" programmed by Bennett. The show kept him almost entirely away from Broadway arranging; Bennett chose the music (composing much of it himself), wrote and narrated the script, and rehearsed and conducted the orchestra. Programming included well-known modern works such as Schoenberg's *Verklärte Nacht* and *Pierrot Lunaire* as well as performances—often premieres—of works by Levant and colleagues Hans Spialek, Dana Suesse, Leigh Harline, Tibor Serly, and Alex North (later to establish himself as a major film composer). Bennett turned out one or more new works for almost every show, some designed for radio presentation and some equally suitable as concert works. It had been his hope to compose a violin concerto for Louis Kaufman, so Bennett completed his

[14]Letter from Bennett to violinist David Sackson, reprinted in Carnegie Recital Hall program [Sackson, violin and Dwight Pelzer, piano], 13 February 1977.

Concerto in 1941, premiering it on the "Notebook" program with concertmaster Joseph Coleman as soloist. Later performances, including the concert premiere, were all by Kaufman.

Bennett's works continued to be at odds with the newer trends in composition; they were tonal and, usually, programmatic—the kind of music he clearly preferred to write—at a time when atonality and abstraction were in vogue. The clever, subtle wittiness that often featured in his scores served to "typecast" him in the sense that critics were sometimes confused by his more serious and abstract works being something other than what they'd expected.

The years 1941 and 1942 were, creatively, some of Bennett's happiest and most productive. He was not shy about expressing his disdain for the popular music industry, and clearly preferred an evening of symphonic music or opera to an opening night on Broadway. He surely perceived the irony in making his living, in large part, from music which he felt to be of little importance. John McGlinn's commentary seems particularly apt:

> He viewed most of the show music he scored with some con-
> tempt, and, paradoxically, this may account for the brilliance of
> his work. The inventiveness of color and counterpoint . . . stems,
> perhaps, from his desire to invest the music with his own stamp,
> to prove himself better than the material he was working with.[15]

Bennett's published firsthand accounts of his work as a theater orchestrator provide a fairly candid assessment of the actual contributions of a show's songwriter(s) and orchestrator(s) to the music as heard by the public. Some songwriters provided him with a fairly detailed piano score, closely resembling that which would eventually appear in the published piano-vocal score. From others would come a "lead sheet" with only the barest harmonic framework. The biggest challenge to Bennett was having to take down and score a songwriter's piano demonstration—sometimes complete, sometimes a "one-finger" melody; this would happen either when the composer lacked notational skills (not an infrequent occurrence) or when, during an out-of-town tryout, time considerations made it necessary to save even a few minutes whenever possible. Published piano-vocal scores, however, are generally a reduction of the completed orchestration and may often differ in many respects from the score as first presented to the orchestrator.

Most of the Broadway public is unaware of the extent of the creative work contributed by Bennett and his colleagues to a show's score. Incidental music was most often composed by the orchestrator, sometimes based on one of the songwriter's melodies. Overtures and entr'actes, too, were usually

---

[15]John McGlinn, "The Original 'Anything Goes'—A Classic Restored," [in liner notes for EMI compact disc CDC 7-49848-2, 1989].

crafted by the orchestrator, beginning only with the songs from the production. The speed with which Bennett typically scored an instrumental overture—often the day before opening night—is quite incredible; Herbert Warren Wind's 1951 *New Yorker* profile of Bennett opens with a description of his preparation of the overture for *The King and I*, beginning the Sunday afternoon just before its Monday night opening. Copying of the orchestra parts and a rehearsal followed the next day, all of this hurried preparation making possible the overture's inclusion in the first performance.[16]

Bennett's working methods remain a continued source of amazement to those who understand the manifold skills necessary to function as a professional orchestrator. He worked almost exclusively in ink, and his scores almost never show "cross-outs" or revisions. He always scored without reference to a piano, even when going from the songwriter's unaccompanied melody to an elaborately harmonized arrangement. The overtures, etc., too were written straight into full score; the only "sketches" he completed first were in his head. One more indication of his remarkable gifts is his ability to score "straight down the page"—flute, oboe, clarinets, bassoon, etc., rather than filling in melody and bass lines first and working out inner voicings and harmonies later. Bennett approached his own composing the same way, with a Mozartean ability to conceive an entire piece mentally, waiting only for an opportunity to transfer it to score paper.

Bennett kept himself busy during the war years with other radio programs, including the Ford Motor Company's "Stars of the Future" show (1944-1945), for which he was again music director. This program featured more popular music than did his "Notebook" show—Frances Greer (later Jo Stafford) and Lawrence Brooks were among the vocal soloists, backed by chorus and orchestra. Still, Bennett turned out some light original works for the program, including the *Cowboy Overture* and *Along the Navajo Trail*, as well as several settings of American folk tunes.

Bennett had scored Rodgers and Hammerstein's *Oklahoma!* in 1943, and would go on to orchestrate almost all of their shows of the 1940s and 1950s, but his commitments to the Ford Show kept him from working on *Carousel* (1945). Hammerstein pleaded with Bennett to do the orchestrations, but Bennett was able only to score early versions of the "Prologue" and "Mister Snow"; credited orchestrator Don Walker evidently reworked these and completed the remainder of the orchestrations.

Bennett's period of highest visibility as an orchestral composer lasted from the mid-1930s through most of the following decade. New works, several of them commissions, received much attention in the musical press and repeated performances by major orchestras—his *Hollywood* (**W21**, 1936),

---

[16]Herbert Warren Wind, "Another Opening, Another Show," *The New Yorker*, 17 November 1951, 46-71.

Eight Etudes for Orchestra (**W18**, 1938), and a symphony, *The Four Freedoms*
(**W19**, 1943), especially.

American composers in general profited from the country's renewed
interest in native works during World War II, and Bennett was no exception.
The 1943-1944 concert season was the one in which he received his highest-
ever number of performances by the country's major orchestras; he placed
seventh on *Musical America*'s ranking of total performances of works by
American composers during that season. The majority of these performances
were of Bennett's unabashedly patriotic *Four Freedoms*.

The *Four Freedoms* symphony was evidently commissioned by *The
Saturday Evening Post*, though this is not mentioned in any of the magazine's
publicity surrounding its premiere. The nation had taken to its heart a set of
four "freedoms" outlined in a Roosevelt speech earlier in the war—"freedom
of speech, freedom of worship, freedom from want, and freedom from fear"—
and the *Post* commissioned a quartet of paintings from Norman Rockwell
representative of these four "freedoms." His illustrations were published in
the magazine early in 1943, exhibited around the country, and reproduced in
quantity for sale to the public. The *Post* commissioned Bennett to translate
each painting's message into music, and he completed the 18-minute work
during three weeks in July 1943. The composition was premiered for the
national radio audience by Frank Black and the NBC Symphony that
September, and performances by other major orchestras soon followed,
including more than ten by the Philadelphia Orchestra, Eugene Ormandy
conducting.

A great many works on patriotic themes were written and highly
publicized during the war, but Bennett's and almost all of the others have
fallen out of the orchestral repertory. Copland seems to have fared the best,
with his *Lincoln Portrait* and *Fanfare for the Common Man* proving to be
especially durable.

Because of rising costs, there were fewer new productions on Broadway
in the postwar years, a trend continuing over several decades as the financial
stakes were continually raised. Bennett was associated with most of the big
hits of the 1940s and 1950s, including Porter's *Kiss Me Kate* and Rodgers's
South Pacific, *The King and I*, and *Flower Drum Song*.

Bennett's career to this point had embraced film, the concert and
theater stage, and radio. As busy as he was with his commercial assigments,
he had managed to complete more than a hundred original compositions,
including six symphonies. As television became a commonplace in American
homes—and while New York still dominated television production—Bennett
found himself increasingly in demand by the networks.

One of Bennett's biggest undertakings was the "Victory at Sea"
television series of 1952-1953. In cooperation with the U. S. Navy, NBC

television produced twenty-six half-hour episodes, each dealing with a different aspect of the Navy's role around the world during World War II. Richard Rodgers's name was then a "household word," with his every activity getting national press coverage; interestingly, for several seasons he was the native composer whose music was most performed by American orchestras (usually in orchestrations by Bennett). He was contracted to compose music for "Victory at Sea" episodes; what he provided were musical themes, which credited arranger Bennett fleshed out, timed, and orchestrated. Bennett also conducted the recording sessions, beginning in the spring of 1952, using Toscanini's NBC Orchestra—an experience he found to be most enjoyable. Following the airing of the twenty-six episodes during 1952-1953, both a long-playing record album of music from the series and a theatrical version were prepared, necessitating much rescoring and rerecording by Bennett. His own composing and orchestrations for Broadway ground almost to a halt simply because of the staggering amount of music to be scored; about twenty-six minutes of all-new music was prepared for each episode, totalling over eleven hours of orchestral score. Bennett would continue to be associated with NBC and their "Project 20" series of television productions, but this was by far his most ambitious assignment.

Because Richard Rodgers was given the "Music by . . . " credit for the "Victory at Sea" series, it was the assumption of all but industry insiders that Rodgers had, in fact, written upwards of eleven hours of music for Bennett to orchestrate. Several of his associates on the project have remarked confidentially, however, that Rodgers provided only a small fraction of the twenty-six minutes of music needed for each episode, and that an overwhelming percentage of the music was of Bennett's invention.

As Bennett's impact as an orchestral composer waned, his notoriety in the band world began to grow. Serious composers were taking a greater interest in the wind band in the postwar years, weaning these ensembles from a steady diet of marches, orchestral transcriptions, and light selections. Listening to an (indoor) concert by the Goldman Band celebrating the 70th birthday of its founder, Edwin Franko Goldman, Bennett was inspired to return to creating original works for the medium. He began sketching out a short score for the *Suite of Old American Dances* [W70] and, over the next year-and-a-half, wrote out individual players' parts from this sketch as time permitted;[17] his scoring of *Kiss Me Kate, South Pacific,* and several other shows—in addition to some in-progress works of his own—kept him from completing the band piece earlier. It was given its premiere by the Goldman Band in June, 1949, beginning an association with them that was to last more than three decades.

---

[17]Frederick Fennell, "Basic Band Repertory: Suite of Old American Dances," *The Instrumentalist* 34:2 (1979), 28.

Bennett always took time to concern himself with issues of interest to himself and other composers and arrangers. He helped form the American Society of Music Arrangers (ASMA) while in Hollywood, and was later active in the National Association for American Composers and Conductors (NAACC), serving as president for several years. He was generous in donating both his time and money to both organizations, ever hoping to raise the professional standing of their members.

As busy as he continued to be with his commercial assignments, Bennett never set aside his composing for long. Frequently pieces were written for one of the fine musicians in New York with whom he had become acquainted or had simply heard in recital; often they were composed "for the asking" or simply presented as gifts; Bennett did not expect his compositions to pay for themselves and wrote most of the noncommisioned works purely for the pleasure of doing so. The *Tema Sporca con Variazoni* was presented to duo-pianists Appleton and Field in 1946,[18] and the *Song Sonata* (violin and piano) was dedicated to Benno and Sylvia Rabinof the following year. Bennett wrote *Five Improvisations on Exotic Scales* (1947) for the Sagul Trio at Edith Sagul's behest;[19] his *Allemande* (1948) for Louis Kaufman, and the *Five Tune Cartoons* (1949) for violinist Marc Brown were other typical gestures. On many an occasion Bennett would present as his gift the original manuscript, not bothering to retain a copy for himself.

By the 1950s, Bennett was increasingly referred to as the "Dean of American Arrangers"—he had already contributed to two or three hundred Broadway shows and finished hundreds of published arrangements. Bennett's typically modest response to this acclaim was, "the way you become the 'dean' of anything is simply to live longer than everyone else in your field." His name was displayed prominently in theater programs and on original-cast albums for his Broadway successes of the period, though he remained philosophical about the less-successful shows—he put just as much creative work into them, and was being paid the same union wage—about $5000 a show in the early 1950s, depending on its length. Asked repeatedly, after the stunning success of *The King and I* in 1951, "what would Richard Rodgers have done without you?", Bennett's reply was again characteristically self-effacing: "He would have engaged another arranger, and the show would probably have run just as long." His writings repeatedly restate his viewpoint that orchestration is merely the adding of color to what either is or is not good music, that a good composition cannot be ruined by inept orchestration and that, similarly, clever orchestration cannot redeem a poorly-composed piece of music. This outlook is very much in keeping with his modesty about his contributions in the field of orchestration.

---

[18]Letter from Vera Appleton to author, December 1989.
[19]Letter from Edith Sagul to author, September 1989.

Bennett's musical acquaintances often expressed to him their conviction that, though he was well paid for his work, he never received the credit due him for his contribution to the success of others' scores. Bennett was aware that his per-page wage for scoring a song was a good one, and evidently preferred the security of a predictable income as measured against the risks involved in writing and producing one's own show. He was perpetually cheerful and uncomplaining on the job, and apparently kept to himself any disgruntlement he might have felt.

Though his large works were becoming fewer in number, and receiving less press attention to their first performances, commissions were continually forthcoming. The Louisville Orchestra, continuing its long series of commissions, hired Bennett to write what would become his *Concert Variations on a Crooner's Theme* of 1949, presented with violinist Aaron Rosand as soloist. The same year he contributed a segment to the collaborative work, *Tribute to James Whitcomb Riley*, written for Fabien Sevitzky's Indianapolis Symphony. Kansas City, celebrating its centennial in 1950, commissioned native son Bennett to write his "seven songs for orchestra," *Kansas City Album*. His 1952 *Madmoiselle (Ballet for Band)*, a commission from the League of Composers, was written for and premiered by the Goldman Band.

Hollywood called once again in the 1950s—Bennett was asked by Rodgers and Hammerstein to score the 1955 film version of *Oklahoma!*, for which he won an Academy Award. When Bennett was hired by Rodgers and Hammerstein to work on their final collaboration, *The Sound of Music*, Bennett announced to several acquaintances that it was to be his farewell to Broadway. Though Bennett had always been disdainful of popular music—he rarely attended opening night performances and called theater music "small voices singing familiar phrases full of familiar emotions"—he spoke of being quite excited about this particular show. It seemed destined to be a surefire success, and Bennett was pleased with the songs and the casting. Although it turned out to be every bit the "hit" he had predicted, Bennett's financial needs, among other things, kept him arranging occasionally afterward for Broadway; *Camelot* and *On A Clear Day You Can See Forever* were two later successes.

By the late 1950s Bennett's creative energies were divided among choice theater assignments (*Bells are Ringing, My Fair Lady*), his "Project 20" television scoring for NBC, and his own composing. The work for NBC he found enjoyable because it afforded him the pleasure of conducting some of New York's best musicians in his own scores. Bennett was a first-rate conductor who took on occasional guest-conducting assignments outside of New York, but these television films and some conducting of recording sessions for RCA long-playing record releases constituted, along with an occasional opportunity to conduct the Goldman Band in one of his works, the extent of conducting opportunities available to him.

Bennett's output of works for band began to increase rapidly. His *Symphonic Songs for Band* [W71], something of a companion piece to the *Suite of Old American Dances*, was the result of a commission from music fraternal organizations Kappa Kappa Psi and Tau Beta Sigma, and he soon was commissioned to write a piece for the newly formed American Wind Symphony (AWS).

AWS conductor and founder Robert Austin Boudreau had been befriended by Bennett while performing in the Goldman Band trumpet section in the late 1940s and early 1950s. Following his formation of the AWS in 1957, Boudreau repeatedly commissioned Bennett to create original works for his ensemble. This series of special works for winds and percussion began with Bennett's *Concerto Grosso for Wind Quintet and Wind Orchestra* in 1958, and continued until Bennett's last year. The AWS used no saxophones or euphoniums, but had available to the composer a plethora of auxiliary woodwinds—several alto flutes, English horns, contrabassoons, etc. were available for the composer's asking. Bennett had always enjoyed the scoring challenge presented by an unusual instrumental combination, and surely enjoyed his work for the AWS. Because of their special instrumentation, however, these "wind orchestra" works are not nearly as well known as Bennett's pieces scored for the more conventionally used American band instrumentation, and thus more widely played.

Bennett, at age 66, had passed what was elsewhere in 1960 considered to be retirement age, but he continued to turn out original works, a growing number of them for wind band. His "Project 20" scores for NBC television continued, lasting into the 1970s. To musicians and the musical public his compositions were seen as expertly crafted and eminently playable, if not innovative. Still, he continued to compose strictly for the pleasure of doing so. His (7th) *Symphony* of 1962, premiered by Fritz Reiner and the Chicago Symphony Orchestra the following year, was seen as a throwback, in no way indebted to the musical avant-garde. It is, however, a logical extension of his highly individual style, and is clearly not a piece he—or another composer— might have written 20 or 40 years earlier. Bennett continued to write based on his inner convictions, using the musical materials he thought could best express what he had to say.

As part of the America's bicentennial celebration, the National Symphony commissioned works from several American composers. Bennett's contribution, *The Fun and Faith of William Billings* [W86], was a chorus-and-orchestra work based on original material by the colonial composer. It was performed by the National Symphony, Antal Dorati conducting, in April 1975 and recorded by them for London Records.

Though a new generation of orchestrators had established their careers on Broadway in the 1950s and 1960s, Bennett's special expertise led to occasional calls to assist in the scoring of new musicals. His last was *Rodgers and Hart* (1975), which seems singularly appropriate—Bennett, after all, had scored their shows a half-century before.

Even late in life, Bennett continued to turn out new works. After hearing a Town Hall recital by Chinese harmonica virtuoso Cham-ber Huang, Bennett wrote his *Concerto for Harmonica and Orchestra* **[W9]** for Huang, who premiered the work with the Hong Kong Philharmonic. Bennett also returned to the operatic field—for which he had not written in decades—and composed a work set in present-day urban America, *Crystal* **[W39]**. Completed in 1972, it remains unperformed, though Bennett did correspond with representatives of the Metropolitan Opera, New York City Opera, and Houston Grand Opera about the possibility of a performance.

Additional evidence that Bennett, to the end of his life, enjoyed writing music purely for the sake of doing so can be seen in his two commissions from the First Presbyterian Church of Orlando, Florida. Having performed his *Many Moods of Christmas* arrangment on several occasions, the church commissioned Bennett to craft a sequel of sorts, the *Carol Cantatas*; a year later, he similarly completed *The Easter Story* at the church's behest. Though a composer of his stature could surely have commanded an impressive fee for the job, Bennett was willing to undertake the assignment for a very reasonable sum—essentially, minimum "union scale."

Such acts of kindness and generosity are in every way typical of Bennett's character. His associates, in interviews with and letters to the author, repeatedly refer to him as "the nicest man in the music business"; his own writings reveal him to be a person of gentle wit and character. Had he been as hard-headed a businessman as his oft-times employer, Richard Rodgers, is reputed to have been, he might have been able to amass more wealth within his lifetime. That, however, does not seem to have been an overwhelming concern to him. He lived comfortably and enjoyed a life that was always filled with what he liked best—writing music.

Bennett's contribution to American music is not easy to quantify and evaluate. Merely assembling a complete list of his output as composer and orchestrator has proven to be a formidable task; his publishers' extant records are very incomplete, Broadway shows did not—for decades—always publicize the names of orchestrators involved, and Bennett himself was often surprisingly casual about his compositional output. Though he felt strongly that an arranger ought to keep going in the field of original composition, he once wrote that "far too much music is written" and was not at all a self-promoter. He composed rarely with publication in mind—sometimes simply giving pieces away to friends—and maintained no elaborate catalog of his works. Several of his manuscripts are being held by his survivors, and a few are in libraries or private hands, but a good many remain unaccounted for. Bennett died on August 19, 1981, and we have only press clippings, programs, or the memories of his acquaintances to establish the existence of some of his compositions.

As a composer, Bennett worked very much against the tide of the times. He wrote tonal music at a time when atonality was the rage among his fellow composers; he wrote programmatic pieces when that, too, was out of fashion. His works are, however, unfailingly original, well-crafted, idiomatically and freshly scored—a pleasure for conductors, performers, and audiences. He certainly deserves respect for his contribution to American theater music—the "Broadway sound" of the middle third of the century is largely his sound—but it would be unfortunate for his achievements and contributions as a composer to go undocumented.

Works and Performances

Individual works are indexed alphabetically under the following headings:

WORKS FOR ORCHESTRA [W1 - 37]
STAGE WORKS [W38 - 45]
INCIDENTAL MUSIC [W46 - 50]
WORKS FOR BAND (and WIND ORCHESTRA) [W51 - 78]
CHORAL WORKS [W79 - 90]
CHAMBER MUSIC [W91 - 120]
KEYBOARD WORKS [W121 - 139]
SONGS [W140 - 148]
WORKS FOR RADIO [W149 - 173]
OTHER COMPOSITIONS [W174 - 175]

Details concerning each composition (if known) are given in this order:

TITLE (composer's subtitle, if any) [genre]; [other titles used in concert programs or reviews]; [date of completion of composition]; [publisher and date of publication]; [dedication, if any]; complete instrumentation for ensemble works; duration in minutes; location of manuscript(s).

WORKS FOR ORCHESTRA [W1 - 37]

Note: other orchestral compositions are listed under WORKS FOR RADIO. Although some of the pieces in this section were first performed as part of a broadcast—usually one of Bennett's radio programs—they were conceived as concert works; almost all were given public performances.

W1   *ABRAHAM LINCOLN: A LIKENESS IN SYMPHONY FORM*
["ABRAHAM LINCOLN" SYMPHONY] (1929) [Harms, Inc. 1931; piano
reduction by Bennett also pub. by Harms, 1931]; 4 (3rd alt. picc.; 4th alt.
alto fl.), 3 (3rd alt. E.h.), 4 (4th alt. b. cl.), 3+cbn. - 6, 4 (3rd alt. E flat tpt.),
3, 1 - timp., perc. (4), cel., 2 hps. - stgs.; 30 min.; Ms. scores in Free
Library of Philadelphia (Edwin A. Fleisher Collection) and
Washington State University (Pullman, WA); *See:* B29, B49, B78,
B164 - 180.
1.   His simplicity and his sadness
2.   His affection and his faith
3.   His humor and his weakness
4.   His greatness and his sacrifice

Premiere

W1a 24 October 1931: Philadelphia; Philadelphia Orchestra;
Leopold Stokowski, conductor; Academy of Music; *See:* B23 - 25,
B166, B170 - 171.

Other selected performances

W1b 7 November 1931: New York; Orchestras from the Juilliard
Graduate School and the Institute of Musical Art; Leopold Stokowski,
conductor; Juilliard School. *See:* B169.

W1c 1-2 April 1932: Philadelphia; Philadelphia Orchestra;
Leopold Stokowski, conductor; Academy of Music [3rd mvt. only].
See: B176.

W1d 23-24 February 1933: Los Angeles; Los Angeles Philharmonic
Orchestra; Arthur Rodzinski, conductor. *See:* B179.

W1e 11 April 1937: Chicago; Illinois Symphony Orchestra; Izler
Solomon, conductor; Great Northern Theatre. *See:* B167, B173, B178.

W1f 19 March 1940: New York: New York Symphony; Izler Solomon,
conductor; Metropolitan Opera House. *See:* B164, B168, B174 - 175,
B177, B180.

This was completed during Bennett's Guggenheim fellowship in
Paris. It, along with his *Sights and Sounds*, was a prize winner in
the 1929 RCA Victor competition for new American works. A piano

reduction of the score by the composer was also published by Harms in 1931.

W2 *ADAGIO EROICO (TO THE MEMORY OF A SOLDIER)* (probably 1932); 8 min.; Ms. ???; *See:* **B181 - 184**.

Premiere

W2a 25 April 1935: Philadelphia; Philadelphia Orchestra; Jose Iturbi, conductor; Academy of Music. *See:* **B181 - 182**.

Other selected performances

W2b 26 July 1936: New York: New York Philharmonic-Symphony; Jose Iturbi, conductor; Lewisohn Stadium. *See:* **B183 - 184**.

W2c 9 August 1937: Robin Hood Dell [Philadelphia]; Philadelphia Orchestra; Jose Iturbi, conductor.

Bennett once wrote that it was "dedicated in a tacet sort of way to the memory of George Washington on his birthday some years ago." This suggests that perhaps the piece was composed at the time of the bicentennial of Washington's birthday (1932).

W3 *AN ADVENTURE IN HIGH FIDELITY* (1954); 2 (2nd alt. picc.), 2 (2nd alt. E. h.), 2+b. cl., 2, AATTB saxes - 4, 3, 3, 1 - hp., pf. (alt. cel.), perc. (3 players, includes timp.), stgs.; c. 16 min.; Ms. ??? (copy in LC); *See:* **D29**.
1.   The Arrival at the Great Gates of the Castle Hi Fi
2.   The Welcome of the Page Boy Prince Dynam
3.   The Variable Pitch of Princess Rhumbamba
4.   The Balinese Ballad of the Tweeter and the Woofer
5.   The Circular Serenade of the Diamond Stylus
6.   The Waltz of the Vinylite Biscuits
7.   The Tomb of the Ogre Distortion
8.   Blasphemy in the Amplifier
9.   The Full Frequency Fountain of Farewell

The piece was commisioned by RCA, released on album LM-1802 [D29]. The titles of the individual movements are as given on the album's liner notes; those on the ms. (in Bennett's hand) differ in detail. The saxophones are scored as "doubles" for the non-principal woodwinds.

W4   *ANTIQUE SUITE FOR CLARINET AND ORCHESTRA* (1941); 1, 1, 1, 4 sax., 1 - 2, 3, 2, 0 - timp., perc. (2), cel. (alt. pf.) - stgs.; 12 min.; ["to Benny Goodman"]; Ms. ???; *See:* **B188**.
   1.   prelude
   2.   allemande
   3.   courante
   4.   sarabande
   5.   gigue

Premiere

W4a 6 April 1941: New York [radio broadcast]; WOR Orchestra; Ralph McLane, clarinet; Robert Russell Bennett, conductor ["Notebook" program]. *See:* **B188**.

Though the work was dedicated to Benny Goodman, there is no evidence that clarinetist Goodman ever performed the piece. Goodman did, however, perform in pit orchestras under Bennett's direction at least once while working as a free-lance musician in New York in the 1920s and early 1930s.

W5   *ARMED FORCES SUITE* [for orchestra, symphonic band, and "combo"] (1959 or 1960); 41 min.; Ms. ???; *See:* **D33, B189 - 190**.
   1.   1776 ("When in the course of human events . . .")
   2.   1812 (". . . What so proudly we hailed . . .")
   3.   1836 ("Hark to the Indian yell ring on the air!")
   4.   1845 ("Near Buena Vista's mountain chain, Hurrah! Hurrah! Hurrah!")
   5.   1861-84 ("That these honored dead shall not have died in vain.")
   6.   1898 ("Remember the Maine")
   7.   1917-18 (". . . to make the world safe for democracy")
   8.   1941-45 ("Blood, sweat, and tears")

"Episodes" 1, 6, and 8 are for orchestra; 2 and 5 for band; 3 and 7 for the "combo" (a "studio orchestra" of brass, saxophones, strings, and expanded percussion section); 4 is for both band and the "combo." This piece was commissioned by the Radio Corporation of America as a recording project (LSC-2445, 1960); only one partial concert performance (of episodes 1 and 8) is known:

W5a 10 November 1981: Washington, DC; U.S. Army Band and U.S. Army Orchestra; D.A.R. Constitution Hall; Col Eugene W. Allen (1) and Edwin McArthur (8), conductors.

W6 *CHARLESTON RHAPSODY* [for small orchestra] (1926, rev. 1933); 12 min.; Ms. in Estate; *See:* **B192 - 194.**

Premiere

W6a 18 February 1931: New York; New York Sinfonietta; Robert Russell Bennett, conductor; Roerich Museum. *See:* **B192.**

Other selected performances

W6b 17 May 1933: New York; New Chamber Orchestra; Bernard Herrmann, conductor; New School Auditorium. *See:* **B193.**

W6c 12 February 1939: Hollywood; Musicians' League for Democracy; Alfred Newman, conductor.

W6d 13 February 1942: New York [radio broadcast]; WOR Orchestra; Robert Russell Bennett, conductor ["Notebook" program]. *See:* **B194.**

The piece exists in two versions—both as scored for chamber ensemble (woodwind quintet, string quintet, and piano) and orchestra (1, 1, 1, 1- 2, 1, 1, 0 - 1 percussion, piano , strings). Both were completed in Paris in 1926; the latter was revised in New York in 1933. Oscar Levant played the prominent piano obbligato at the first performance.

W7 *CLASSIC SERENADE FOR STRINGS (Portraits Of Three Friends)*[string orchestra] (1941); 12 min.; Ms. ???; *See:* **B196.**

Premiere

W7a 30 March 1941: New York [radio broadcast]; WOR Orchestra; Robert Russell Bennett, conductor ["Notebook" program]. *See:* **B80.**

Other selected performance

W7b 2 August 1945: Toronto; Toronto Philharmonic; Fritz Mahler, conductor [first public performance]. *See:* **B196**.

Some details about the work are provided in **B80**; one of the movements is described as a portrait of *New Yorker* music critic Robert A. Simon, who was also Bennett's librettist for *Maria Malibran* [**W44**].

W8   *A COMMEMORATION SYMPHONY: STEPHEN COLLINS FOSTER* [SATB chorus, soprano and tenor soloists, and orchestra] (1959); 3, 3, 3, 2 - 4, 3, 3, 1 - timp., perc., hp. - stgs.; [Chappell, 1960]; 22 min.; Ms. ???; *See:* **D12, B197 - 198**.

Premiere

W8a 30 December 1959; Pittsburgh; Pittsburgh Symphony; Mendelssohn Choir of Pittsburgh; William Steinberg, conductor.

Other selected performance

W8b 31 August 1961; Los Angeles; Hollywood Bowl Orchestra; William Steinberg, conductor.

The piece was commissioned for the Pittsburgh centennial celebration. It was based on melodies by Pittsburgh native Foster, with choral parts (optional) in the final movement. Rather than being subjected to symphonic development, the melodies are orchestrated with introductory and linking passages of Bennett's. His aim was to work in a mid-19th-century style, as if he were a contemporary of Foster's. Bennett did not consider himself the "composer" of the piece; program credits for the first performance are as follows: "specially arranged and orchestrated by Robert Russell Bennett."

W9   *CONCERTO FOR HARMONICA AND ORCHESTRA* (1971 or 1972); Ms. in Estate.

Premiere

W9a February or March 1981: Hong Kong; Hong Kong Philharmonic Orchestra; Cham-ber Huang, harmonica; Karel Husa, conductor.

W10 *CONCERTO FOR HARP, VIOLONCELLO, AND ORCHESTRA* (1959 or 1960); Ms. in Estate; *See:* **B199.**

Premiere

W10a 31 July 1960: New York; Naumburg Orchestra; Assunta Dell'Aquila, harp; Daniel Vandersall, cello; Robert Russell Bennett, conductor; The Mall (Central Park). *See:* **B199.**

This piece is a revision of the 1941 *Concerto for Viola, Harp and Orchestra* [**W11**].

W11 *CONCERTO FOR VIOLA, HARP AND ORCHESTRA* (1940 or 1941); 2, 2, 2, 2 - 4, 3, 2, 0 - perc., pf., gtr. - stgs. - solo viola, solo harp; Ms. in Estate (copy in LC).

Premiere

W11a 27 February 1941: New York; WOR Orchestra; Milton Katims, viola; Laura Newell, harp; Robert Russell Bennett, conductor ["Notebook" program].

This piece was was later revised as the *Concerto for Harp, Cello, and Orchestra* [**W10**].

W12 *CONCERTO FOR VIOLIN IN A MAJOR (IN THE POPULAR STYLE)* (1941); 21 min.; Ms.: Estate and Louis Kaufman, Los Angeles; *See:* D2, D3, D23, D36; B200 - 225.

1. Allegro moderato
2. Andante moderato (Meditation)
3. Vivace (Humoresque)
4. Marziale (Finale)

Premiere

W12a 26 December 1941: New York [radio broadcast]; WOR Symphony; Joseph Coleman, violin; Robert Russell Bennett, conductor ["Notebook" program]. *See:* **B215**.

Other selected performances

W12b 1 March 1942: Los Angeles; Louis Kaufman, violin; Theodore Saidenberg, piano; Wilshire-Ebell Theater. *See:* **B213**.

W12c 25 March 1942: New York; Louis Kaufman, violin; Robert Russell Bennett, piano; Carnegie Hall. *See:***B201, B203, B209, B211, B214, B218, B221**.

W12d 14 February 1944: New York; Louis Kaufman, violin; National Orchestral Association; Leon Barzin, conductor; Carnegie Hall. *See:* **B200, B205 - 208, B212, B217, B220, B222 - 223, B225**.

W12e 19 May 1956: London; Louis Kaufman, violin; London Symphony Orchestra; Bernard Herrmann, conductor; Royal Festival Hall. *See:* **B202, 204, 216, 224**.

W13   *CONCERTO FOR VIOLIN, PIANO AND ORCHESTRA* (1958 or 1959); [Chappell, rental]; 2, 2, 2, 2 - 4, 2, 3, 0 - timp., pf. - stgs.; 24 min.; Ms. in Estate; *See:* **B226 - 227**.

Premiere

W13a 18 March 1963: Portland, OR; Benno Rabinof, violin; Sylvia Rabinof, piano; Portland Symphony Orchestra; Jacques Singer, conductor. *See:* **B227**.

W14   *CONCERTO GROSSO FOR DANCE BAND AND ORCHESTRA (Sketches From An American Theatre)* (1932); 2 (2nd. alt. picc.), 2 (2nd alt. E.h.), 2+b. cl., 1 - 3, 2, 2, 0 - timp., perc. (2-3), mar. - stgs.; *concertino* is AAT saxes (all alt. clarinets); 2 tpts., trb., guitar, piano, drums (traps); 13 min.; Ms.: Free Library of Philadelphia (Edwin A. Fleisher Collection); *See:* **D37; B29, B228 - 242**.

1. Praeludium (Opening chorus, vigoroso e con brio)
2. Moderato con amina (Dialogue, ingenue and juvenile)
3. Andante con moto (Theme song)
4. Allegro scherzando (Comedy scene and blackout)
5. Marcia (Finale with flags)

Premiere

W14a 9 December 1932: Rochester; Rochester Philharmonic; Howard Hanson, conductor; Eastman Theatre. *See:* **B230 - 235, B240, B242.**

Other selected performances

W14b 7 January 1933: Berlin; Berlin Philharmonic; Howard Hanson, conductor. *See:* **B228 - 229, B233, B238.**

W14c 4 July 1934; New York; New York Philharmonic-Symphony; Robert Russell Bennett, conductor; Lewisohn Stadium. *See:* **B231 - 232, B234.**

W14d 24 April 1945: Rochester; Eastman School Senior Symphony Orchestra; Howard Hanson, conductor; Eastman Theatre. *See:* **D37; B237, B241.**

W15 *CONCERT VARIATIONS ON A CROONER'S THEME FOR VIOLIN AND ORCHESTRA* (1949); 2, 2 (2nd. alt. E.h.), 2, 2 - 4, 2, 3, 1 - timp., perc. (2), cel. (alt. pf.) - stgs.; 12 min.; ["to Aaron Rosand and the Louisville Philharmonic Society"]; Ms. in Estate (copy in LC); *See:* **B244 - 253.**

Premiere

W15a 30 November and 1 December 1949: Louisville, TN; Aaron Rosand, violin; Louisville Orchestra; Robert Whitney, conductor; Columbia Auditorium. *See:* **B244, B247, B249 - 250, B252 - 253.**

Other selected performance

W15b 9 February 1951: New York; Aaron Rosand, violin; Eileen Flisser, piano; Town Hall.

Mr. Rosand performed the piece with a piano reduction of the orchestra score; the piece was retitled *Theme and Variations* [**W115**]. *See:* **B245 - 246, B251**.

W16 *A DRY WEATHER LEGEND* [flute and orchestra] (1946); 2 (2nd. alt. picc.), 2 (2nd alt. E.h.), 2 (2nd. alt. b. cl.), 2 - 2, 2, 1, 0 - timp., perc., mar., xyl., hp. - stgs.; ["to Lamar Stringfield"]; 7 min.; Ms. in Estate (copy in LC); *See:* **B257 - 262**.

Premiere

W16a 19 February 1947: Knoxville, TN; Knoxville Symphony Orchestra; Lamar Stringfield, flute; Robert Russell Bennett, conductor; Knoxville H.S. Auditorium. *See:* **B257 - 262**.

W17 *AN EARLY AMERICAN BALLADE ON MELODIES OF STEPHEN FOSTER* [small orchestra, "30 or fewer instruments"] (1932); c. 5 min.; Ms. ???; *See:* **B263**.

Premiere

W17a 15 April 1932: New York [radio broadcast]; CBS Orchestra; Nathaniel Shilkret, conductor.

The work was commissioned for performance on the "Chesterfield Music That Satisfies" radio program. Short works—approximately five minutes in length—were similarly commissioned from Grainger, Cadman, Carpenter, Respighi, and others.

W18 *EIGHT ETUDES FOR SYMPHONY ORCHESTRA* (1938); 2, 2 (2nd. alt. E.h.), 2+b. cl., 1 - 3, 3, 2, 0 - timp., perc. (2), hp. - stgs.; 18 min.; Ms. ???; *See:* **D39; B264 - 278**.
1.   Allegro con brio (to Walter Damrosch)
2.   Andantino (to Aldous Huxley)
3.   Allegretto scherzando (to Noel Coward)
4.   Ben animato, quasi una fantasia (to Carl Hubbell)
5.   Alla marcia (to all dictators)
6.   Adagio e sincero (to the Grand Lama)
7.   Con grazia (to Eugene Speicher)
8.   Allegro animato (to the ladies)

Premiere

W18a 17 July 1938: New York [radio broadcast]; CBS Orchestra; Howard Barlow, conductor; Liederkranz Hall. *See:* **D39; B267, B272, B278.**

Other selected performances

W18b 10-11 January 1941: Philadelphia; Philadelphia Orchestra; Eugene Ormandy, conductor; Academy of Music. *See:* **B266, B275.**

W18c 6 January 1942: New York; Philadelphia Orchestra; Eugene Ormandy, conductor; Carnegie Hall. *See:* **B264 - 265, B268 - 270, B276.**

W18d 5-6-7 November 1942: New York; New York Philharmonic-Symphony Orchestra; Howard Barlow, conductor; Carnegie Hall.

W18e 20 and 22 November 1942: Pittsburgh; Pittsburgh Symphony Orchestra; Fritz Reiner, conductor.

W18f 13-14 November 1958: Chicago; Chicago Symphony Orchestra; Fritz Reiner, conductor; Orchestra Hall. *See:* **B277.**

This piece was comissioned by the Columbia Broadcasting System as part of its "Everybody's Music" series of new works by American composers. As noted above, each movement bears a separate dedication.

W19   *"THE FOUR FREEDOMS"; A SYMPHONY AFTER FOUR PAINTINGS BY NORMAN ROCKWELL* (1943); [Contemporary Music, 1943 and Robbins, 1943]; 2 (2nd. alt. picc.), 2, 2+b. cl., 1 - 4, 3, 3, 1 - timp., perc. (2), hp. - stgs.; 18 min.; Ms.???; *See:* **D41; B114, B294 - 311.**

1.   Allegro vigoroso (freedom of speech and expression)
2.   Lento (freedom of every person to worship God in his own way)
3.   Scherzo: allegro vivace (freedom from want)
4.   Molto tranquillo; poco a poco piu marziale (freedom from fear)

Premiere

W19a 26 September 1943: New York [radio broadcast]; NBC Symphony; Frank Black, conductor. *See:* **B294, B300, B302 - 303, B307.**

Other selected performances

W19b 13 December 1943: Philadelphia; Philadelphia Orchestra; Eugene Ormandy, conductor; Academy of Music. *See:* **B294 - 299, B306 - 307.**

W19c 16 December 1943: Los Angeles; Los Angeles Philharmonic Orchestra; Alfred Wallenstein, conductor. *See:* **B294 - 295, B301, B304 - 305, B307 - 308.**

W19d 26 March 1944: Cleveland; Cleveland Orchestra; Frank Black, conductor; Severance Hall. *See:* **B309.**

W19e 13 May 1944 [two-piano and percussion version]: New York; Teen-Age Dance Workshop; Times Hall; performers unknown. *See:* **B310.**

The orchestra score was published by Robbins, although G. Schirmer's advertisement in 1944 lists their firm as "sole selling agents." A piano reduction by Helmy Kresa, and a simplified "adaptation" for piano by Tibor Serly, were both published by Contemporary. The Ms. of Bennett's two-piano-with percussion setting—unpublished—is held by his survivors (copy in LC).

W20   *HOLLYWOOD (Introduction and Scherzo)* (1936); 2+picc., 2+E.h., 2+b. cl., 2 - 4, 3, 3, 1 - timp., perc. (2), 2 pf. - stgs.; 15 min.; Ms. in Free Library of Philadelphia (Edwin A. Fleisher Collection); *See:* **B29, B353 - 359.**

Premiere

W20a 15 November 1936: New York [radio broadcast]; NBC Symphony; Frank Black, conductor.

Other selected performance

W20b 15 February 1943: New York; National Orchestral Association; Leon Barzin, conductor; Carnegie Hall. *See:* **B355 - 358.**

The piece was a League of Composers commission.

W21 *KANSAS CITY ALBUM (Seven Songs for Orchestra)* (1949); 3 (3rd. alt. picc.), 2 (2nd alt. E.h.), 2+b. cl., 2 - 4, 3, 3, 1 - timp., perc. (3), xyl., hp. - stgs.; Ms. in Estate; *See:* **B360**.
1. Prelude (Westport Landing)
2. Allegro (Missouri Pacific)
3. Allegretto (The Cable Car Ride)
4. Nocturne (A City Under Trees)
5. Scherzo (12th Street)
6. Religioso (The Gallery)
7. Finale (The Big Town Today)

Premiere

W21a 6 February 1950: Kansas City, MO; Kansas City Philharmonic; Robert Russell Bennett, conductor.

The piece was commissioned by the Philharmonic to commemorate the city's centennial.

W22 *A MARCH FOR AMERICA* (1941); Ms. in Estate (copy in LC); *See:* **D44**.

Premiere

W22a 4 July 1941: New York; WOR Orchestra; Robert Russell Bennett, conductor ["Notebook" program].

Other selected performances

W22b 22 February 1943: New York [radio broadcast]; NBC Symphony; Alfred Wallenstein, conductor.

W22c 5 July 1943; New York (radio broadcast]; NBC Symphony; Gustave Haenschen, conductor.

W23 *MARCH FOR GENERAL MACARTHUR* (1942); Ms.???

Premiere

W23a 20 March 1942: New York [radio broadcast]; WOR Orchestra; Robert Russell Bennett, conductor ["Notebook" program].

W24 *MARCH FOR TWO PIANOS AND ORCHESTRA* (1930, rev. 1950); 14 min.; Ms. in Estate (copy in LC); *See:* **B368 - 370**.

Premiere

W24a 18 July 1930: Los Angeles; Oscar Levant and Robert Russell Bennett, pianos; Los Angeles Symphony Orchestra; Karl Krueger, conductor; Hollywood Bowl. *See:* **B56, B369**.

Other selected performance

W24b 13 August 1931: New York; Oscar Levant and Robert Russell Bennett, pianos; New York Philharmonic-Symphony Orchestra; William Daly, conductor; Lewisohn Stadium. *See:* **B46, B368, B370**.

The piece was revised in 1950 and retitled *Three Marches for Two Pianos and Orchestra.*

W25 *NOCTURNE AND APPASSIONATA, FOR PIANO AND ORCHESTRA* (1941); 2, 2, 2, 2 - 2, 3, 2, 0 - timp., perc. (2), hp., solo pf. - stgs.; 14 min.; Ms. ???; *See:* **B398 - 399**.

Premiere

W25a 18 August 1941: New York ; WOR Orchestra; Milton Kaye, piano; Robert Russell Bennett, conductor ["Notebook" program].

Other selected performance

W25b 21-22 November 1941: Philadelphia; Milton Kaye, piano; Philadelphia Orchestra; Saul Caston, conductor; Academy of Music. *See:* **B398 - 399**.

W26 *ORCHESTRAL FRAGMENTS FROM THE AMERICAN OPERA*
"MARIA MALIBRAN" (1934); 2, 2 + E. h., 2 + b. cl., 2 - 4, 3, 3, 1 -
timp., perc. (2-3), hp., pf. - stgs.; 30 min.; Ms. ???; *See:* **B400 - 403**.

1. Bouree
2. Fugue
3. Gavotte
4. Pastorale
5. Gigue

Premiere

W26a 7 February 1935: Los Angeles; Los Angeles Philharmonic
Orchestra; Alfred Wallenstein, conductor. *See:* **B400 - 403**.

This suite of music (some of it evidently underscoring for dialogue)
from Bennett's opera *Maria Malibran* **[W44]** was prepared at
Wallenstein's request and premiered two months before the opera's
first staging.

W27 *OVERTURE TO AN IMAGINARY DRAMA* (1946) ["for Fritz
Mahler"]; 2, 2, 2+b. cl., 2 - 4, 3, 3, 1 - timp., perc. (2-3), hp. - stgs.; 7 min.;
Ms. in Estate; *See:* **B404 - 409**.

Premiere

W27a 14 May 1946: Toronto; Toronto Symphony; Fritz Mahler,
conductor; Varsity Arena. *See:* **B408**.

Other selected performances

W27b 27 June 1946: New Orleans; New Orleans Symphony;
Jacques Singer, conductor; Beauregard Square.

W27c 23 February 1947: Washington, D.C.; National Symphony
Orchestra; Hans Kindler, conductor. *See:* **B406 - 409**.

W27d 2 November 1947: Washington, D.C.; National Symphony
Orchestra; Howard Mitchell, conductor.

W27e 5-6 April 1949: Erie, PA; Erie Philharmonic Orchestra; Robert
Russell Bennett, conductor; Strong Vincent Auditorium.

W27f 26 November 1949: New York; New York Philharmonic-Symphony Orchestra;   Leopold Stokowski, conductor; Carnegie Hall. *See:* **B404 - 405, B407.**

W28   *OVERTURE TO THE MISSISSIPPI*   (1950); [Chappell, 1977]; 2 (2nd. alt. picc.), 2 (2nd. alt. E.h.), 3 (3rd. alt. b. cl.), 2 - 4, 3, 3, 1 - timp., perc. (3), hp., banjo - stgs.; 9 min.; Ms. ???; *See:* **B410.**

Premiere

W28a 14 January 1950: Boston; Indianapolis Symphony Orchestra; Fabien Sevitzky, conductor; Symphony Hall. *See:* **B410.**

W29   *PAYSAGE (Landscape)* (1927 or 1928); 3 (3rd alt. picc.), 2+E.h., 2+b. cl., 2 - 4, 3, 3, 1 - timp., perc. (1-2), hp. - stgs.; 15 min.; Ms. in Estate (copy in LC); *See:* **B411 - 413.**

Premiere

W29a 15 December 1933: Rochester; Rochester Philharmonic Orchestra; Howard Hanson, conductor; Eastman Theatre. *See:* **B411 - 413.**

W30   *PIANO CONCERTO IN B MINOR* (1947); Ms. in Estate; *See:* **B414.**

Performance

W30a October or November 1952; Stuttgart; Andor Foldes, piano; orchestra unknown [Stuttgart Radio Music Festival]. *See:* **B414.**

Rigdon **[B129]** mentions a premiere in Helsinki in 1948; correspondents in Helsinki are unable to confirm this date/location. There is no indication whether this is the concerto that Jose Iturbi commissioned from Bennett in the early 1930s. According to **B414**, however, performance **W30a** is *not* the work's premiere.

W31   *SIGHTS AND SOUNDS (AN ORCHESTRAL ENTERTAINMENT)* (1929) 2+2 picc., 3+E.h., 3+b. cl., 4 saxes, 3+cbn. - 6, 4, 3, 2 - timp., perc. (4), hp., cel., pf. - stgs.; [Harms, 1931; piano reduction by Bennett also published 1931]; 28 min.; Ms. in Free Library of Philadelphia (Edwin A. Fleisher Collection); *See:* **B29, B49, B78, B420 - 426.**

1. Union Station
2. Highbrows
3. Lowbrows
4. Electric signs
5. Night club
6. Skyscraper
7. Speed

Premiere

W31a 13 December 1938: Chicago; Illinois Symphony; Izler Solomon, conductor; Great Northern Theatre. *See:* **B423.**

Other selected performance

W31b 22-23 January 1943: Boston; Boston Symphony Orchestra; Richard Burgin, conductor; Symphony Hall. *See:* **B420 - 422, B424 - 425.**

W32 *SIX VARIATIONS IN FOX-TROT TIME ON A THEME BY JEROME KERN* [chamber orchestra] (1933); ["to Benny"]; 1, 1, 2, 1 - 2, 2,1, 0 - timp., perc. (1), pf. - stgs.; 10 min.; Ms. in Estate (copy in LC); *See:* **B427 - 429.**

Premiere

W32a 3 December 1933: New York; New Chamber Orchestra; Bernard Herrmann, conductor; Town Hall. *See:* **B427 - 429.**

Other selected performances

W32b 15 July 1934: Chapel Hill, NC; North Carolina Symphony; Lamar Stringfield, conductor.

W32c 15 November 1934: New York [radio broadcast]; Little Symphony Orchestra; Phillip James, conductor.

W32d 15 January 1935: Washington, D.C.; New Chamber Orchestra; Library of Congress; Bernard Herrmann, conductor.

The dedicatee is Bernard Herrmann. The "theme" is Kern's song, "Once in a Blue Moon," from *Stepping Stones* (1923).

W33   *SUITE OF OLD AMERICAN DANCES* (1949) [Chappell, 1950]; 2 (2nd alt. picc.), 2 (2nd alt. E.h.), 2+b. cl.; 2 - 4, 3, 3, 1 - timp., perc. (2-3), xyl., vibra. - stgs.; 15 min., Ms. ??? [published score is reproduction of Bennett's holograph]; *See:* **D6**, **D13**, **D18** [all are recordings of original scoring for *band*, however].
1.   Cakewalk
2.   Schottisch
3.   Western one-step
4.   Wallflower waltz
5.   Rag

Bennett first wrote the piece for band [**W70**], in which scoring it is more frequently played. Many sources erroneously credit the piece as being originally for orchestra, perhaps because the band score was published later (1952) than the copyright and publication dates for the orchestral setting (December 1950). Fennell relates that he was assured by Bennett that the *band* scoring was the work's original form.

W34   *SYMPHONY* ["Uke" Symphony, First Symphony] (1926); ["To Carl Busch"]; Ms. in Estate; *See:* **B477 - 479**.

Unpublished and, apparently, unperformed. This piece, composed while studying with Nadia Boulanger, won Bennett an honorable mention in the 1927 *Musical America* competition. The alternate title refers to the second movement, in which four of the violins are to "double" on ukeleles, *ad lib.*

W35   *SYMPHONY* [Sixth Symphony] (1946); 38 min,; Ms. ???

Bennett made mention of the piece in several published accounts, and it is included in *Goss* [**B117**] and other works lists, but no public performances or other details are known.

W36   *SYMPHONY* [Seventh Symphony, "Reiner" Symphony] (1962); 3 (3rd. alt. picc.), 2 + E.h., 2 + b. cl., 2 + cbn. - 4, 4, 3, 1 - timp., perc., hp., pf. - stgs.; ["to Fritz Reiner"]; Ms. in Estate (copy in LC); *See:* **B480 - 482**.

1. Allegro
2. Lento cantabile
3. Con gioia
4. Grave—Rondo—Allegro con brio

Premiere

W36a 11-12 April 1963: Chicago; Chicago Symphony Orchestra; Fritz Reiner, conductor; Orchestra Hall. *See:* **B480 - 482.**

Other selected performance

W36b 25 May 1966: Terre Haute, IN; Indiana State University Symphony Orchestra; Robert Russell Bennett, conductor.

W37 *SYMPHONY IN D FOR THE DODGERS* [Third Symphony] (1941); 2, 2, 2, 2 - 2, 3, 2, 0 - timp., perc. (2), hp., pf. - stgs.; 20 min.; Ms. ???; *See:* **D47; B483 - 492.**
1. Dodgers win
2. Dodgers lose
3. Hunting for a pitcher
4. Giants come to town

Premiere

W37a 16 May 1941: New York [radio broadcast]; WOR Orchestra; Walter Lanier ("Red") Barber, narrator [in last movement]; Robert Russell Bennett, conductor ["Notebook" program]. *See:* **B487 -488, B490.**

Other selected performance

W37b 3 August 1941: New York; New York Philharmonic-Symphony; Hans Wilhelm Steinberg, conductor, Walter Lanier ("Red") Barber, narrator; Lewisohn Stadium [first concert performance]. *See:* **B483 - 486, B489, B491 - 492.**

STAGE WORKS [W38 - 45]

W38   *COLUMBINE (pantomine ballet with theater orchestra)* (1916); Ms. in Estate (copy in LC).

Performance

W38a 6 February 1942: New York [radio broadcast]; WOR Orchestra; Robert Russell Bennett, conductor ["Notebook" program].

This performance, of one of Bennett's earliest large-scale works, *may* be the premiere; it is the only known performance.

W39   *CRYSTAL* [opera] (1972); Ms. in Estate [copy in LC]; *See* **B115**.

This unperformed work tells the story of "a girl named Crystal and the conflict between the Western civilization of today and a more primitive time—the Stone Age [**B115**]."

W40   *THE ENCHANTED KISS* [opera] (1944 or 1945); 75 min.; Ms. in Estate. *See:* **B80, B124, B279 - 280.**

Premiere

W40a 30 December 1945: New York (radio broadcast); WOR Orchestra; Miriam Berg and Harriet O'Rourke, sopranos; Robert Marshall, tenor; Hugh Thompson, baritone; Sylvan Levin, conductor. *See:* **B280.**

The work is based on an O. Henry story; the libretto is by Robert A. Simon. The work was begun in the late 1930s, but published articles from late 1943 describe the piece as still unfinished; this suggests the date of completion as given above. The work has apparently never been staged.

W41   *ENDIMION* [operetta-ballet in five acts] (1926 or 1927); 2, 2, 2, 2, - 2, 2, 0, 0 - perc. (1, includes timp.) - 8, 6, 6, 4, 4 stgs.; [piano-vocal score, Eastman School, 1934]; 105 min.; *See:* **B281 - 286.**

Premiere

W41a 5 April 1935: Rochester; Rochester Civic Orchestra; Eastman School Chorus; Howard Hanson, conducting; Eastman Theater. *See:* **B281 - 286.**

Based on a poem by Bernard le Bovier de Fontenelle; English version is by Bennett and Robert A. Simon. In American newspapers and other publications, the title is invariably given as *Endymion*.

W42 *HOLD YOUR HORSES* [musical play; words and music by Russell Bennett, Robert A. Simon and Owen Murphy] (1933); [piano-vocal folio pub. Harms, 1933]; Ms. ??? [NYPL has typewritten script]; *See:* **B339 - 352.**

Premiere

W42a 25 September 1933: New York; Wintergarden Theater; the run of the show was 88 performances.

W43 *AN HOUR OF DELUSION (an anecdote with music, for opera ensemble)* (one-act opera] (1928); 30 min.; Ms. in Estate; *See:* **B124.** The story was by Arthur Kissane Traine, Jr. The work is apparently unperformed.

W44 *MARIA MALIBRAN* [opera] (1934); 2-1/2 hrs.; Ms. of piano-vocal score in Estate (incomplete); *See:* **B124, B371 - 394.**

Premiere

W44a 8-9-10-11 April 1935: New York; The Juilliard School; Albert Stoessel, conductor. *See:* **B371 - 376, B379 - 380, B383 - 385, B387 - 388, B391 - 394.**

Other selected peformances

W44b 16 and 19 August 1935: New York; Chautauqua Opera Association; Norton Memorial Hall; Albert Stoessel, conductor. *See:* **B374, B382, B386.**

W44c 16-17-18 October 1964: New York; Community Opera, Inc.; Bart Ferrara, music director; P. S. 75 Auditorium.

W45   *PRINCESS CHARMING* [musical play; words and music by Russell Bennett, Jack Waller, Harry Ruby and Albert Sirmay] (1926) [piano-vocal folio published by Chappell (London), c. 1926]; *See:* **B415**.

Premiere

W45a 21 October 1926: London; 362 performances.

The score is mostly Sirmay's (spelled "Szirmai" at the time; he was for several decades a principal editor of theater music for Chappell); Bennett and Waller are credited with "additional songs."

INCIDENTAL MUSIC [W46 - 50]

This list includes only those stage productions for which Bennett was credited with the incidental music. He composed underscoring, etc. for most of the musical plays he orchestrated; this, however, was an understood part of his duties and he was credited only as "orchestrator."

W46   *THE FIREBRAND* (1924); Ms. ???

First production

W46a 15 October 1924: New York; Morosco Theatre; 287 performances.

The play was written by Edwin Justus Mayer; incidental music is credited to Maurice Nitke and Russell Bennett. The plot revolves around the adventures of Benvenuto Cellini; it was turned into a musical play, *The Firebrand of Florence*, in New York in 1945, though Bennett was apparently not involved.

W47   *HAMLET* (1922); 3 tpts., timp., stg. quartet, and musical saw; Ms. ???; *See:* **B318 - 319**.

First production

W47a 16 November 1922: New York; Sam. H. Harris Theatre; produced and directed by Arthur Hopkins; starred John Barrymore; 101 performances. *See:* **B318 - 319.**

Revival

W47b 26 November 1923: New York; Manhattan Opera House; produced and directed by Arthur Hopkins; starred John Barrymore; 24 additional performances.

W48   *HAPPY BIRTHDAY* (1946); Ms. ???

Original production

W48a 31 October 1946: New York; Broadhurst Theatre; 564 performances.

The play was written by Anita Loos and produced by Rodgers and Hammerstein, who wrote one song for the production.

W49   *MACBETH* (1921); Ms. ???; *See:* **B361 - 363.**

First production

W49a 17 February 1921: New York; Apollo Theatre; produced and directed by Arthur Hopkins; starred Lionel Barrymore; 28 performances. *See:* **B361 - 363.**

W50   *ROMEO AND JULIET* (1922); Ms. ???; *See:* **B417 - 418.**

First production

W50a 27 December 1922: New York; Longacre Theatre; produced and directed by Arthur Hopkins; starred Ethel Barrymore; 29 performances. *See:* **B417 - 418.**

WORKS FOR BAND (and WIND ORCHESTRA) [W51 - 78]

The works listed as "wind orchestra" compositions were written for the American Wind Symphony (renamed the American Waterways Wind Orchestra in the 1980s), conducted by its founder, Robert Austin Boudreau, who commissioned each composition. The slightly unorthodox instrumentation of this fine ensemble—no saxophones or euphoniums, and a multiplicity of auxiliary woodwinds—was surely a creative challenge for Bennett, though this has limited somewhat the number of performances of these pieces by other wind ensembles.

Detailed instrumentation is given for the wind orchestra works, but not for all of the remaining band scores. Their instrumentation—not specific as to the number of players on a part—is typically as follows:

Flutes I, II, Piccolo; Oboes I, II (English Horn in some works); Bassoons I, II (contrabassoon is not specified); E flat clarinet; B flat clarinets I, II, III; E flat alto clarinet (in some works); B flat bass clarinet; EE flat or BB flat contrabass clarinet (in some of the later works); E flat alto saxophones I, II; B flat tenor saxophone; E flat baritone saxophone; B flat bass saxophone (in a few earlier scores); trumpets/cornets in 3 to 5 parts; E flat and/or F horns, I, II, II, IV, trombones I, II, III, baritone/euphonium (one part), tuba, and percussion. When Bennett was writing for a specific ensemble—the Goldman Band or the 1939-1940 New York World's Fair Band —exact details of instrumentation are included when known.

ARMED FORCES SUITE [for orchestra, symphonic band, and "combo"]
See: **W5.**

W51 *AUTOBIOGRAPHY (Part One: 1894-1900; Part Two: 1916-1935);*
(1976 or 1977) [Schirmer, 1979]; c. 15 min.; Ms. ???; See: **B191.**
1.   1894: Cherry Street (Allegretto)
2.   1899: South Omaha (Con anima)
3.   1900: Corn, Cows and Music (Jig)
4.   1916: Mo. to N.Y. (Tempo di "Missouri Waltz")
5.   1919: The Merrill Miracle (Bright march)
6.   1926: A Parisian in Paris (Poco allegretto)
7.   1935: What Was the Question? (Moderato maestoso)

Premiere

W51a 22 June 1977: New York; Guggenheim Concert Band; probably Ainslee Cox, conductor; Lincoln Center Library Auditorium. *See:* **B191**.

W52 *CHRISTMAS OVERTURE* [wind orchestra]; (1980 or 1981); 3, 3, 3, 3 - 4, 4, 4, 2 - timp., perc. (4), cel., hp.; 5 min.; Ms. ???; *See:* **B195**.

Premiere

W52a 7 June 1981: Pittsburgh (Point State Park); American Wind Symphony; Robert Austin Boudreau, conductor.

Other selected performance

W52b 25 July 1982: New York; Guggenheim Concert Band; Ainslee Cox, conductor; Damrosch Park, Lincoln Center; *See:* **B195**.

W53 *CONCERTO GROSSO FOR WIND QUINTET AND WIND ORCHESTRA* [solo flute/oboe/clarinet/bassoon/horn and wind orchestra] (1957); [Henmar]; 5+2 picc., 5+2 E.h., 5+e flat cl., alto cl., b. cl, c-b. cl.), 5+2 cbn. - 5, 3+2 cornets, flugelhorn, 6, 1 - timp., perc., contrabass, and solo quintet; 16 min.; Ms. ???; *See:* **D1, D37; B243**.
1.   Adagio; con brio
2.   Andante con moto
3.   Moderato
4.   Allegro moderato ma energico

Premiere

W53a 6 July 1958: Pittsburgh (Point State Park); American Wind Symphony; Robert Russell Bennett, conductor.

W54 *DARTMOUTH OVERTURE* (1972 or 1973); Ms.: Dartmouth College.

Premiere

W54a 17 April 1973: Hanover, NH; Dartmouth College Concert Band; Spaulding Auditorium; Donald Wendlandt, conductor.

W55 *DOWN TO THE SEA IN SHIPS* (1968) [Warner Brothers, 1969]; 13 min.; Ms. ???; *See:***B88, B89.**
  1.   The Way of a Ship
  2.   Mists & Mystery
  3.   Songs in the Salty Air
  4.   Waltz of the Clipper Ships
  5.   Finale, introducing the *S.S. Eagle March*

Premiere

W55a 16 July 1969: Brooklyn (NY); Goldman Band.

Other performance

W55b 10 November 1981: Washington, D.C.; U.S. Army Band; Col Eugene W. Allen, conductor; D.A.R. Constitution Hall.

This is a suite of excerpts from his score for an NBC production of the same name, first televised on 11 December 1968.

W56 *THE FABULOUS COUNTRY (concert march)* (1975) [Warner Brothers, 1975]; 2-1/2 min.; Ms. ???

W57 *FANFARE FOR THE AMERICAN WIND SYMPHONY* [wind orchestra] (1981); 0, 0, 0, 0 - 5, 5, 5, 2 - timp., perc. (3); 3 min.; Ms. ???

Premiere

W57a 7 June 1981: Pittsburgh (Point State Park); American Wind Symphony; Robert Austin Boudreau, conductor.

W58 *FOUNTAIN LAKE FANFARE (MARCH)* (1939) [Chappell, 1940]

Premiere

W58a 1939 or 1940: New York (Flushing Meadows); New York World's Fair Band; probably Joseph Littau, conductor.

W59 *FOUR PRELUDES FOR BAND* (1974) [Belwin-Mills, 1975]; 13 min.; Ms. ???; *See:* **B80, B312**.
1. George (Vigoroso)
2. Vincent (Allegretto)
3. Cole (Moderato, thoughtfully)
4. Jerome (Vivo, alla tarantella)

Selected performance

W59a 22 June 1978: New York; Goldman Band; probably Ainslee Cox, conductor. *See:* **B312**.

The movements' titles refer to songwriters Gershwin, Youmans, Porter, and Kern.

W60 *GENERAL DOUGLAS MACARTHUR (MARCH)* [Chappell, 1965]; 4 min.

The march is from his music for the NBC-Project 20 television production, "That War in Korea," of 1965. It is undetermined whether the music is identical to his orchestral *March for Douglas MacArthur* of 1942.

W61 *JAZZ?* (1969); Ms. in Estate.

Premiere

W61a 16 July 1969: New York; Goldman Band; probably Richard Franko Goldman or Robert Russell Bennett, conductor.

W62 *KENTUCKY ("FROM LIFE")* [wind orchestra] (1961); 3+picc., alto fl., 3+E.h., 2+e flat, b. cl., 2+2 cbn., 4, 4, 4, 1, - timp., perc., hp., cel., pf.; [pub. Henmar]; 17 min.; Ms. in Estate.

Premiere

W62a 13 June 1965: Pittsburgh; American Wind Symphony; Robert Austin Boudreau, conductor.

W63 *MADEMOISELLE (BALLET FOR BAND)* (1952) 2+picc., 2, 9+e flat, b. cl., 2, ATB saxes - 4, 3 tpts., 4 cornets, 3, 2 (bar.), 4 (tubas) - timp., perc. (2) ["for the Goldman Band"]; 11 min.; Ms. ??? (copy in LC); *See:* **B28, B364 - 367.**

Premiere

W63a 18 June 1952: New York; Goldman Band; The Mall (Central Park); Robert Russell Bennett, conductor. *See:* **B364 - 367.**

Other selected performance

W63b 13 July 1955: Evanston, IL; Northwestern University Summer Session Concert Band; Robert Russell Bennett, conductor.

The piece was commissioned for the Goldman Band by the League of Composers. The instrumentation given above, including the numbers of players on each part, is written in Bennett's hand on the score; it is presumably the precise makeup of the Goldman Band at the time.

W64 *THE MARCH FOR MIGHT* (1955) [Chappell, 1956); Ms. ???

This is from his score for the NBC television production, "A Nightmare in Red," first televised on 27 December 1955.

W65 *OHIO RIVER SUITE* [wind orchestra] (1959); 6+2 picc., 6+2 E.h., 6+ e flat cl., alto cl., b. cl., c-b. cl., 6+2 cbn., 6, 3+ 2 cornets, flugelhorn, 6, 1 - timp., perc., contrabass; [Henmar, 1977]; 20 min.
  1.   The Allegheny 1859 (Prelude; andante—"prayer meeting song"; allegro—"Saturday night jig")
  2.   The Monongahela 1909 (Prelude; allegretto—"banjos across the river"; moderato—"the ballad of the mines")
  3.   The Ohio 1959 (Prelude; tranquillo—"counterpoint of two rivers"; allegro con ritmo—"this is it")

Premiere

W65a 5 June 1959: Pittsburgh; American Wind Symphony; Robert Austin Boudreau, conductor.

W66 *OVERTURE TO TY, TRIS AND WILLIE* [wind orchestra] (1961); 3+ 2 picc., 2 alto fl., 3+3 E.h., 3+3 b. cl., 3+3 cbn. - 6, 6, 6, 0 - perc. [Henmar, 1977]; 10 min.; Ms. ???

Premiere

W66a 15 June 1961: Pittsburgh; American Wind Symphony; Robert Russell Bennett, conductor.

The title makes reference to Pittsburgh baseball greats Ty Cobb, Tris Speaker, and Willie Stargell.

W67 *"PICKLE" OVERTURE* [wind symphony] (1969) [pub. Peters, 1969?]; 2 min.; *See*: **D28**.

Premiere

W67a ??? 1969: Pittsburgh; American Wind Symphony; Robert Austin Boudreau, conductor; Samuel Hazo, narrator.

H. J. Heinz Company, headquartered in Pittsburgh, observed its 100th anniversary in 1969. To celebrate the occasion, R. A. Boudreau commissioned several poets to write pickle-related poems, which were scored for narrator and wind orchestra by Bennett, Oliver Nelson, Shulamit Ran, Jacques Casterede, and Henk Badings. Bennett's contribution was a two-minute scoring of Sara Henderson Hay's poem, "The Pickle"; Bennett also composed this *Overture* for the set, collectively titled *The Pickle Suite*.

W68 *ROSE VARIATIONS* [trumpet or cornet and band] (1955) [Chappell, 1955; also pub. with piano reduction, probably by Bennett]; Ms. ???; Introduction [The Garden Gate]; Theme [Carolina (wild) rose]; Var. I [Dorothy Perkins (rambler) rose]; Var. II [Frau Karl Druschki (white) rose]; Var. III [Cinnamon rose (with humming birds)]; Var. IV [American Beauty (red) rose]. *See*: **D7**; [**B13**].

Premiere

W68a Summer 1955: New York; Goldman Band; James Burke, cornet; probably Robert Russell Bennett, conductor.

Selected Performance

W68b 10 November 1981: Washington, D.C.; U.S. Army Band; Sgt. Robert Ferguson, trumpet; D.A.R. Constitution Hall; Col. Eugene W. Allen, conductor.

W69   *SOAP BOX DERBY MARCH* (1966) [Chappell, 1966]; Ms. ???; *See:* **B430**.

Premiere

W69a 6 August 1966: Akron, OH: massed bands from several Akron high schools; Robert Russell Bennett, conductor. *See:* **B430**.

The piece was commissioned by officials of the Soap Box Derby for performance at the 1966 National Finals in Akron.

S. S. EAGLE MARCH—See: DOWN TO THE SEA IN SHIPS [**W55**].

W70   *SUITE OF OLD AMERICAN DANCES* (1949) [Chappell, 1952];
      15 min.; Ms.: Private Collection?; *See:* **D6, D13, D18, D31; B457 - 466**.
      1.   Cakewalk
      2.   Schottisch
      3.   Western one-step
      4.   Wallflower waltz
      5.   Rag

Premiere

W70a 17 June 1949: New York; Goldman Band; Robert Russell Bennett, conductor; The Mall (Central Park). *See:* **B89, B460 - 462, B464 - 465**.

Other selected performances

W70b 9 July 1950: New York; Goldman Band; Edwin Franko Goldman, conductor; The Mall (Central Park).

W70c 22 February 1953: Evanston (IL); Northwestern University Concert Band; Glenn Cliffe Bainum, conductor; Cahn Auditorium.

W70d 2 August 1957: New York; Goldman Band; Robert Russell Bennett, conductor; The Mall (Central Park). *See:* **B458**.

W70e 10 November 1981: Washington, D.C.; U.S. Army Band; Col. Eugene W. Allen, conductor; D.A.R. Constitution Hall.

W70f 21 July 1982: New York; Guggenheim Concert Band; H. Robert Reynolds, conductor; Damrosch Park, Lincoln Center.

Bennett's most popular work for band; many who are unaware of his *Tone Poems* of 1939-1940 assume that the *Suite* was his first piece for winds. According to Fennell [**B457**], there is no full score; Bennett made a condensed "sketch" score c. early 1948 and copied out the individual parts from it over a period of almost two years.

W71   *SYMPHONIC SONGS FOR BAND* (1957) [Chappell, 1958]; 13 min., Ms.???; *See:* **D15, D19, D20, D24; B80, B467 - 476.**
   1.   Serenade
   2.   Spiritual
   3.   Celebration

Premiere

W71a 24 August 1957: Salt Lake City; The National Intercollegiate Band; Lt. Col. Santelmann, conductor; Salt Lake Tabernacle. *See:* **B468, B476**.

Other selected performances

W71b 27 July 1958: New York; Goldman Band; Robert Russell Bennett, conductor; The Mall (Central Park). *See:* **B471**.

W71c 9 January 1959: Ann Arbor, MI; University of Michigan Symphonic Band; Robert Russell Bennett, conductor; Hill Auditorium

W71d 20 June 1979: New York; Goldman Band; Richard Franko Goldman or Ainslee Cox, conductor. *See:* **B469**.

The National Intercollegiate Band was comprised of members Kappa Kappa Psi and Tau Beta Sigma, the fraternal organizations that commissioned the piece.

W72   *THREE HUMORESQUES* [wind orchestra] (1961?) [Henmar, 1977]; 9 min.; Ms. ???

Premiere

W72a 15 June 1961: Pittsburgh; American Wind Symphony; Robert Russell Bennett, conductor.

The first is scored for 2 harps, piano, timpani and 4 percussionists; the second for woodwinds—2 piccolos, 3 flutes, 3 alto flutes, 3 oboes, 3 english horns, 3 clarinets, 3 bass clarinets, 3 bassoons, 3 contrabassoons. The third is for brass—6 horns, 6 trumpets, 6 trombones, tuba—with percussion.

W73   *A TNT COCKTAIL* (1939); Ms. at University of Iowa (Goldman Band Collection); *See:* **B500**.

Premiere

W73a April 1939: New York (Flushing Meadows); New York World's Fair Band; probably Joseph Littau, conductor. *See:* **B500**.

Other selected performance

W73b 21 July 1982: New York; Guggenheim Concert Band; Ainslee Cox, conductor; Damrosch Park, Lincoln Center.

W74 *TONE POEMS FOR BAND (For the Lagoon of Nations)* (1939);
4 (all alt. picc.), 1, 7 + e flat cl., b. cl., AATB saxes - 4, 9, 4, 2 (euph.), 2 -
perc. (4), hp.; Duration—see below; Ms. in Estate (copy in LC)—but see
note below; *See:* **B56, B501 - 511**.

1. The Call to the Nations (30 sec.)
2. The Spirit of George Washington (15 min.)
3. The Hunt (15 min.)
4. The Garden of Eden [alternate title is "Adam and Eve"] (15 min.)
5. The Story of Three Flowers—Morning Glory, Daffodil at Noon,
   Moonflower (15 min.)
6. The Dance of Life (15 min.)
7. From Clay to Steel (15 min.)
8. The World and the Cathedral (15 min.)
9. The Lagoon of Nations Postlude (c. 2 min.)

Composed for the 1939-1940 New York World's Fair, these works were
written to be synchronized with fountain and lighting displays at the
Lagoon of Nations "choreographed" by Jean Labatut. They were
presented almost daily, with the band a short distance away from the
Lagoon. The band's performance, picked up by microphone(s), was
amplified and played over a special public-address system near the
fountains. Each performance began with the "Call to the Nations" and,
apparently, ended with the "Postlude," with one of the 15-minute tone
poems played in between. The "Dance of Life" and "From Clay to
Steel" segments, mentioned repeatedly in the contemporary press, do
not survive; copies of the others are at the Library of Congress. A few
of the movements have optional choral parts, but it is unclear
whether these were ever performed.

Premiere

W74a 30 April 1939: New York (Flushing Meadows); New York
World's Fair Band; Joseph Littau, conductor. *See:* **B502**.

Other performances

W74b 27 June 1951: New York; Goldman Band; Edwin or Richard
Franko Goldman, conductor; The Mall (Central Park) ["The World and
The Cathedral" only]. *See:* **B507**.

W74c 27 July 1958: New York; The Goldman Band; Robert Russell Bennett, conductor; The Mall (Central Park) ["Adam and Eve" only].

W75   *TRACK MEET* (1960) [Chappell, 1961]; 9 min.; Ms. in LC.
   1.   Grand entry
   2.   Pole Vault
   3.   Rival team
   4.   Double date
   5.   The big race

W76   *TWAIN AND THE RIVER* [narrator and wind orchestra] (1968); 2+picc., alto fl., 2+E.h., 4+b. cl, 2 c-b. cl., 2+2 cbn. - 4, 4, 4, 1 - timp., perc., hp., cel., pf.; [Henmar, 1977]; 8 min.

Premiere

W76a 9 June 1968: Pittsburgh; American Wind Symphony

W77   *WEST VIRGINIA EPIC* [wind orchestra] (1960); 3+3 alto fl., 3+3 E.h., 3+3 b. cl., 3+3 cbn. - 6, 6, 6, 1 - perc. (3), hp., cel.; [Henmar, 1977]; 10 min.; Ms. ???

Premiere

W77a June 1963: Fairmont, WV; American Wind Symphony; Robert Austin Boudreau, conductor.

W78   *ZIMMER'S AMERICAN GREETING* [narrator and wind orchestra] (1974); 3+picc., 2+2 E.h., 3+b. cl., 3+cbn. - 5, 5, 5, 1 - timp., perc. (3); [Henmar]; 12 min.; *See:* B530 - 531.

Premiere

W78a 26 May 1974: Pittsburgh; American Wind Symphony; Robert Russell Bennett, conductor. *See:* B530 - 531.

Text is by Pittsburgh poet Paul Zimmer.

CHORAL WORKS [W79 - 90]

W79 *AUX QUATRE COINS (pour quatre femmes)* [for two sopranos and two altos] (1929); c. 4 min.; Ms.: New York Public Library.

W80 *CAROL CANTATAS I-II-III-IV* [SATB chorus and orchestra or piano] (1977) 2, 2, 2, 2 - 4, 3, 3, 0 - timp., perc., hp. - stgs.; [Lawson-Gould, 1978; each published separately]; Ms. in Estate.; *See:* B27.

> *CAROL CANTATA I:* Jesus Love Me; How Far Is It to Bethlehem; The Friendly Beasts; We Three Kings of Orient; We Wish You a Merry Christmas.
> *CAROL CANTATA II:* Carol of the Birds; The Twelve Days of Christmas; While Shepherds Watched Their Flocks; A Virgin Unspotted.
> *CAROL CANTATA III:* The Virgin Mary Had a Baby Boy; O Come, O Come Emmanuel; Wassail Song; Carol of the Birds.
> *CAROL CANTATA IV:* God Rest Ye, Merry Gentlemen; It Came Upon a Midnight Clear; Now is Born; O Holy Night.

Premiere

W80a 24 December 1977: Orlando, FL; First Presbyterian Church of Orlando; Chancel Choir; members of the Florida Symphony; Jack Wilson, conductor [*Cantatas I-IV*].

Each is "an original suite based upon traditional Christmas carols." They were commissioned by the First Presbyterian Church to celebrate its 100th anniversary.

W81 *CHESTER* [SATB chorus, contralto and baritone soloists, and orchestra] (1945); Ms. ???; *See:* D35.

Premiere

W81a 21 October 1946: New York [radio broadcast]; Jo Stafford and Lawrence Brooks, probable vocal soloists; Robert Russell Bennett, conductor. *See:* D35.

The work is based on the William Billings hymn of the same name.

A COMMEMORATION SYMPHONY See **W8**.

W82   *CRAZY CANTATA #1* [SAATTBB chorus, alto and baritone soloists, piano (1945) [Chappell, 1947]; Ms. ???; *See:* **B27**.

Premiere

W82a 29 April 1945: New York [radio broadcast]; The Ford Chorus; Kay Armen, contralto; Lawrence Brooks, baritone; Robert Russell Bennett, conductor [Ford Motor Co. "Stars of the Future" program].

Other selected performances

W82b 23 April 1946: New York; Mendelssohn Glee Club; Cesare Sodero, conductor; Waldorf-Astoria Hotel.

W82c 20 December 1946: New York; Teachers College Choir; Harry Wilson, conductor; Times Hall.

Based on the song, "Three Blind Mice."

W83   *CRAZY CANTATA #2* (*"I Took a Spanish Lesson"*) [SATB soloists, piano, percussion] (c. 1947); Ms. ??? (copy in LC).

W84   *THE EASTER STORY* [SATB chorus with orchestra or piano] (1978) [Lawson-Gould, 1978]; Ms. in Estate.

Premiere

W84a 8, 12, and 15 April 1978; Orlando, FL; First Presbyterian Church of Orlando; Chancel Choir; members of the Florida Symphony; Jack Wilson, conductor.

Words taken from the Bible and various hymn tunes. This work, like **W80**, was commissioned by Orlando's First Presbyterian Church.

W85? *EPITHALAMIUM* [SATB chorus and orchestra] (Date?) [Theodore Presser?]; *See:* **B28**

Eagon is the only published source [**B28**] that lists this as a Bennett work, supposedly available as a rental from Presser; staff members at Presser, however, have found no mention of the piece in the firm's files. The text, according to *Eagon*, is by John Milton.

W86 *THE FUN AND FAITH OF WILLIAM BILLINGS , AMERICAN* [SATB chorus and orchestra] (1975); 3, 3, 3, 2 - 4, 3, 3, 1 - timp., perc., hp. - stgs.; [Chappell, 1975]; 30 min.; Ms. in Estate;*See:* **D16**; **B316 - 317**.

W86a 29 April 1975: Washington, D.C.; National Symphony Orchestra; University of Maryland Chorus; Antal Dorati, conductor; Kennedy Center for the Performing Arts. *See:* **B316**.

The piece was one of twelve commissions by the National Symphony, premiered during their 1975-76 season, to commemorate the American bicentennial.

W87 *NIETSCHZE VARIATIONS* [women's chorus and piano] (1929); Ms. ???; *See:* **B397**.

Premiere

W87a 8 May 1930: New York; Women's University Glee Club; Gerald Reynolds, conductor; Town Hall. *See:* **B397**.

W88 *THEME AND VARIATIONS IN THE FORM OF A BALLADE ABOUT A LORELEI* [SSAA chorus, soprano, mezzo-soprano and contralto soloists, and piano] (1929); Ms. in Estate (copy in LC); *See:* **B497**.

Premiere

W88a 1 May 1929: New York; Women's University Glee Club; Gerald Reynolds, conductor; Town Hall.

Other selected performance

W88b 18 December 1930: New York; Women's University Glee Club; Gerald Reynolds, conductor [Town Hall?]. *See:* **B497**.

W89 *UNITED NATIONS ALL FAITH PRAYER FOR PEACE* [SATB chorus. solo voice, and orchestra or piano] (1953); 2, 2, 2+b. cl., 2 - 4, 3, 3, 1 - timp., hp. - stgs.; [Chappell, 1953]; Ms. ???

The text is by John Golden.

W90? *VERSES 1-2-3* [SATB chorus and orchestra] (Date?) [Theodore Presser?]; *See:* **B28**.

Eagon is the only published source [**B28**] that lists this as a Bennett work, supposedly available as a rental from Presser; staff members at Presser, however, have found no mention of the piece in the firm's files.

CHAMBER MUSIC [W91-120]

W91 *ALLEMANDE* [violin/piano] (1947 or 1948); Ms.: Louis Kaufman, Los Angeles; *See:* **B185 - 187**.

Premiere

W91a 25 March 1948: New York: Louis Kaufman, violin; Erich Itor Kahn, piano; Town Hall. *See:* **B185 - 187**.

W92 *ARABESQUE* [2 trumpets/horn/trombone/bass trombone] (1978); ["for the American Brass Quintet"]; Ms. in Estate; 3 min.

Premiere

W92a 27 March 1979: New York; American Brass Quintet—Louis Ranger and Raymond Mase, trumpets; Edward Birdwell, horn; Herbert

Rankin, trombone; Robert Biddlecome, bass trombone; Carnegie Recital Hall.

W93 *AT SUNDOWN: ROMANCE* [violin/piano] (1912 or 1913) [pub. in *Etude* 32:1, January 1914, p. 44-45]; 3 min.; Ms.???

W94 *CLARINET QUARTET* (1941); Ms. in Estate.

Premiere

W94a 18 August 1941: New York; members of WOR Orchestra; Robert Russell Bennett, conductor ["Notebook" program].

W95 *DANCE* [flute/piano] (1928); Ms. ???; *See:* **B254**.

Premiere

W95a Summer 1928: Paris (Fontainebleau): Quinto Maganini, flute and Robert Russell Bennett, piano [private performance].

Other selected performance

W95b 9 February 1930: New York; Quinto Maganini, flute and Robert Russell Bennett, piano; Steinway Hall (Copland-Sessions Concert) [first public performance]. *See:* **B254**.

W96 *DANCE SCHERZO* [flute/oboe/clarinet/horn/bassoon] (1937); Ms.: Robert Austin Boudreau, Pittsburgh, PA; *See:* **B255 - 256**.

Premiere

W96a 14 March 1938: Los Angeles; Sylvia Ruderman, flute; Gordon Pope, oboe; Franklyn Stokes, clarinet; Arthur Frantz, horn; Ray Nowlin, bassoon; Biltmore Hotel (Pro Musica concert); Biltmore Music Room. *See:* **B255 - 256**.

Other selected performance

W96b 20 April 1941: New York [radio broadcast]; members of WOR Orchestra. *See:* **[B188]**.

W97   *FIVE IMPROVISATIONS ON EXOTIC SCALES* [flute/cello/piano] (1947); Ms.: Ingrid Dingfelder, Ridgewood, NJ; *See:* **B287**.

Premiere

W97a 14 February 1947: New York; The Sagul Trio (Edith Sagul, flute; Maryjane Thomas, cello; Geraldine Winnett, piano); Town Hall. *See:* **B287**.

Other selected performance

W97b 20 December 1947: New York; Blaisdell Trio; Times Hall (NAACC Concert).

The piece was written for the Sagul Trio; the first performance was a part of the 1947 WNYC [radio] American Music Festival.

W98   *FIVE TUNE CARTOONS* [violin/piano] (1948); Ms. ???; *See:* **B226**, **B288 - 291**.
   1.   After Al Capp (L'il Abner)
   2.   After Peter Arno ("Modern" ladies and gentlemen)
   3.   After Edgar Martin (Pug sings Boots' baby to sleep)
   4.   After Charles Addams (Danse Macabre)
   5.   After Walt Disney (Tempo di samba) (The animals at dancing school)

Premiere

W98a 27 February 1949: New York; Marc Brown, violin and Brooks Smith, piano; Carnegie Hall. *See:* **B288 - 291**.

W99   *A FLUTE AT DUSK* [flute solo] (1952) [Chappell, 1952]; Ms. ???; 4 min.

W100 *FOUR DANCES FOR PIANO TRIO* (1953 or 1954); Ms. ???;
   See: **B292 - 293**.
   1.   Dance of life
   2.   Dance of love
   3.   Dance of cats (hep)
   4.   Dance of delerium

Premiere

W100a ?? October 1954: Scranton, PA; The Columbia Concert Trio.
See: **B293**.

The piece was written for the Columbia Concert Trio—Teresa Testa,
violin; Ardyth Alton, cello; and Richard Gregor, piano. It was
performed on each of their 1954-1955 Community Concerts tour
programs.

W101 *HEXAPODA (five studies in jitteroptera)* [violin/piano] (1940)
   [Chappell, 1941]; 8 min.; *See:* **D3, D4, D8, D9, D11, D17, D23, D26, D43;**
   B226, B320 - 338.
   1.   Gut-Bucket Gus (Very slow and sustained in rhythm)
   2.   Jane Shakes Her Hair (Animated)
   3.   Betty and Harold Close Their Eyes (Lazily)
   4.   Jim Jives (Fast and very strict)
   5.   . . . Till Dawn Sunday (Vivo caldo)

Premiere

W101a 20 March 1940: New York; Louis Kaufman, violin and Robert
Russell Bennett, piano; Town Hall. *See:* **B320, B327, B330, B332**.

Other selected peformances

W101b 29 October 1940: New York; Jascha Heifetz, violin and Emanuel
Bay, piano.; Carnegie Hall. *See:* **B4, B323 - 324, B326, B331, B334 - 336**.

W101c 30 November 1945: New York; Benno Rabinof, violin and
Robert Russell Bennett, piano; Carnegie Hall. *See:* **B321**.

W101d May-June 1946: Prague (International Music Festival), Vienna,
Rome, The Hague; Carroll Glenn, violin and Eugene List, piano.

W101e 13 February 1977: New York; David Sackson, violin and Dwight Pelzer, piano; Carnegie Recital Hall.

W101f 3 May 1985: Washington, D.C.; David Sackson, violin and Leon Pommers, piano; Library of Congress; Coolidge Auditorium (The 1985 Festival of American Chamber Music).

Written in Los Angeles for Louis Kaufman, early 1940. The piece is a virtuoso challenge, appearing frequently on recital programs—or as an encore piece—by Kaufman, Heifetz, and other prominent American violinists in the 1940s and 1950s.

W102 *NOCTURNE* [flute/piano] (1928); Ms. ???; *See:* **B254**.

Premiere

W102a Summer 1928: Paris (Fontainebleau): Quinto Maganini, flute and Robert Russell Bennett, piano [private performance].

Other selected performances

W102b 9 February 1930: New York; Quinto Maganini, flute and Robert Russell Bennett, piano; Steinway Hall (Copland-Sessions Concert) [first public performance]. *See:* **B254**.

W102c 3 October 1953: Washington, D.C.; American University; Lamar Stringfield, flute and Jean Robinson Callaghan, piano; Clendenen Auditorium.

W103 *PIANO TRIO IN F (Op. 1)* (1915); Ms. in Estate.

This early work was composed in Kansas City while Bennett was a student of Carl Busch.

W104 *QUINTETTE ("Psychiatry")* [accordion and string quartet] (1962 or 1963); Ms. ??? (copy in LC); *See:* **B416**.

1.   Recitativo, con brio (. . . trying to find oneself . . .)
2.   Andante e mesto (. . . not loved and wanted . . .)
3.   Allegro (. . . crazy, mixed-up kid . . .)
4.   Vivo (. . . well adjusted—to what?)

Premiere

W104a 21 April 1963; Kansas City, MO; Joan Cochran, accordion; Hugh Brown and Helen Hollander, violins; Lucinda Gladics, viola; Catherine Farley, cello; University of Missouri-Kansas City; Pearson Hall. *See:* **B416**.

W105 *RHYTHM SERENADE* [solo percussion: triangle, wood block, 4 temple blocks, 2 suspended cymbals, 2 cowbells, 2 snare drums, bass drum with foot pedal] (1968) [pub. in *Studies in Solo Percussion*, ed. by Ralph Satz, Chappell, 1968]; 1 -1/2 min.

W106 *RONDO CAPRICCIOSO* [four flutes] (1916) [New York Flute Club, 1922; revised edition, Chappell, 1962]; 6 min.; Ms. of revision in LC; *See:* **D22**; **B419**.

Premiere

W106a 1916 or 1917: New York; Georges Barrère, William Kincaid, George Posselt and Lamar Stringfield, flutes.

Other selected performances

W106b 6 February 1942: New York [radio broadcast]; members of WOR Orchestra; probably with Robert Russell Bennett conducting ["Notebook" program]. *See:* [**B194**].

W106c 21 March 1976: New York; Eleanor Lawrence, Wendy Heckler-Denbaum, Susan Stewart, and Sue Ann Kahn, flutes; CAMI Hall. *See:* **B419**.

Barrère and other members of the New York Flute Club programmed the piece often in the 1920s. Bennett later made an adaptation for two flutes and two clarinets [**W106b**].

ROSE VARIATIONS [trumpet or cornet with band or piano acc.]
See: **W68**.

W107 *SEVEN POSTCARDS TO OLD FRIENDS* [flute/viola/piano] (probably 1966); Ms. in Estate.

Written for the Musical Arts Trio: John Wummer, flute; David Sackson, violin and viola; Joseph Wollman, piano.

W108 *SIX SOUVENIRS* [two flutes/piano] (1948); Ms. ???

Premiere

W108a 29 February 1948: New York; John Wummer and Mildred Hunt Wummer, flutes; Robert Russell Bennett, piano; Chamber Music Hall, City Center.

W109 *SONATA FOR VIOLIN AND PIANO* (1927); 25 min.; Ms. ???

Premiere

W109a Summer 1928: Paris; Société Musical Indépendante; (unknown violinist; Bennett was likely the pianist).

W110 *A SONG SONATA* [violin/piano] (1947) ["to Benno and Sylvia Rabinof"] [Chappell, 1958]; 15 min.; Ms. in Estate (copy in LC); *See:* D3, **D5, D23, D27, D30, D46; B446 - 454**.

1.   Quiet and philosophic
2.   Same tempo, but belligerent
3.   Slow and lonely
4.   Madly dancing
5.   Gracefully strolling

Premiere

W110a 24 November 1947; New York; Benno Rabinof, violin; Sylvia Rabinof, piano. *See:* **B447, B451 - 453**.

Other selected performance

W110b 15 February 1955: New York; Jascha Heifetz, violin; Brooks

Smith, piano; Carnegie Hall [movements 2, 3, and 4]. *See:* **B4, B448 - 449, B454.**

W111 *STRING QUARTET* (1956) ["to the memory of Hugo Grunwald"]; Ms. in Estate; *See:* **B455 -456.**
1.   con brio, moderato in tempo
2.   andante alla serenata
3.   rondo allegro con ritmo

Premiere

W111a 13 December 1956: New York; Guilet String Quartet; Brooklyn Academy of Music. *See:* **B455.**

Other selected performance

W111b 22 December 1958: New York; Guilet String Quartet; Hunter College Assembly Hall (NAACC concert). *See:* **B456.**

W112 *SUITE* [violin/piano] [Chappell, 1945]; Ms. ???
1.   Warm up
2.   Serenade
3.   March
4.   Blues
5.   Hoe down

W113 *SUITE FOR FLUTE AND B FLAT CLARINET* (1973) [Warner Brothers, 1973]; 9 min.; Ms. ???
1.   toe dance
2.   medium bounce
3.   panama
4.   cowboy song
5.   low-down-hoedown
6.   Strauss waltz
7.   horse race

Selected performance

W113a 8 July 1973: Palo Alto, CA; Stanford University; William Mencken, clarinet and Joseph Bruneau, flute [possibly the premiere?].

W114 *TEMA SPORCA CON VARIAZONI* [two pianos, four hands] (1946); Ms.: Vera Appleton; *See:* **B493 - 496.**

Premiere

W114a 17 October 1946: New York; Vera Appleton and Michael Field, pianos; Town Hall. *See:* **B493 - 496.**

[W115] *THEME AND VARIATIONS* [violin/piano]—*See CONCERT VARIATIONS ON A CROONER'S THEME* **[W15]**.

W116 *TOY SYMPHONY* [flute/oboe/clarinet/horn/bassoon] (1928); 18 min., Ms. ???; *See:* **B512.**

Premiere

W116a 7 January 1931: Philadelphia; Society for Contemporary Music; Alexander Smallens, conductor. *See:* **B512.**

Bennett composed the piece while in Paris. Its premiere was delayed because it had been submitted to the Elizabeth Sprague Coolidge Prize competition (which it didn't win), limited to yet-unperformed works. According to **[B512]**, the performers at the first performance were the (unnamed) principals from the Philadelphia Orchestra.

W117 *TRIO* [flute/cello/piano] (1950 or 1951); Ms. ???; *See:* **B514.**

Premiere

W117a 12 February 1951: New York; Helimi Trio—Mildred Hunt Wummer, flute; Livis Manucci, cello; Helmuth Wolfes, piano; Town Hall. *See:* **B514.**

W118 *TRIO FOR HARP, CELLO AND FLUTE (SONATINA)* (c. 1960); Ms. ???
1.   slow (alle breve)
2.   andante semplice (alla berceuse)
3.   rondo

Selected performance

W118a 6 February 1961: Bloomfield Hills [Detroit], MI; New York Concert Trio; Cranbrook House (Cranbrook Music Guild).

Written for the New York Concert Trio: Cynthia Otis, harp; Ardyth Alton, cello; Paul Boyer, flute.

W119 *A VALENTINE* [flute/harp/string quartet] (1942); Ms. ???

Premiere

W119a 13 February 1942 (Valentine's Day): New York [radio broadcast]; members of WOR Orchestra; Robert Russell Bennett, conductor ["Notebook" program].

W120 *WATER MUSIC* [string quartet] (1937); Ms. in Estate (copy in LC); *See:* **B527 - 528.**

Premiere

W120a 20 April 1941: New York [radio broadcast]; members of WOR Orchestra ["Notebook" program].

Other selected performance

W120b 12 May 1945: New York; Walden Quartet (Homer Schmitt and Bernard Goodman, violins; George Poinar, viola; Robert Swenson, cello); Festival of Contemporary Music, McMillin Academic Theatre, Columbia University [first public performance]. *See:* **B527 - 528.**

The piece is based on the "Sailor's Hornpipe."

KEYBOARD WORKS [W121 - 139]

For solo piano unless otherwise noted.

W121 *A BELASCO SONATA* (1917) [by David Belasco, Winifred Merrill, and Robert Russell Bennett]; Ms.: New York Public Library.

Belasco was among the most prominent theatrical producers of the early 20th century; Merrill, who ran a girls'school, Oaksmere, in New York, became Bennett's mother-in-law in 1919.

W122 *CELEBRATION FESTIVE (dance joyeuse for piano solo)* (c. 1915); Ms. in Estate (copy in LC).

W123 *ECHOES OF PALERMO* (1913) [pub. in *Etude* 33:9, September 1913, p. 652); 3 min.; Ms. ???

W124 *A FLEETING FANCY* (c. 1914); c. 4 min.; Ms. in Estate.

W125 *FOUR NOCTURNES* [accordion] (1959) ["to my friend Tony"]; [Chappell, 1960]; Ms. ???
   1.   Moderato alla serenata
   2.   Un piu blu
   3.   Lento e pianissimo
   4.   Allegro

Premiere

W125a 21 November 1959: New York; Carmen Carrozza, accordion; Carnegie Recital Hall.

Commissioned by the American Accordionists' Association.

IDA'S FOX TROT [piano roll, possibly spurious] *See:* **D50?**

W126 *JUNE TWILIGHT* (1912 or 1913) [pub. in *Etude* 33:7, July 1913, p. 500-501); 3 min.; Ms. ???

W127 *MELODY* (c. 1911-1915); 3 min.; Ms. in Estate.

W128 *NOCTURNE IN A FLAT* (1911); c. 4 min.; Ms. in Estate.

W129 *THE OAKSMERE SPIRIT (a march for piano solo)* (c. 1917-1919); c. 4 min.; Ms. in Estate.

This was probably composed while Bennett was teaching at Oaksmere, the private school run by Winifred Merrill in New York.

W130 *SEVEN FOX TROTS IN CONCERT FORM* (1928); Ms. in Estate.

Premiere

W130a 30 November 1932: New York; Jose Iturbi, piano; Carnegie Hall [selections].

W131 *SONATA IN G FOR ORGAN* (1929) ["to Barrett Spake"]; [Cos Cob, 1934]; Ms. in Estate (copy in LC); *See:* [D21], **D25**; **B26**.
1.   Con fuoco
2.   Allegretto grazioso
3.   Rondo: allegro molto

W132 *SONATA (RAGTIME)* (early 1970s?); Ms. in Estate.

W133 [First] *SONATINA* (1941?); Ms. ???

Published references to this work are limited to listings in some works lists; there are no accounts of public performances.

W134 *SECOND SONATINA* (1944); 9 min.; ["to M. P."]; Ms. in Estate; *See:* D14; B432 - 439.

Selected performances

W134a late Fall 1944: Los Angeles; Jakob Gimpel, piano [may be first performance]. *See:* **B439.**

W134b 13 December 1944: New York; Jakob Gimpel, piano; Town Hall. *See:* **B434 - 435, B437.**

W134c 1 October 1945: New York; Milton Kaye, piano; Town Hall. *See:* **B432 - 433, B436, B438.**

W135 *SPIRIT OF THE DANCE* (1914); Ms. in Estate.

W136 *SPRING SPIRITS (scherzo caprice)*(c. 1914-1915); Ms. in Estate.

Submitted to "Miss Anna Pavlova's dance music contest."

TEMA SPORCA CON VARIAZONI [two pianos]; *See:* **W114.**

W137 *TRAVEL SKETCHES* (1916); Ms. in Estate (copy in LC).
1. in a Missouri woodland
2. rolling fields
3. Indiana villages

The three movements are descriptive of Bennett's journey from Kansas to New York City in 1916, and may have been composed along the way.

W138 *"VU (See in Paris)" (20 etudes in miniature, from the 20 arrondissements* [precincts] *of Paris)* (1929) [Editions Raoul Breton, Paris, 1934]; c. 20 min.; Ms. ???; *See:* **D44; B70, B520 - 526.**
1. Louvre; 2. Bourse; 3. Temple; 4. Hôtel de Ville; 5. Panthéon; 6. Luxembourg; 7. Palais Bourbon; 8. Elysée; 9. Opéra; 10. Enclos St. Laurent; 11. Popincourt; 12. Reuilly; 13. Gobelins; 14. Observatoire;

15. Vaugirard; 16. Passy; 17. Batignolles; 18. Montmartre;
19. Buttes-Chaumont; 20. Ménilmontant.

Premiere

W138a 30 November 1932: New York; Jose Iturbi, piano; Carnegie Hall [selections]. *See:* **B70, B525 - 526.**

Other selected performances

W138b 29 April 1935: Philadelphia; Jose Iturbi, piano; Academy of Music [selections?]. *See:* **B522.**

W138c 25 February 1938: Rochester; Jose Iturbi, piano; Eastman Theatre [selections]. *See:* **B524.**

W138d 20 January 1942: New York; Amparo Navarro, piano; Town Hall [selections]. *See:* **B520 - 521, B523.**

W139 *WILDWOOD (scherzo for piano)* (c. 1914-1915); c. 5 min.; Ms. in Estate.

SONGS [W140 - 148]

All are for voice and piano unless otherwise noted.

W140 *FOUR SONGS (TEASDALE)* (1928); Ms. in Estate; *See:* **B313 - 315.**
1. The tune
2. I could snatch a day
3. On the south downs
4. An end

Premiere

W140a 1 March 1931: New York; Radiana Pazmor, mezzo-soprano; Robert Russell Bennett, piano; Art Centre (League of Composers concert). *See:* **B313 - 315.**

W141 *KISSELBERRY PIE* [popular song; words by Harold Orlob] (1956) [Chappell, 1956]; Ms. ???

W142 *MY GARDEN* [text: Thomas Edward Brown] (c. 1916); ["to Miss Eunice Sexton"]; Ms. in Estate.

Written to be submitted to an *Etude* magazine composition contest.

W143 *MY STAR* [text: John Browning] (c. 1917); Ms. in Estate.

W144 *ROMANCE* [text: John Moroney] (1917); Ms. in Estate.

W145 *SEVEN LOVE SONGS* [w/ukelele accompaniment—or piano *ad lib.*] (1929) [Harms, 1931]; Ms. ???

W146 *SONATINE POUR SOPRAN ET HARPE* (1947); Ms. in Estate; *See:* **B440 - 445**.

Premiere

W146a 1 October 1947: New York; Jean Love, soprano and Laura Newell, harp; Town Hall. *See:* **B441 - 445**.

Other performance

W146b 20 December 1950: New York; Florence Vickland, soprano and Margaret Ross, harp; Times Hall. *See:* **B440**.

The text, in French, is by Bennett.

W147 *SUE ANN* [popular song; words by Bennett] (1942) [Chappell/Harms, 1942); Ms. ???; *See:* [**B131**].

W148 *THREE CHAUCER POEMS* [women's voice or voices with string
quartet or piano acc.] (1926) ["to Percy E. Fletcher"]; Ms. in Estate;
See: **B498 - 499**.
1. captivitity
2. rejection
3. escape

Premiere

W148a [probably Spring] 1927: Paris; Société Musicale Indépendante;
personnel unknown.

Other selected performances

W148b 30 April 1932: Saratoga Springs, NY; Ada MacLeish, soprano;
Hans Lange Quartet—H. Lange and A. Schuller, violins; Z. Kurthy,
viola; P. Such, cello; (Yaddo Festival of Contemporary Music).
See: **B498 - 499**.

W148c 18 December 1932: New York; Women's University Glee Club.
See: [**B497**].

WORKS FOR RADIO [W149 - 173]

Works listed in this section, for orchestra with or without vocal soloists and
chorus, are those pieces written specifically for broadcast presentation on one
of the radio programs for which Bennett was serving as musical director.
They tend to have been designed for the artificial balances possible using one
or more microphones (alto flute with full orchestra in the *Grey Flute Song*, for
example), are of a somewhat lighter nature than most of Bennett's concert
works, and were generally *not* played on the concert stage.

W149 *ALONG THE NAVAJO TRAIL (double concerto for bass clarinet and
temple blocks)* [orchestra] (1945); Ms. in Estate; *See:* **D47**.

Premiere

W149a 9 October 1945: New York; Ford Symphony Orchestra; Robert Russell Bennett, conductor [Ford Motor Co. "Stars of the Future" program]. *See:* **D47**.

The piece satirizes Ferde Grofé's "On The Trail" from his 1931 *Grand Canyon Suite*.

W150 *BETTY WAVE* [narrator and orchestra] (1944); Ms. ???

Premiere

W150a 11 June 1944: New York; WOR Orchestra; Carol Thurston, narrator [the WOR "Music for an Hour" program].

W151 *CANZONETTA FOR STRINGS* [string orchestra] (1942?); Ms. in Estate.

Premiere

W151a 4 July 1942: New York; WOR Orchestra; Robert Russell Bennett, conductor ["Notebook" program].

W152 *COWBOY OVERTURE* [orchestra] (1945) ["to a son-in-law"]; c. 5 min.; Ms. in Estate (copy in LC); *See:* **D47**.

Premiere

W152a 2 February 1945: New York; Ford Symphony Orchestra; Robert Russell Bennett, conductor [Ford Motor Co. "Stars of the Future" program]. *See:* **D47**.

W153 *FIVE DANCES FOR THE CAMP FIRE GIRLS* [orchestra] (1942); Ms. in Estate.

Premiere

W153a 20 March 1942: New York; WOR Orchestra; Robert Russell Bennett, conductor ["Notebook" program].

W154 *GIVE ME LIBERTY* [narrator and orchestra] (1942); Ms. in Estate.

Premiere

W154a 20 March 1942: New York; WOR Orchestra; Robert Russell Bennett, conductor ["Notebook" program].

This is Bennett's setting of Patrick Henry's "give me liberty or give me death" speech. Bennett may have been observing its "anniversary," as it was delivered by Henry on 23 March 1775.

W155 *THE GREY FLUTE SONG (based on a Hopi Indian song)* [alto flute and orchestra] (1940); 2, 2, 3 (3rd alt. b. cl.), 1 sax - 2, 3, 2, 0 - perc. (1), hp., pf. - stgs.; 6 min.; Ms. in Estate; *See:* **D41**.

Premiere

W155a 17 November 1940: New York: WOR Orchestra; Robert Russell Bennett, conductor. *See:* **D41**.

This piece was written for the first of the "Notebook" radio shows.

W156 *KREUTZER DUO* [orchestra—or string orchestra?] (1941); Ms. ???

Premiere

W156a 20 April 1941: New York; WOR Orchestra; Robert Russell Bennett, conductor ["Notebook" program].

The piece is apparently an elaboration upon one or more of Rodolphe Kreutzer's violin studies.

W157 *MILL POTATOES* [orchestra] (1940 or 1941); Ms. ???; *See:* **B16**.

Premiere

W157a Early 1941: New York [radio broadcast]; WOR Orchestra; Robert Russell Bennett, conductor ["Notebook" program]. *See:* **B16**.

W158 *MUSIC BOX OPERA #1 (CLEMENTINE)* (1940); c. 25 min.; Ms. in Estate (copy in LC); *See:* **B395**.

Premiere

W158a 8 December 1940: New York; WOR Orchestra and Chorus; vocal soloists unknown [probably the same as in **W158b**, below]; Robert Russell Bennett, conductor ["Notebook" program]. *See:* **B395**.

Other performance

W158b 13 April 1941: New York; WOR Orchestra and Chorus; Jean Merrill, soprano; Pauline Pierce, mezzo; Robert Stuart, tenor; Jack Kitty, bass; Robert Russell Bennett, conductor ["Notebook" program].

W159 *MUSIC BOX OPERA #2 (THE MAN ON THE FLYING TRAPEEZE)* (1941); c. 25 min.; Ms. in Estate (copy in LC); *See:* **B80**, [**B188**],

Premiere

W159a 23 March 1941: New York; WOR Orchestra; Jean Merrill, Robert Stewart and Hardesty Johnson, vocal soloists; Robert Russell Bennett, conductor ["Notebook" program].

Other performance

W159b 7 July 1941: New York; WOR Orchestra; vocal soloists probably same as **W159a**; Robert Russell Bennett, conductor ["Notebook" program].

W160 *MUSIC BOX OPERA #3 (THE BAND PLAYED ON)* (1941); c. 25 min.; Ms. in Estate (copy in LC).

Premiere

W160a 4 May 1941: New York; WOR Orchestra; vocal soloists unknown; Robert Russell Bennett, conductor ["Notebook" program].

W161 *MUSIC BOX OPERA #4 (KEFOOZELUM, METHUSELUM)* (1941); c. 25 min.; Ms. in Estate (copy in LC).

Premiere

W161a 30 May 1941: New York; WOR Orchestra; vocal soloists unknown; Robert Russell Bennett, conductor ["Notebook" program].

This is evidently Bennett's setting of Marion L. Langham's children's story, *The High Cockalorum of Kafoozalem* [sic] (J. B. Lippincott, 1941).

W162 *MUSIC BOX OPERA #5 (MY OLD KENTUCKY HOME)* (1941); c. 25 min.; Ms. in Estate (copy in LC); *See:* **B396**.

Premiere

W162a early Fall 1941: New York; WOR Orchestra; vocal soloists unknown; Robert Russell Bennett, conductor ["Notebook" program]. *See:* **B396**.

W163 *PRAYER FOR FRITZ KREISLER* [orchestra?] (1941?); Ms. ???

This work is mentioned only in the works list in *Goss* [**B179**]. Kreisler, a close friend of Bennett's, was involved in a traffic accident on 26 April 1941 that permanently damaged his vision and hearing and required an extended convalescence. The *Prayer* was likely performed on one of the "Notebook" shows in mid-1941.

W164 *RAILROAD CANTATA (on "Casey Jones")* [vocal quartet and orchestra] (1941); Ms. in Estate (copy in LC).

W164a 27 June 1941: New York; WOR Orchestra; vocal soloists unknown; Robert Russell Bennett, conductor ["Notebook" program].

Similar in style to his "Music Box Operas."

W165 *SIX PARAGRAPHS FROM SODOM BY THE SEA* (1941); c. 18 min.; Ms. in Estate (copy in LC); *See:* **B431**.
1.   The Lying Pirates
2.   Righteous Wrath
3.   Weber and Fields
4.   Luna Park
5.   The Old Mill
6.   Bathing Beauties

W165a 21 July 1941: New York; WOR Orchestra; Robert Russell Bennett, conductor ["Notebook" program]. *See:* **B431**.

Based on a contemporary essay of the same name about New York's Coney Island by New York journalists Jo Ranson and Oliver Pilat.

W166 *A SMATTERING OF IGNORANCE* [five clarinets and strings] (1940); c. 5 min.; Ms. ???; *See:* **D45**.

W166a 22 December 1940: New York [radio broadcast]; WOR Orchestra; Robert Russell Bennett, conductor ["Notebook" program]. *See:*D44.

The piece opened a "Notebook" radio broadcast on which Oscar Levant was featured as guest pianist and composer. The title is taken from Levant's then-recently-published memoirs of his association with Gershwin. Aural evidence suggests that one or two bass clarinets are used during the course of the work.

W167 *A STUDY IN ORCHESTRATION* (1941); Ms. ???; *See:* [**B188**].

Premiere

W167a 6 April 1941; New York; WOR Orchestra; Robert Russell Bennett, conductor ["Notebook" program]. *See:* [**B188**].

The piece was a demonstration of the Broadway arranger's craft, beginning with a hypothetical songwriter's "one-finger" piano melody and ending with an elaborate full orchestration. The unnamed tune used as the subject for the exercise was evidently Bennett's own, as this broadcast took place during the 1941 ASCAP strike.

W168 *SYMPHONY ON COLLEGE TUNES* [Fourth Symphony] (1941); Ms. ???

Premiere

W168a 24 November 1941: New York [radio broadcast]; WOR Orchestra; Robert Russell Bennett, conductor ["Notebook" program].

The piece, based on "fight songs" of a number of American colleges, was written at WOR's request as part of its celebration of "Football Day," 1941.

W169 *THEME AND VARIATIONS ("FATHER, DEAR FATHER")* [reader and orchestra] (1941); Ms. in Estate (copy in LC).

Premiere

W169a 6 June 1941: New York; WOR Orchestra; Robert Russell Bennett, conductor ["Notebook" program].

W170 *THEME AND VARIATIONS ("MY LOST YOUTH")* [reader and orchestra] (1941); Ms. ???; *See:* [**B188**].

Premiere

W170a 30 March 1941: New York; WOR Orchestra; Robert Russell Bennett, conductor ["Notebook" program]. *See:* [**B188**].

Stanzas of the Longfellow poem were read between each of the individual orchestral variations.

W171 *VOCAL VARIATIONS ON "THE YOUNG OYSTERMAN"* [mezzo-soprano, baritone and orchestra] (1945); Ms. in Estate (copy in LC); *See:* **D47**.

Premiere

W171a ??? 1945: New York; Ford Symphony Orchestra; probably Kay Armen or Jo Stafford, mezzo-soprano; Lawrence Brooks, baritone; Robert Russell Bennett, conductor [Ford Motor Co. "Stars of the Future" program]. *See:* **D47**.

W172 *THE WEDDING SEXTET* [SATB soloists, oboe and alto saxophone and orchestra] (1941 or 1942); 24 min.; Ms. in Estate (copy in LC).

According to Bennett's annotations on the score, the piece was performed on one of the "Notebook" broadcasts, though the precise date is not known; the piece is not mentioned in any published radio program listings.

W173 *WOR ANNIVERSARY OVERTURE* [orchestra] (1947); Ms. ???; *See:* **B529**.

Premiere

W173a 22 February 1947; New York; WOR Orchestra; Robert Russell Bennett, conductor. *See:* **B529**.

Commissioned by WOR, it was composed to celebrate the twenty-fifth anniversary of the station's founding.

OTHER COMPOSITIONS [W174 - 175]

W174 *VICTORY AT SEA* (score for NBC television series, 1952-1953); Ms. in Estate (Copy in LC); credited as "Original Musical Score by Richard Rodgers; Music Arranged by Robert Russell Bennett, conducting the NBC Symphony Orchestra." *See:* **D34; B59, B75, B515 -519.**

The Episodes/Air Dates: "Design for War" (26 Oct. 1952); "The Pacific Boils Over" (2 Nov.); "Sealing the Breach" (9 Nov.); "Midway is East" (23 Nov.); "The Mediterranean Mosaic" (30 Nov.); "Guadalcanal" (7 Dec.); "Rings Around Raboul" (14 Dec.); "Mare Nostrum" (21 Dec.); "Sea and Sand" (28 Dec.); "Beneath the Southern Cross" (4 Jan. 1953); "Magnetic North" (11 Jan.); "Conquest of Micronesia" (18 Jan.); "Melanesian Nightmare" (25 Jan.); "Roman Renaissance" (1 Feb.); "D-Day" (8 Feb.); "Killers and the Killed" (15 Feb.); "The Turkey Shoot" (22 Feb.); "Two If By Sea" (1 Mar.); "The Battle for Leyte Gulf" (8 Mar.); "The Return of the Allies" (15 Mar.); "Full Fathom Five" (22 Mar.); "The Fate of Europe" (29 Mar.); "Target Suribachi" (5 Apr.); "The Road to Mandalay" (12 Apr.); "Suicide for Glory" (19 Apr.); "Design for Peace" (26 Apr. 1953).

The twenty-six episodes, each calling for about 26 minutes of orchestral score, resulted in Bennett's scoring about 11-1/4 *hours* of music for the series from Rodgers' thematic sketches. A theatrical version of the series, again orchestrated and conducted by Bennett, was released in 1954.

W175 *A TRIBUTE TO JAMES WHITCOMB RILEY* [orchestra] (1949); Ms. ???; *See:* **B513.**

Premiere

W175a 12-13 November 1949: Indianapolis, IN; Indianapolis Symphony; Fabien Sevitzky, conductor; Murat Theatre. *See:* **B513.**

The piece, a collaborative tribute to Indiana poet Whitcomb on his 100th birthday, consists of a sequence of "musical sentences" written by Bennett, Frederick Jacobi, Morton Gould, Paul Creston, Paul White, Indiana songwriter Hoagy Carmichael, Sevitzky, and Deems Taylor.

Discography

COMMERCIAL RECORDINGS [D1 - 34]

This list includes all commercial recordings of Bennett's compositions—
and the *Victory At Sea* suites—whether or not currently "in print."
Recordings of his Broadway "symphonic pictures" and other arrangements,
along with original-cast theater scores, are not included. Date of release is
given for most recordings; **D1** through **D34** are all 12" LP's unless otherwise
noted.

Though most of these recordings contain non-Bennett works as well, only
the Bennett compositions included on each disc, tape, or compact disc are
listed.

D1   American Wind Symphony AWS-109 (1985?); *CONCERTO GROSSO
FOR WOODWIND QUINTET AND WIND ORCHESTRA*; American
Wind Symphony Orchestra; Robert Austin Boudreau, cond. [compact
disc]

D2   Bay Cities 1008 (1989): *CONCERTO FOR VIOLIN*; Louis Kaufman,
violin; London Symphony Orchestra; Bernard Herrmann, cond.
(reissue of CONCERTO recording on D3). [compact disc]

D3   Citadel CT-6005 (1976): Louis Kaufman, violin; *HEXAPODA* and *A
SONG SONATA* (w/Annette Kaufman, piano); *CONCERTO FOR*

VIOLIN with London Symphony Orchestra; Bernard Herrmann, cond. (*CONCERTO* recorded 1956, others in 1975). *See:* **B210, B219, 450, D2, D23.**

D4   Columbia 70727D (1941): *HEXAPODA*; Louis Kaufman, violin and Robert Russell Bennett, piano. [12", 78 rpm] *See:* **B325, B333, D11, D26.**

D5   Concert Hall CHS-1062 (1951): *A SONG SONATA*; Louis Kaufman, violin and Theodore Saidenberg, piano.

D6   Cornell CUWE-4 (1971): *SUITE OF OLD AMERICAN DANCES*; Cornell Univ. Wind Ensemble; Marice Stith, cond. *See:* **B463.**

D7   Crystal S-363 (1978): *ROSE VARIATIONS*; David Hickman, trumpet and Pauline Soderholm, piano. *See:* **[B13]**.

D8   Decca DA-23659 (in set DA-454) (1940s): *HEXAPODA*; Jascha Heifetz, violin and Emmanuel Bay, piano. [12", 78 rpm] *See:* **D17.**

D9   Decca DL-9760 (1955): *HEXAPODA*; Jascha Heifetz, violin and Milton Kaye, piano. *See:* **B322, B328.**

D10   Decca DL79093: *THE COMING OF CHRIST* (soundtrack of the NBC production, first telecast 21 December 1960); orchestra cond. by Robert Russell Bennett [*See* Appendix B, Film/Television Scores].

D11   Discopaedia/Masters of the Bow MB-1032 (late 1970s): *HEXAPODA*; Louis Kaufman, violin and Robert Russell Bennett, piano. (reissue of **D4**)

D12   Everest LPBR 6063 (1960): *A COMMEMORATION SYMPHONY*; Pittsburgh Symphony Orchestra; Mendelssohn Choir of Pittsburgh (in last mvt.); William Steinberg, cond. *See:* **B197 - 198.**

D13   Fidelity Sound Recordings FSR-1209 (1958): *SUITE OF OLD AMERICAN DANCES*; College of the Pacific Band; cond. ????

D14   Golden Crest CRDG 4195 (1978?): *SECOND SONATINA*; Milton Kaye, piano.

D15   Kosei Records (Japan) KOCD 3562 (1988): *SYMPHONIC SONGS FOR BAND*; Tokyo Kosei Wind Orchestra; Frederick Fennell, cond. [compact disc]

D16   London OS 26442 (1975): *THE FUN AND FAITH OF WILLIAM BILLINGS, AMERICAN*; National Symphony Orchestra; University of Maryland Chorus; Antal Dorati, cond.

D17   MCA MCAD 42212 (1988): *HEXAPODA*; Jascha Heifetz, violin and Milton Kaye, piano. (reissue of **D8**) [compact disc]

D18   Mercury MG 40006 (1953); MG 50079 (1957); SRI 75086 (1977): *SUITE OF OLD AMERICAN DANCES*; Eastman Wind Ensemble; Frederick Fennell, cond.

D19   Mercury MG50220, SR 90220 (1960): *SYMPHONIC SONGS FOR BAND*; Eastman Wind Ensemble; Frederick Fennell, cond. *See:* **B467, B472, B474**.

D20   Mercury MG-50361, SR-90361 (1964): "Celebration" (final movement of *SYMPHONIC SONGS FOR BAND*); Eastman Wind Ensemble; Frederick Fennell, cond.

[D21]   Mirrosonic DRE-1012 (1958): *SONATA FOR ORGAN*; David Craighead, organ. [though listed in several discographies, this recording—from a London recital performance—was never released, according to Craighead]

D22   Musical Heritage Society MHS 3578 (1977): *RONDO CAPRICCIOSO*; Eleanor Lawrence, Wendy Heckler-Denbaum, Susan Stewart, and Sue Ann Kahn, flutes.

D23   Musical Heritage Society MHS 3974 (1978): *HEXAPODA; A SONG SONATA; CONCERTO FOR VIOLIN*; (reissue of **D3**). *See:* **B450**.

D24   New World NW 211 (1977): *SYMPHONIC SONGS FOR BAND*; Northwestern University Symphonic Wind Ensemble; John P. Paynter, cond. *See:* **B473**.

D25   Organ Historical Society F-MS-I-II (1965): *Allegretto Grazioso* from *SONATA FOR ORGAN*; Melville Smith, organ.

D26   Orion OC 800 (c. 1980): *HEXAPODA*; Louis Kaufman, violin and Robert Russell Bennett, piano. (reissue of **D4**) [cassette] *See:* **B450**.

D27   Orion ORS 82439 (1982): *A SONG SONATA*; Malan-Sutherland Duo (Roy Malan, violin and Robin Sutherland, piano). *See:* **B446**.

D28   Point Park College KP-102 (1969): *PICKLE OVERTURE* and *THE PICKLE*; American Wind Symphony Orchestra; Robert Austin Boudreau, cond.

D29   RCA LM-1802 (1954), SRL-12-1 (1958): *AN ADVENTURE IN HIGH FIDELITY*; members of the NBC Symphony Orchestra; Robert Russell Bennett, cond. [SRL-12-1 was 4-track tape cartridge]

D30   RCA LM-2382 (1960): *A SONG SONATA*; Jascha Heifetz, violin and Brooks Smith, piano. (mvts. 2, 3, 4 only) *See:* [B13].

D31   RCA LMP-1133 (1955): "Western One-Step" (final movement of *SUITE OF OLD AMERICAN DANCES*); Cities Service Band of America; Paul Lavalle, cond.

D32   RCA LOC/LSO-1055 (1960): *NOT SO LONG AGO* (soundtrack of the NBC production, first telecast 19 February 1960); orchestra cond. by Robert Russell Bennett [*See* Appendix B, Film/Television Scores].

D33   RCA LSC-2445 (1960): *ARMED FORCES SUITE*; RCA Victor Symphony Orchestra and Symphonic Band; Robert Russell Bennett, cond. *See:* B189 - 190.

D34   RCA (2) VCS-7064: *VICTORY AT SEA* (Three suites: "The Pacific," "The Atlantic and Other Oceans," and "The End in Sight"; NBC Symphony Orchestra; Robert Russell Bennett, cond.

Additional recordings of *VICTORY AT SEA* music, conducted by Bennett, are on RCA LM- 1779 (1954), LM-2226 (1958), and various re-releases of these, with many duplications between them. Also, the published orchestral suite has been recorded by several other orchestras/conductors.

ARCHIVAL RECORDINGS [D35 - 49]

This is a listing of radio air checks and researchers' interviews with Bennett. They may be listened to at the Motion Picture, Broadcasting and Recorded Sound Division Library of Congress (**LC**) or the New York Public Library's Rodgers and Hammerstein Archive of Recorded Sound (**NYPL**), as noted.

D35　*CHESTER*: Rec. 21 October 1946; apparently an aircheck of **W80a**. (**LC**: LWO 9670 R9 B10)

D36　*CONCERTO FOR VIOLIN*: Louis Kaufman, violin; Bernard Herrmann, conductor; CBS Orchestra. Rec. probably mid-1940s. (**LC**: NCP 1442/1443)

D37　*CONCERTO GROSSO (Sketches From An American Theater)*: Eastman School Senior Symphony Orchestra; Howard Hanson, conductor. This must be the 24 April 1945 performance [**W14d**]. (**LC**: NCP 1151/1152; also **NYPL**: 16-p-424, catalogued as *Sketches From...*)

D38　*CONCERTO GROSSO FOR WIND QUINTET AND WIND ORCHESTRA*: Eastman Wind Ensemble; Interlochen Arts Quintet; A. Clyde Roller, conductor; rec. 30 April 1964. (**LC**: LWO 17707 R15 B2)

D39　*EIGHT ETUDES*: CBS Symphony Orchestra; Howard Barlow, conductor. This is a partial recording of the 17 July 1938 premiere, **W18a**. (**LC**: 5242 R2 A2)

D40　"THE FORD SHOW": Bennett's weekly half-hour program, sponsored by the Ford Motor Company, which ran weekly from 8 December 1944 to 25 December 1945 on NBC radio. **LC** has an apparently complete collection of airchecks, which should include **W148, 151,** and **170**, as well as various American folk song arrangments (not included in the Works and Performances section) for orchestra written by Bennett specifically for performance on this program. (LWO 7364)

D41　*THE FOUR FREEDOMS*: probably NBC Orchestra; Frank Black, conductor. (**LC**: NCP 1186/1187 and B-13 R3 A1; possibly two different performances; at least one is almost certainly the 26 September 1943 premiere, **W19a**)

D42　*THE GREY FLUTE SONG*: WOR Orchestra; Robert Russell Bennett, conductor. Aircheck of **W154a**, the 17 November 1940 "Notebook" broadcast. (**NYPL**: 10"-1449; also included is Schoenberg's *Pierrot Lunaire*, same program/personnel/date.)

D43　*HEXAPODA*: Louis Kaufman, violin; Robert Russell Bennett, piano. Dated 21 October 1946. (**LC**: IWO 9670 R9 B9)

D44 *MARCH FOR AMERICA*: San Francisco Symphony Orchestra; Alfred Wallenstein, conductor. Probably 1942 or 1943. (**LC**: NCP 1161/1162; also **NYPL**: 16-F-312)

D45 *A SMATTERING OF IGNORANCE*: WOR Orchestra; Robert Russell Bennett, conductor. Aircheck of the 22 December 1940 "Notebook" broadcast, **W165a**, with Bennett's guest Oscar Levant, who also plays three movements from Bennett's *VU*.

D46 *A SONG SONATA*: Louis Kaufman, violin; pianist unknown. (**LC**: LWO 12968 R4 B1)

D47 *SYMPHONY IN D FOR THE DODGERS*: An aircheck of either **W37a** or **W37b**; the recording is incomplete, but it does include the fourth movement, with "Red" Barber's narration. (**LC**: RWB 6851)

D48 Interview with Bennett by author Max Wilk, in preparation for his 1973 study of popular songwriters, *They' re Playing Our Song*. About 35 min. in length; Bennett recalls his associations with Kern, Berlin, Gershwin, and others. It was recorded in New York on 12 November 1971, perhaps at Bennett's apartment. (**NYPL** 10"-2156)

D49 Mary Margaret McBride's radio program of 3 May 1951; she interviews Gertrude Lawrence, Oscar Hammerstein II and Bennett about Rodgers and Hammerstein's new musical play, *The King and I*. (**LC**: RWA 1480)

PIANO ROLLS RECORDED BY BENNETT [D50?]

According to *Who is Who* [**B120**], Bennett recorded one or more piano rolls for Aeolian-Vocalion during his first years in New York. The Aeolian catalogs of the period list a "Bennett" (no first name given) as performer in only one instance—their July-August 1917 catalog:

[D50?] *IDA'S FOX TROT* [piano roll]; performer is listed simply as "Bennett"; performance is "played by the composer." Listed in Aeolian's July-August 1917 catalog as *Universal Hand-Played* #203047; its last known listing is in their January 1920 catalog as *Metro-Art* #203046. It can not be ascertained whether this is Robert Russell Bennett's work. Its first catalog appearance suggests that it was recorded shortly before July 1917—at which time Bennett had been in New York for about a year, but shortly before his entering the U. S. Army later in 1917.

Bibliography

GENERAL REFERENCES [B1 - 100]
BIOGRAPHICAL REFERENCES [B101 - 145]
WRITINGS BY ROBERT RUSSELL BENNETT [B146 - 163]
REFERENCES TO INDIVIDUAL WORKS [B164 - 531]

Titles of some New York newspapers are abbreviated as follows: *NYT* = *New York Times*; *NYH-T* = *New York Herald-Tribune*; *NYW-T* = *New York World Telegram*; *NYJ-A* = *New York Journal-American*.

GENERAL REFERENCES [B1 - 100]

B1 [American Film Institute]. *Catalog of Motion Pictures Produced in the United States*. New York: Bowker, 1971.
Includes detailed production information, credits, etc. concerning Bennett-scored Hollywood films (listed in Appendix B).

B2 Arvey, Verna. *In One Lifetime*. Fayetteville, AK: The University of Arkansas Press, 1984, 123.
Many details of Bennett's warm professional and personal relationship with composer William Grant Still as recalled by Still's wife.

B3 "ASCAP Goes On Air With List of Hits." *NYT*, 26 January 1941, 34.
Details of radio programming during the ASCAP strike that began in January 1941; a few weeks into the strike, Bennett was chosen to be musical director for an ASCAP-sponsored weekly program beginning late in January—the only radio program on which ASCAP songwriters' music was heard.

B4   Axelrod, Herbert R., ed. *Heifetz*. Neptune City, NJ: Paganiniana
      Publications, Inc., 1976.
      Contains reprints of many Heifetz concert reviews, including his
      performances of Bennett's *Hexapoda* [**W101b**] and *A Song Sonata*
      [**W110b**].

B5   B. C. "NAACC Concert: Town Hall, Nov. 15, 5:30." *Musical America*
      72:15 (1 December 1952), 27.
      Review of a concert of new music sponsored by the National
      Association for American Composers and Conductors. Article also
      gives an account of Bennett's introductory speech that evening (he was
      then president of the NAACC): "Mr. Bennett told members of the
      audience that each work they were to hear . . . was a deathless utterance
      written in the belief that it represented an advance in musical thought
      and was the equal, as a personal expression of the composer, of the
      works of Beethoven or Brahms. This last assertion may well have
      been true . . ."

B6   Beckerman, Bernard, comp. *ON STAGE: selected theater reviews from
      the New York Times, 1920-1970*. New York: Quadrangle, 1973.
      A comprehensive selection of reviews of plays and musicals produced
      in New York over five decades. Many of the shows for which Bennett
      did orchestrations are reviewed, though his work is not consistently
      given special mention.

B7   "Bennett, Bernstein to get ASMA Awards." *Variety*, 13 June 1979.
      Concerns his "Golden Score Award" from the American Society of
      Music Arrangers. *See:* **B162**.

B8   "Bennett is Honored by Composers' Unit." *NYT*, 17 February 1970, 34.
      An account of the NAACC's awarding of the Henry Hadley Medal to
      Bennett at their 16 February Alice Tully Hall concert in New York.

B9   Blitzstein, Marc. "Popular Music—An Invasion: 1923-1933." *Modern
      Music* 10:2 (January-February 1933), 96-102.
      An overview of the preceding decade's best and most influential
      musical comedies, popular songs, dance steps, etc. and their impact
      upon "serious" works. Bennett is praised for his scoring of "I've [*sic*]
      Got Rhythm" from Gershwin's *Girl Crazy*, "surely the high-water mark
      of a highly-developed, perfectly mature craft."

B10 Bordman, Gerald. *Jerome Kern: His Life And Music*. New York:
Oxford University Press, 1980.
Easily the most comprehensive and thoroughly-researched study of
Kern and his career. Includes many details of Bennett's professional
and personal relationship with Kern, along with accurate Broadway
and film credits.

B11 "The Boys That Make The Noise." *Time*, 5 July 1943, 65.
Discussion of leading Broadway arrangers of the period—Bennett,
Hans Spialek, Ted Royal, and Don Walker. While the Broadway stage
was given considerable attention by such national weeklies as *Time*,
Life, etc., at this time—songwriters included—this is one of the rare
mentions of the vital work of Bennett and his lesser-known colleagues.
The four featured orchestrators are pictured.

B12 Chapman, John. "Mainly About Manhattan." *NY Daily News*, 17 May,
1937.
He remarks: "A program credit, instead of stating 'Orchestrations by
Russell Bennett,' should read: 'You can thank Mr. Bennett for the
music sounding nice. All he had to start with was a one-finger piano
outline of eight song choruses.'"

B13 Cohn, Arthur. *Recorded Classical Music: A Critical Guide to
Compositions and Performances*. New York: Schirmer Books, 1981.
Reviews of **D7**, **D19**, and **D30**.

B14 Collinson, Francis M. *Orchestration for The Theatre*. London: John
Lane, The Bodley Head, 1941.
The standard reference on theater scoring until Bennett's
Instrumentally Speaking [**B155**] appeared in 1974. Orchestrator
Collinson's emphasis is on British shows and fellow orchestrators (I. E.
de Orellana, Charles W. "Jock" Prentice, Arthur Rule, Kennedy
Russell, etc.), but Bennett's work for Porter's *Anything Goes* and
Kern's *Music in the Air*—both of which played in New York and
London—is also discussed. Many of the scoring examples are taken
from actual London musical comedy and operetta productions; a few of
the uncredited ones are likely Bennett's work.

B15 [Columbia Broadcasting System, Inc.] *Serious Music on the Columbia
Broadcasting System: A Survey of Series, Soloists and Special
Performances From 1927 Through 1938*, n.d.

Thoroughly detailed reference concerning each season's nationally-aired radio programs on which many of Bennett's works were presented. Includes personnel listings, etc.

B16   "Composing is Hard Work." *NY Sun*, 12 April 1941.
Bennett is interviewed concerning his preparations for and philosophy behind his "Notebook" radio programs, for which he composed new works weekly. He provides background on his piece *Mill Potatoes* [W157]—not published elsewhere—and shares his thoughts on introducing the general listening public to " 'serious' modern music."

B17   Copland, Aaron. *Copland On Music*. Garden City, NY: Doubleday & Co., Inc., 1960.
In one chapter, "America's Young Men—Ten Years Later," [reprinted from *Modern Music* 8:4 (May 1936), 3-11] Copland "follows up" on those composers he had considered "promising" in the mid-1920s. He notes that Bennett, like Piston, was not included in the earlier essay because his works were not yet known publicly. Bennett is described as "well known now as the composer of music that is light in touch and deftly made, with a particular eye on orchestral timbre, of which he is a past master."

B18   _____. "Serge Koussevitsky and the American Composer." *Musical Quarterly* 30 (July 1944), 261-269.
Boston Symphony performances of Bennett's and others' works during the period 1923-1943 are listed.

B19   Copland, Aaron, and Perlis, Vivian. *Copland: Volume I, 1900-1942*. London and Boston: Faber and Faber, 1984.
Bennett's involvement in the first (1930) Copland-Sessions Concert, as well as the first two Yaddo Festivals (1932 and 1933, the latter as member of the Central Music Committee) is discussed.

B20   [Coward, Noel]. *The Noel Coward Diaries*. ed. Graham Payn and Sheridan Morley. Boston and Toronto: Little, Brown and Co., 1982.
Spanning the years 1941-1969, Coward's diaries provide a wealth of "inside" information about musical theater on both sides of the Atlantic. Bennett, who did the orchestrations, is included in diary entries relating to the 1963 production of Coward's show *Blithe Spirit*.

B21   Daly, William. "Gershwin as Orchestrator." *NYT*, 15 January 1933.

Daly responds to Allan Lincoln Langley's published suggestion [B53] that Daly, and possibly others, are anonymously scoring Gershwin's works for orchestra.

B22   Downes, Olin. *Olin Downes on Music: A Selection from His Writings during the Half-Century 1906 to 1955.* Downes, Irene, ed., New York: Simon and Schuster, Inc., 1957; reprint ed., New York: Greenwood Press, 1968.
Most of the reprinted essays were originally published in the *New York Times.* His criticism of Rodgers's music for *Oklahoma* is included; of Bennett's scoring, he comments: "It is an orchestration valuable principally, not for its treatment of sonorities and its carrying power in the theater, but for its imaginative suggestion, underlying situation and text."

B23   Downes, Olin. " 'Porgy' Fantasy: R. R. Bennett Makes Symphonic Work From Gershwin Opera." *NYT*, 15 November 1942, VIII:7.
Details Fritz Reiner's commissioning of, and Bennett's scoring of, the *Porgy and Bess "Symphonic Picture."*

B24   Duke, Vernon. [Vladimir Dukelsky] "The Composer's Lot in America." *Music Publishers Journal* 2:5 (September-October 1944), 6-7, 44-45.
A candid chronicle of burdens, financial and otherwise, faced by American composers of concert music. Also reprinted in its entirety is a lengthy manifesto establishing the "Composers Protective Society" in 1933. Among the 29 composers listed who had signed the document are Bennett, Blitzstein, Cowell, Gershwin, Grainger, Douglas Moore, Riegger, Salzedo, and William Grant Still.

B25   _____. *Listen Here! A Critical Essay On Music Depreciation.* New York: Ivan Obolensky, Inc. and Toronto: George J. McLeod Ltd., 1963.
Duke's strongly opinioned essay discusses twentiety-century concert and theater music and their standing with critics and audiences at mid-century. Bennett's important role as America's premiere theater orchestrator is discussed in Chapter Eight, "The American Musical Here and Abroad."

B26   _____. *Passport to Paris.* Boston and Toronto: Little, Brown and Co., 1955, 234, 274.
Passing references to Bennett's work as orchestrator for Duke's 1932 show, *Walk a Little Faster.* Also, writing of his years in Paris (late 1920s), Duke mentions "Robert Russell Bennett, whom I met in Paris,

where he showed me an interesting organ sonata [W131] of his [and] promised every assistance [in establishing himself as a composer]."

B27   Dux, Thurston J. *American Oratorios and Cantatas: A Catalog Of Works Written In The U.S. From Colonial Times to 1985*. Metuchen, NJ and London: Scarecrow Press, 1986.
Details concerning Bennett's *Carol Cantatas I-IV* [W80] and his *Crazy Cantata #1* [W82].

B28   Eagon, Angelo. *Catalog of Published Concert Music by American Composers*. Second edition. Metuchen: Scarecrow Press, 1969.
Lists only a small portion of Bennett's published output. Also includes the only published mention of two works for chorus and orchestra he attributes to Bennett: *Epithalamium* [W85] and *Verses 1, 2, 3* [W90]. Though both are listed as rental works available from Theodore Presser, that publisher has no listing for either in any of its files pertaining to current or out-of-print works.

B29   *The Edwin A. Fleisher Collection of Orchestral Music in the Free Library of Philadelphia: A Cumulative Catalog, 1929-1973*. Boston: G. K. Hall and Co., 1979, 79.
Detailed information on the four manuscript Bennett scores— *Abraham Lincoln* [W1], *Concerto Grosso* [W14], *Hollywood* [W20], and *Sights and Sounds* [W31]—in the Collection.

B30   Eells, George. *The Life That Late He Led*. New York: G. P. Putnam's Sons, 1967.
General information about Bennett's role in preparing orchestrations for Cole Porter's Broadway shows. Also, the hurried, overnight scoring of a new song for *Jubilee* (the night before the dress rehearsal) by Bennett is described—typical of the deadlines faced by Bennett and his colleagues.

B31   Ewen, David. *The Story of Irving Berlin*. New York: Henry Holt and Co., 1950, 71.
Bennett's orchestrations for Berlin are briefly noted.

B32   Farish, Margaret K., ed. *Orchestral Music in Print*. Philadelphia: Musicdata, 1979.

B33   _____. *Orchestral Music in Print: 1983 Supplement*. Philadelphia: Musicdata, 1983.

B34   Fiese, Richard K. "College and University Wind Band Repertoire 1980-
       1985." *Journal of Band Research* 23:1 (Fall 1987), 17-42.
       A study of frequency of performance of band pieces at two- and four-
       year colleges and universities in the U.S. The author identifies a group
       of twenty-two "Most Frequently Performed Composers," of which
       Bennett is 20th.

B35   Fordin, Hugh. *Getting To Know Him*. New York: Random House,
       1977; reprint ed., New York: Ungar, 1986.
       A study of Oscar Hammerstein II; includes Bennett in discussions of
       the many Broadway works for which Hammerstein was lyricist, both
       before and after forming his partnership with Richard Rodgers. Much
       detail on the 1943 Hammerstein-Bennett collaboration, *Carmen Jones*.

B36   Gelatt, Roland. "Music Makers: Bruckner and a Loewe-Bennett Fair
       Lady From Pittsburgh." *High Fidelity*, July 1968, 20, 22.
       Interview with Bennett, who had completed special symphonic
       arrangements of the music from *My Fair Lady* and *Sound of Music*
       to be recorded by William Steinberg and the Pittsburgh Symphony.

B37   Gill, Brendan., ed. by Kimball, Robert. *Cole: A Biographical Essay*.
       New York: Holt, Rinehart and Winston, 1971.
       General details concerning Bennett's orchestrations for Cole Porter's
       Broadway scores.

B38   Goldman, Richard Franko. "A New Day For Band Music." *Modern
       Music* 23:4 (Fall 1946), 261-265.
       A discussion of Bennett and other "noted composers" who have
       written band works. This essay appeared also in Goldman's *The
       Concert Band* (Rinehart and Co., 1946).

B39   _____. *The Wind Band: Its Literature and Technique*. Boston: Allyn
       and Bacon, Inc., 1961.
       In addition to the general observation that Bennett is among those
       "by now fairly prolific composers of band works," Bennett's 1952
       Mademoiselle [W63] is included in a discussion of works for the
       Goldman Band commissioned by the League of Composers.

B40   Gould, Jack. "A Prize Package? Emmy Grab Bag Yields a Thought;
       How State of TV Has Declined." *NYT*, 2 June 1963, II:13.
       In reviewing the annual award by the Academy of Television Arts and
       Sciences, Gould singles out Bennett's contributions to NBC television's

"Project 20" documentary films: "In entertainment, much the most deserved award was won by . . . Bennett. . . . That he received the night's most sustained ovation in New York was fitting."

B41   Greenbaum, Lucy. "About an Arranger." *NYT*, 24 October 1943, II:1. Bennett discusses his craft and, in particular, his work in adapting Bizet's score for *Carmen Jones*, in collaboration with Oscar Hammerstein II.

B42   "Guggenheim Fund Gives Awards to 82." *NYT*, 25 March 1928, 13. Includes notice of the renewal of Bennett's fellowship for an additional three-month period.

B43   Hanson, Howard. "Twenty Years' Growth in America." *Modern Music* 20:2 (January-February 1943), 95-101. A evaluation of progress in creating a uniquely "American school" of composition; Copland, MacDowell, Griffes, Gershwin, Bennett, Bloch, etc. are discussed. Hanson writes of the "urban group centering around New York City," including (the late) George Gershwin, Copland, Bennett, Gould and others and discusses characteristics of the works written by these composers.

B44   Hutchens, John. "Mr. Kern and the Melodious Seasons." *NYT*, 18 October 1931, VIII:1. No direct mention of Bennett, but this lengthy essay gives valuable descriptions of the orchestrations and unique pit instrumentation for several Kern shows orchestrated by Bennett, many of them the intimate productions written for New York's Princess and Globe theaters. *The Cat and the Fiddle* is given particular attention.

B45   Jablonski, Edward. *Gershwin: A Biography*. New York: Doubleday, 1987. Useful information, otherwise unavailable, about Gershwin's social and professional associations with Bennett in Paris in the late 1920s. Bennett's contributions to the RKO films *Shall We Dance* and *A Damsel In Distress* are thoroughly detailed, but almost no references are made to Bennett's work on Gershwin's stage musicals.

B46   Jablonski, Edward, and Stewart, Lawrence D. *The Gershwin Years*. Garden City, NY: Doubleday and Co., 1958. Gershwin's ability to orchestrate his own shows is discussed. While acknowledging that Gershwin left almost all of this to others more capable than he—Bennett and William Daly, especially—the authors note that Gershwin, in his later shows, spent considerably more time discussing and making suggestions to Bennett regarding the scoring of individual musical numbers. Also included is a photograph of Gershwin, Bennett, Fritz Reiner, and Deems Taylor, dating to mid-August 1931, at rehearsals for a Lewisohn Stadium concert [W24b].

B47   Jacobi, Frederick. "America's Popular Music." *Modern Music* 18:2 (January-February 1941), 76-80.
A critical overview of the commercial music scene, with substantial praise for the "incomparable brilliance of our expert arrangers, of whom Ace No. 1 seems to be Russell Bennett."

B48   Kirstein, Lincoln. *Choreography by George Balanchine: A Catalogue of Works*. New York: Viking Penguin, Inc., 1982.
Details Bennett's involvement with the 1936 *Ziegfeld Follies*, as well as *Louisiana Purchase* and *Dream With Music*.

B49   Kolodin, Irving. "American Composers and the Phonograph." *Modern Music* 11:3 (March-April 1934), 131-133.
Kolodin, critical of the shortage of American works on commercial disc recordings, criticizes the Victor company; though their 1929 competition offered $25,000 in awards ($10,000 of this received by Bennett for *Sights and Sounds* [W31] and *Abraham Lincoln* [W1]) and generated considerable publicity for the firm, not one of the works had yet been recorded by Victor.

B50   Krasker, Tommy, and Kimball, Robert. *Catalog Of The American Musical*. National Institute for Opera and Musical Theater, 1988.
Using as its subject the musical comedies by Irving Berlin, George Gershwin, Cole Porter, and Richard Rodgers (his shows with Larry Hart), the authors have compiled a complete catalog of all authentic performance materials extant for each show, including said materials' current location. For each show, detailed information is given separately for individual songs, even those later cut from the show. The authors have been able to positively identify—in almost every case—individual orchestrators for each musical number; a great many Bennett-orchestrated items are included in the *Catalog*.

B51   Kreuger, Miles. *Show Boat: The Story Of A Classic American Musical*. New York: Oxford University Press, 1977.
Discussion of Bennett's involvement with and contributions to the

original (1927) production, 1936 Paramount film, and later theatrical revivals.

B52 _____. "Some Words About 'Show Boat'." [liner notes for Angel compact disc CDS7-49108 and 12" LP A1-49108], 13-24.
Kreuger recalls his 1978 visit with Bennett to the West 52nd Rodgers & Hammerstein warehouse in New York, where they located orchestra parts from the show's 1927 production and 1946 revival. The album is an attempt to present *all* of the music written for the play by Kern, in Bennett's original orchestrations when available.

B53 Langley, Allan Lincoln. "The Gershwin Myth." *The American Spectator* 1:2 (December 1932), 1-2.
The author questions Gershwin's ability to orchestrate his own concert works (other than *Rhapsody in Blue*, for which Grofé was credited). Bennett is included as Kern's acknowledged orchestrator; Langley suggests that William Daly—and possibly others—are anonymously aiding Gershwin in this regard. **B21** is Daly's published response to these accusations.

B54 Lasky, Betty. *RKO: The Biggest Little Major Of Them All.* Englewood Cliffs, NJ: Prentice-Hall, Inc., 1984.
Detailed discussion and credits for individual RKO film productions are provided, including those for which Bennett composed, orchestrated, and/or conducted in the 1930s.

B55 Lees, Gene. "The Lees Side—Odds and Ends: Eavesdropping in Purgatory." *High Fidelity*, November 1968, 126.
Lees reports on a recent conversation with Bennett, who reflects on his musical interests and working procedures.

B56 Levant, Oscar. *A Smattering of Ignorance.* Garden City, NY: Garden City Publishing Co., Inc., 1940.
Levant provides much detail regarding Bennett's contributions in discussing film scoring in Hollywood in the late 1930s, Kern's *I Dream Too Much* specifically. He also discusses performing the *March for Two Pianos and Orchestra* with Bennett in New York [**W24a**], the 1932 Yaddo Festival, and Bennett's band scores for the 1939-1940 New York World's Fair [**W74**].

B57 Lowe, Donald Robert. *Sir Carl Busch: his life and work as a teacher, conductor and composer.* DMA dissertation, University of Missouri-Kansas City, 1972.

Lengthy discussion of Busch's career in Kansas City, including his tutelage of Bennett c. 1910-16.

B58   Lynch, Richard Chigley, comp. *Broadway on Record: A Directory of New York Cast Recordings of Musical Shows, 1931-1986*. Westport, CT: Greenwood Press, 1987.
As the Discography in the present volume does *not* include recordings of Bennett-orchestrated shows, Lynch's compilation is recommended as one of the most accurate and comprehensive guides to such commercial releases.

B59   "Man Behind the Tune." *Newsweek*, 20 July 1953, 86.
A profile with emphasis on Bennett's scoring of Rodgers' music for the 1952-53 "Victory at Sea" NBC television production [W174]; Bennett and Rodgers are pictured together at a recording session for the series.

B60   Marx, Samuel and Clayton, Jan. *Rodgers and Hart: Bewitched, Bothered and Bedeviled*. New York: G. P. Putnam's Sons, 1976.
Bennett's orchestrations for Rodgers and Hart shows are briefly noted; Bennett's comments about a theater orchestrator's duties are included also.

B61   McCarty, Clifford. *Film Composers In America: A Checklist Of Their Work*. Glendale, CA: Valentine, 1953; reprint ed.; Da Capo, 1972.
Detailed credits for composers and orchestrators of American film scores through the early 1950s; one of the very best such indexes available. His research goes beyond the official credits for each film, including uncredited orchestrators, etc.

B62   McGlinn, John. "The Original 'Anything Goes'—A Classic Restored." [in liner notes for EMI compact disc CDC 7-49848-2, 1989].
Porter's 1934 *Anything Goes*, orchestrated by Bennett and Hans Spialek, was "restored" by Spialek, along with McGlinn and orchestrator Russell Warner, for this recording. McGlinn's essay details the original orchestrators' contributions and makes this observation about Bennett: "He viewed most of the show music he scored with some contempt, and, paradoxically, this may account for the brilliance of his work. The inventiveness of color and counterpoint . . . stems, perhaps, from his desire to invest the music with his own stamp, to prove himself better than the material he was working with."

B63   Mehr, Linda Harris, comp. and ed. *Motion Pictures, Television and Radio : a union catalogue of manuscript and special collections in the western United States.* Boston: G. K. Hall & Co., 1977.
Details the whereabouts of many of the scores and other production materials for theatrical films with which Bennett was associated.

B64   Mielziner, Jo. *Designing For The Theatre: A Memoir and a Portfolio.* New York: Bramhall House, 1965, 45.
Mielziner, designer for many of the Rodgers and Hammerstein shows, recalls the 11 December 1948 first reading of the *South Pacific* score at Rodgers' apartment. In attendance were the principals, Bennett, and several members of the production staff.

B65   Morgan, Alfred Lindsay. "Music on the Ether Waves." *Etude* 59:5 (May 1941), 301.
A general overview of Bennett's career, with specific emphasis on his work for radio and the "Russell Bennett's Notebook" program.

B66   Morton, Lawrence. "On The Hollywood Front." *Modern Music* 21:4 (May-June 1944), 264-266.
Morton reviews recent film scores. Of Weill's *Lady In The Dark*, he writes: "The excellence of Robert Russell Bennett's arrangements . . . could have been forecast, and of course they proved to be, as one expected, superior in skill and taste to anything that has been turned out for similar pictures."

B67   *The New York Times Directory of the Theater.* Introduction by Clive Barnes. New York: Arno Press/New York Times Book Co., 1973.
A guide to *Times* articles mentioning Bennett's Broadway work; articles are indexed separately according to his contribution (composer, lyricist, etc.) and then by individual productions.

B68   Oja, Carol J. *American Music Recordings: A Discography of 20th-Century U. S. Composers.* Brooklyn, NY: Institute for Studies in American Music, 1982.
The Bennett discography, as extensive as any in print, is carefully researched and generally accurate, though not without error.

B69   "One-Man Concert on MBS." *Newsweek* 16:23 (2 December 1940), 52.
Outlines Bennett's career to 1940 and debut of the "Notebook" show on 17 November 1940.

B70   "Orchestrator on His Own." *Time* (12 December 1932), 33.
An account of Bennett's current activites as both composer and
orchestrator, along with a biographical sketch. Also includes an
account of **W138a**, Iturbi's premiere of the *"Vu"* etudes. Mention is
made of the concertos commissioned by Kreisler and Iturbi.

B71   Pakenham, Compton. "Recorded Music: Casals As Conductor." *NYT*,
14 September 1930, VIII:7.
Includes an account of the award of $25,000 in prizes in the Victor
symphonic contest of 1929, including names of the panel of judges.
With $5,000 going to the others, and $10,000 to Bennett for his *Sights
and Sounds* **[W31]** and *Abraham Lincoln* **[W1]**, Pakenham quotes the
judges as "assuring the winners of at least a year's security and leisure
for creative work," and "Bennett for two years by reason of two of his
compositions being chosen . . . "

B72   Parrent, Amy. "From 'The Beggar's Opera' to 'Sweeney Todd': The Art
of the Broadway Orchestrator." *Music Educators Journal* 66 (May 1980),
32-35.
Bennett is featured prominently in this overview of theater scoring.
Past and present trends in pit instrumentation, along with vocal
amplification and other technical considerations, receive considerable
attention. Regrettably, almost no musical examples are given; excerpts
from orchestrations by Bennett, Jonathan Tunick, and other arrangers
profiled in the article would have added much to its value.

B73   Rasponi, Lanfranco. "Pages From A Notebook: American Music Is
on The Title Page of Russell Bennett's Program Guide." *NYT*, 27 April
1941, IX:10.
Bennett discusses his "Notebook" program, including his thoughts
about his programming as well as the weekly regimen of writing and
rehearsing new works.

B74   Raymond, Jack. *Show Music On Record From The 1890s To The 1980s*.
New York: Ungar, 1982.
A very comprehensive listing of New York "original cast" recordings,
as well as revivals, foreign and studio cast albums, etc. The volume is
arranged chronologically (by original production date) and extensively
indexed; orchestrators' credits are included where known.

B75   Rodgers, Richard. *Musical Stages: An Autobiography*. New York:
Random House, 1975.

Bennett's role in the creation of Rodgers's shows, as well as the music for the "Victory at Sea." television series, receives surprisingly little mention. Of the latter [**W174**], he writes (p. 279): "what I composed were actually musical themes. For the difficult technical task of timing, cutting and orchestrating, I turned to my old friend Russell Bennett, who has no equal in this kind of work. He fully deserves the credit, which I give him without undue modesty, for making my music sound better than it was."

B76   _____. "Music for the American Theatre." *Music Publishers Journal* 1:5 (September-October 1943), 13.
Rodgers defends musical theater as a commercial product and, by describing the theater as a "collaborative medium," defends the near-universal practice among he and his songwriting colleagues of hiring orchestrators. He notes that "it is extremely doubtful that years of study and experience would find [the songwriter] as satisfactory in scoring his own show as Robert Russell Bennett, who has devoted his life to the business and brings to it a rare and high talent."

B77   Rosensteil, Leonie. *Nadia Boulanger—A Life in Music.* New York: W. W. Norton, 1982.
Bennett is included in discussions of Boulanger's American students.

B78   "Russell Bennett at the Top." *Kansas City Times*, 19 September 1930.
Article profiles Kansas-City-native Bennett's success as an arranger and composer at the time of his award of $10,000 for *Sights and Sounds* [**W31**] and *Abraham Lincoln* [**W1**] in the Victor competition.

B79   "Russell Bennett Begins New Air Program Today." *NYH-T*, 17 November 1940.
Discussion, with captioned photograph of Bennett, of the premiere of his "Notebook" radio program.

B80   "Russell Bennett's Notebook." *Time*, 7 April 1941 [37:14], 67.
Details the return of the "Notebook" show to the WOR schedule on 23 March; it had been discontinued as part of the ASCAP strike beginning in January 1941. Bennett is described as the "first ASCAP man" returning to the airways, as his show is considered "non-commercial." Also discusses the *Classic Serenade for Strings* [**W7**] and *Music Box Opera #2* [**W159**].

B81 J. S. "Goldman Band Opens Guggenheim Concerts." *Musical America*
75:9 (July 1955), 7.
Bennett's new arrangement of "The Star Spangled Banner,"
commissioned by Goldman, is reviewed.

B82 Sanjek, Russell. *American Popular Music and Its Business: The First
Four Hundred Years; Volume III: From 1900 to 1984.* New York:
Oxford University Press, 1988, 99.
Bennett's promotion (c. 1925) to head of the music staff at New York
publisher Harms, Inc.—by Max Dreyfus—is discussed.

B83 Schwartz, Charles. *Cole Porter: a biography.* New York: Dial Press,
1977.
Bennett's involvement is mentioned briefly during discussions of a
number of individual shows.

B84 _____. *Gershwin: His Life And Music.* Indianapolis: Bobbs-Merrill Co.,
Inc., 1973.
A few passing references to Bennett's orchestrations for Gershwin and
to the Gershwin-Bennett *Symphonic Picture of Porgy and Bess.*

B85 Shackelford, Rudy. "The Yaddo Festivals of American Music; 1932-
1952." *Perspectives of New Music*, 92-103.
Some discussion of Bennett's involvement in the 1932 and 1933
festivals.

B86 Shavin, Norman. "Television Discovers Music." *Music Journal*
January 1957, 40, 55-56.
Includes Bennett's comments about his work for two of the NBC
television "Project 20" films, *Nightmare in Red*, and *The Great War.*

B87 Siegmeister, Elie, ed. *The Music Lover's Handbook.* New York:
William Morrow and Co., 1943, 644, 782.
Bennett is mentioned in a discussion of the CBS Columbia
Composers' Commission program (1937), and as one of many
American composers who do commercial work to supplement their
income.

B88 Smith, Norman E. *March Music Notes.* Lake Charles, LA: Program
Note Press, 1986, 34-35.
A one-page biographical sketch, along with details about the *S. S.
Eagle March* [*See:* **W55**] and *Down To The Sea In Ships* [**W55**].

B89   Smith, Norman E., and Stoutamire, Albert. *Band Music Notes*. rev. ed. San Diego: Kjos West, 1979, 22-23.
Brief biographical sketch, along with background on Bennett's *Down to the Sea in Ships* [W55], *Four Preludes* [W59], *Suite of Old American Dances* [W70], and *Symphonic Songs for Band* [W71].

B90   "Stars of the Future." *NYT*, 24 December 1944, II:7.
Discusses Bennett's Ford-sponsored radio show [*See:* D40] of the same name shortly after the show's debut.

B91   Stravinsky, Igor, and Craft, Robert. *Dialogues And A Diary*. Garden City, NY: Doubleday & Co., Inc., 1963, 83.
Producer Billy Rose's cable to Stravinsky (1944) is reprinted, suggesting that Stravinsky allow his *Scenes de Ballet* score to be re-orchestrated by Bennett, presumably in a more "commercial" style.

B92   Stuart, Robert W. "The Joys and Headaches of Show's Uncrowned Hero—the Orchestrator." *NYW-T*, 15 June 1943, II:21.
Discussion of his composing and arranging work in New York, Hollywood, and London; many details about his work on *Oklahoma!* Some material also on his Kansas City childhood.

B93   Summers, Harrison B. *Radio Programs Carried on National Networks, 1926-1956*. Columbus, OH: Department of Speech, Ohio State University, 1958.
Useful reference for data (network, date, time, first airing, etc.) concerning radio shows for which Bennett was composer and music director in New York in the 1940s.

B94   Taylor, Deems. *Of Men And Music*. New York: Simon and Schuster, 1937, 265-266.
Taylor remarks on Bennett's succeeding Frank Saddler as the premier musical comedy arranger in New York in the 1920s.

B95   Ussher, Bruno David. "Composing For Films." *NYT*, 28 January 1940, IX:7.
Bennett is included in a discussion of "personages of the strictly symphonic and operatic realm who have been accepted in Hollywood."

B96   _____. "The Hollywood Bowl." *NYT*, 22 August 1937, X:7.
Announces Bennett's recent appointment to the RKO music staff and the necessary delay in his completion of *The Enchanted Kiss* [W40].

B97   "Veteran Handles Music For Cooper's Biography." *Wooster* [OH]
      Record, 22 March 1963.
      Appears to be a verbatim reprint of an NBC press release concerning
      the NBC "Project 20" production, *The Tall American—Gary Cooper*.
      This lengthy article is devoted almost entirely to a recounting of
      Bennett's professional career as composer and arranger; Bennett is
      quoted extensively.

B98   Walker, Don. "Who Says 'Arranger'?" *Theatre Arts* 34:11 (November
      1950), 53-54.
      Though Bennett is not mentioned, his colleague and onetime office-
      mate Walker discusses the deadline pressures and considerable creative
      work involved in theater scoring. It is all very much in accord with
      Bennett's many published descriptions of his Broadway work.

B99   Weil, Irving. "The American Scene Changes." *Modern Music* 4:4
      (May-June 1929), 3-9.
      Bennett is included, along with Copland, Harris, Thomson, Antheil,
      etc. in a discussion of composers of "growing notoriety": "Young
      Bennett, not yet well known, has nonetheless already proved himself
      to be interesting and two of his latest works, unperformed thus far we
      believe, undoubtedly will be heard before long. One of them was a
      close second to . . . [Bloch] . . . in the *Musical America* prize
      competition."

B100 Wildbihler, Hubert and Völklein, Sonja. *The Musical: An
      International Annotated Bibliography*. Munich, London, New York,
      Oxford and Paris, 1986.

BIOGRAPHICAL REFERENCES [B101 - 145]

B101 Anderson, Ruth E. *Contemporary American Composers: A
      Biographical Dictionary*. Second Edition. Boston: G. K. Hall, 1982, 40.

B102 *The ASCAP Biographical Dictionary of Composers, Authors and
      Publishers, 1966 Edition*. S.v. "Bennett, Robert Russell." Compiled
      and ed. by The Lynn Farnol Group, Inc. New York: The American
      Society of Composers, Authors, and Publishers, 1966.
      Concerned almost exclusively with Bennett's career as composer.

B103   *Baker's Biographical Dictionary of Musicians.* S.v. "Bennett, Robert
        Russell."

B104   Bauer, Marion. *Twentieth Century Music.* Revised Edition. New York:
        G. P. Putnam's Sons, 1947, 330-331.
        Overview of Bennett's career and major works.

B105   "Bennett, Robert Russell." *Current Biography Yearbook* 1942; 1962;
        1981.

B106   *Bio-Bibliographical Index of Musicians in the United States of
        America from Colonial Times.* Foreward by Harold Spivacke.
        Washington, D.C.: WPA Historical Records Survey, 1941.

B107   Bordman, Gerald. *The Oxford Companion To American Theatre.*
        S.v. "Bennett, Robert Russell." New York and Oxford: Oxford
        University Press, 1984.
        Concentrates upon Bennett's work as a theater orchestrator.

B108   Butterworth, Neil. *A Dictionary of American Composers.* New York
        and London: Garland, 1984, 33-34.

B109   *Celebrity Register, Third Edition.* S.v. "Bennett, Robert Russell." Ed.
        by Earl Blackwell. New York: Simon and Schuster, 1973.

B110   "Double-Life Bennett." *NYT,* 1 January 1933, IX:3.
        A lengthy portrait with equal emphasis on the two sides of Bennett's
        professional career, both well established by this time.

B111   Ewen, David. *American Composers: A Biographical Dictionary.*
        New York: G. P. Putnam's Sons, 1982, 52-54.
        A very substantial entry. The article is flawed, however, by a
        considerable number of errors—dates and titles of compositions,
        specifically.

B112   _____. *Composers Since 1900.* New York: H. W. Wilson, 1969, 55-57.

B113   _____. *Ewen's Musical Masterworks: The Encyclopedia of Musical
        Masterpieces.* New York: Arco Publishing Co., 1954, 83-85.
        A retitled second edition of **B114**. The "Bennett" entry is reprinted
        without revision.

B114 _____. *Music for the Millions: The Encyclopedia of Musical Masterpieces.* New York: Arco Publishing Co., 1944, 79-81.
Only the barest of biographical sketches. Of value, however, are Bennett's own detailed essays describing his *Abraham Lincoln* [W1] and *Eight Etudes for Symphony Orchestra* [W19].

B115 Ferriss, John. "Mr. Music And His Pal." *NY Sunday News*, 29 December 1968, 3, 21, 25, 28.
Extensive interview/profile of Bennett, with much detail on both his early years and then-current projects. Includes a rare published reference to his opera, *Crystal* [W39], completed a few years later. Encompasses both his composing and commercial work.

B116 Fields, Sidney. "Only Human: Robert Russell Bennett, Broadway's Music Doctor." *NY Daily Mirror*, 2 August 1951.
An interview with the composer, containing many anecdotes about his career; emphasized is his theater arranging.

B117 Goss, Madeline. *Modern Music Makers.* New York: Dutton, 1952; reprint ed., Westport: Greenwood Press, 1970, 180-193.
Probably the most detailed discussion of his life and works published during Bennett's lifetime; appears to have involved one or more interviews with the composer. His Broadway scoring receives only slight attention. The works list, some errors notwithstanding, is fairly complete through 1950.

B118 Howard, John Tasker. *Our American Music.* Third Edition, Revised [1946] and Fourth Edition [1965]. New York: Thomas Y. Crowell Company, 1946, 485-487.
Good overview of Bennett's career and major works; the earlier edition gives somewhat more details.

B119 Hughes, Rupert, comp. *Music Lovers' Encyclopedia.* Completely revised and newly edited by Deems Taylor and Russell Kerr. Garden City, NY: Garden City Books, 1950, 56-57.

B120 *The International Who Is Who In Music.* 5th ed., 1951. S.v. "Bennett, Robert Russell."
Includes many details—Bennett's vital statistics, religious preference, etc.—that were otherwise unpublished. Like many such references, these details appear to have been provided by the composer. *See:* D50?

B121   *Die Musik in Geschichte und Gegenwart.* S.v. "Bennett, Robert
Russell," by Karl H. Wörner.

B122   *The New Grove Dictionary of American Music.* S.v. "Bennett, Robert
Russell," by Ronald Byrnside and Robert Skinner.

B123   *The New Grove Dictionary of Music and Musicians.* S.v. "Bennett,
Robert Russell," by Ronald Byrnside.

B124   Northouse, Cameron. *Twentieth Century Opera in England and the
United States.* Boston: G. K. Hall & Co., 1976.
Information on librettists and premieres of *Maria Malibran* [W44],
The Enchanted Kiss [W40], and *An Hour of Delusion* [W43].

B125   *Notable Names in the American Theatre.* Clifton, NJ: James T. White
and Co., 1976, 559.
This is the second edition of the Rigdon *Biographical Encyclopedia*
[B129]; has much information on Bennett's concert works in addition
to his theater credits.

B126   Peck, Ira. "The Double Life Of Russell Bennett." *This Week,* 26 April
1950, 8-9, 25.
Discusses both his serious composing and his commercial work. Based
upon interviews with Bennett, it is rich with anecdotes and Bennett's
comments and opinions on a variety of topics. Of particular note is
Bennett's recollection of the last-minute changes made to *Oklahoma!*
during its New Haven tryout.

B127   Reis, Claire. *Composers in America.* London: Macmillan & Co., 1947,
26-28.

B128   _____. *Composers in America.* revised and enlarged ed., New
York: Macmillan Co., 1947.

B129   Rigdon, Walter, ed. *The Biographical Encyclopedia of Who's Who
In The American Theatre.* New York: James H. Heineman, Inc. 1966,
288.
A surprisingly thorough discussion of Bennett's credits, with the
balance not at all tilted toward his Broadway work, as one might expect.

B130   "Who Is Who Among Famous American Composers of Instrumental
Music." *The Instrumentalist* 8:6 (February 1954), 30-31.

B131   Wind, Herbert Warren. "Another Opening, Another Show." *The New Yorker*, 17 November 1951, 46-71.
Based on interviews with Bennett and many of his associates; a richly-detailed study with its emphasis shifted slightly toward Broadway scoring. One of the longest essays about Bennett and his career in print, and engagingly written. Includes comments about Bennett's work by Richard Rodgers, Cole Porter, Albert Sirmay, and others.

[OBITUARIES]

B132   Hanser, R. "Robert Russell Bennett—A Sound for All Seasons (In Memoriam)." *Television Quarterly* 18 (1981):43.

B133   [Obituary] *Billboard* 93:76 (29 August 1981).

B134   [Obituary] *Central Opera* 23:57 n3 (1982).

B135   [Obituary] *Gramophone* 59:496 (October 1981).

B136   [Obituary] *High Fidelity/Musical America* 32:Ma25 (January 1982).

B137   [Obituary] *Instrumentalist* 36:115 (November 1981).

B138   [Obituary] *International Musician* 86:11 (January 1982).

B139   [Obituary] *Musical Times* 122:695 (October 1981).

B140   [Obituary] *Musik und Gesellschaft* 31:640 (October 1981).

B141   [Obituary] *NYT*, 19 August 1981.

B142   [Obituary] *School Musician* 53:36 (October 1981).

B143   [Obituary] *Time*, 118 (31 August 1981), 53.

B144   [Obituary] *Variety*, 304:93-94 (26 August, 1981).

B145   "Robert Russell Bennett, 1894-1981." *The Instrumentalist* 36:4 (November 1981), 115.

WRITINGS BY ROBERT RUSSELL BENNETT [B146 - 163]

B146 "All I Know About Arranging Music." *International Musician,*
February 1949, 9, 33.

B147 "Another Chapter On Arranging Music." *International Musician,*
March 1949, 16, 33.

B148 "Another Chapter On Arranging Music." *International Musician,*
April 1949, 49.
In this three-part series [B146, 147, 148] Bennett gives a concise yet
valuable overview of each orchestral instrument, with advice
regarding effective scoring procedures. The first article [B146] profiles
the orchestral strings; woodwinds [B147] and brass/percussion [B148]
are covered in the succeeding installments. His advice is concerned
with both concert and popular music.

B149 "Backstage With The Orchestrator." *Etude* 61:4 (April 1943), 233,
273, 288.
Bennett discusses the behind-the-scenes aspects of his show arranging,
with advice for those interested in becoming professional arrangers
and composers.

B150 "Eight Bars and a Pencil." *NYT,* 8 June 1947.
A lengthy discussion of the orchestrator's role in the preparation of a
new musical production. Bennett recounts in detail the preparation
of the ensemble's presentation of the title song in *Oklahoma!* (1943),
from composition through rehearsal, staging, orchestration, and later
revision.

B151 "Fools Give You Reasons." *Music Journal,* 25:5 (May 1967), 44, 88.
The title is taken from the song "Some Enchanted Evening" (*South
Pacific*). Using that portion of the song lyric as his topic, Bennett
ponders many not-easily-explained aspects of the art of music—the
unique skills of great performing artists, composers' gift for melody (or
lack thereof), etc., and concludes: "it all comes back to what can't be
taught, bought, or imitated: talent, that miserable word that accounts
for tears, laughter, and monuments."

B152 "From Composer of Malibran." *NYT*, 7 April 1935.
Extended discussion of music for his opera, Maria Malibran [W44], at the time of its Juilliard School premiere.

B153 "From the Notes of a Music Arranger." *Theater Arts* 40 (Nov. 1956), 88-89.
Bennett elaborates upon a theme that appears often in his writing, *"No combination of orchestral instruments can change the quality of a tune."* Also, he shares many anectodes about theatre scoring assignments (beginning in the 1920s) and his work in Hollywood in the late 1930s. Another item of interest is Gershwin's evaluation of *Maria Malibran* [W44], as recalled by Bennett.

B154 "How to Become an Arranger of Hit Musicals." *Toronto Globe and Mail*, 1 Feb. 1956.
An autobiographical essay, beginning with his Kansas City childhood.

B155 *Instrumentally Speaking.* Melville, NY: Belwin Mills, Inc., 1975.
An instrumentation/orchestration text emphasising arranging for musical theater. Bennett takes the reader through the scoring of a hypothetical new production, *Madame Cinq à Sept*, including both vocal accompaniments and dance music. Sections on individual orchestral instruments, as well as symphony orchestra and concert band writing and transcribing—using Beethoven's Sonata, Op. 106 ("Hammerklavier") as his subject—are also included. A great deal of practical information is shared by Bennett in his typically unassuming prose.

B156 "A Look at Music Arranging." *Music Journal* 22 (March 1964), 37, 88-89.
Bennett's article deals mostly with his thoughts about theater scoring rather than how-to-do advice for the novice. He opines that "no orchestration should be bigger or better than the music. The tune is the thing . . ." Turning to concert works, he criticizes the "marvellous naivete of serious composers [because their scores contain] tiny melodic chirps and grunts plus a lot of col legno, sulla tastiera . . . extreme registers . . . whole hardware stores of percussion . . . in short, all of the effects most of the good arrangers threw out years ago, and do not recall unless they are needed for some (usually very cheap) special reason."

B157 "A Master Arranger Speaks." *The Musical Digest*, October-November 1948, 5, 20.

Subtitled "Philosophy of the Composer-Arranger Who Rejuvenated Our Music Stage," his thoughts on scoring extend both to popular music and to concert works. He explains his preference for Beethoven over Mozart and others he terms "natural melodists," and advises composers who come to him with their orchestration dilemmas: "*Recompose it*. If the sound disappoints you even when well conducted and played, recompose it."

B158 "Music of *Carmen Jones*." [in the souvenir program for the 1943 original production].
He discusses at length his adaptation of the Bizet score and collaboration with lyricist Oscar Hammerstein II.

B159 "On Writing Harp Music." *Harp News* 1:10 (Fall 1954), 2-3.
A technical, yet practical, guide to idiomatic scoring for the harp. Interestingly, it is aimed at composers and orchestrators, rather than the harpists who comprise the majority of the journal's subscribers.

B160 "Orchestrating for Broadway." *Modern Music* 9:4 (May-June 1932), 148-152.
Bennett describes his musical training and how he came to be involved in commercial music in New York, sharing many anecdotes about the theater arranger's trade. Also included is an extended discussion of then-contemporary theater scoring practices in New York—orchestra make-up, woodwind "doubling," etc.

B161 "A Pretty Girl Is Like a Melody." *Music Publishers Journal* 2:5 (September-October 1944), 15, 30-31.
Bennett expounds upon the need for professional arrangers in the popular music industry and the unpredictablility of the public as far as determining which popular songs become "hits." He also makes some slightly veiled critical remarks aimed at Broadway songwriters who fail to give their orchestrators proper credit for their contributions.

B162 "To A. S. M. A. from R. R. B." *Overture*, September 1979.
Bennett received the American Society of Music Arrangers' "Golden Score" award in 1979; this poem, published in the A. S. M. A.'s monthly newsletter, was part of his letter of thanks sent to the Society. *See:* **B7.**

B163 [program notes]. Carnegie Hall recital (Louis Kaufman, violin), 20 March 1940.

Bennett's program notes for the premiere of *Hexapoda* briefly essay his ideas about nationalism in music, as well as the piece itself. Remarking upon the dual nature of his arranging-composing career, he charmingly remarks that he "studied with Carl Busch . . . and with Nadia Boulanger in Paris, can write double counterpoint invertible in the octave, tenth, and twelfth—and Fred Astaire likes my saxophone parts."

REFERENCES TO INDIVIDUAL WORKS [B164 - 531]

This section is arranged alphabetically **by title** rather than by genre. Second citations of previously listed sources are enclosed in brackets, giving the "B" number and the author's last name, e.g., [**B13**, Cohn].

ABRAHAM LINCOLN (Symphony) [W1]

B164 L.B. "City Orchestra Plays American Works." *NYW-T*, 20 March 1940, 21.
Louis Biancolli's brief account of **W1f**.

B165 Burrows, Raymond and Redmond, Bessie Carroll. *Symphony Themes*. New York: Simon and Schuster, 1942.
Includes thematic incipits from *Abraham Lincoln*.

B166 M.M.C. "Philadelphia Orchestra Plays Modern Works." *Musical Courier*, 103:18 (31 Oct. 1931), 24.
Review of the premiere, **W1a**: "It was a likeable work, although perhaps a bit too much alike in the mood of the first two and the last movements. The third was entirely different and essentially brighter."

B167 Chotzinoff, Samuel. "WPA Music Project Gives American Concert At Met." *NY Post*, 20 March 1940.
Review of **W1f**: "Mr. Bennett's Symphonic Likeness of the Emancipator constitutes, I think, a more than ordinary abuse of the freedom of musical speech."

B168 Devries, René. "Chicago Concert Halls in Active Weekend Program." *Musical Courier* 115:17 (24 April 1937), 16.

W1e is briefly reviewed: "[Bennett' s] graphic composition . . . admirably depicts the characteristics and life of the martyred president."

B169   "November 7: Dedicatory Orchestral Concert." *Musical Courier* 103:20 (14 November 1931), 17, 19.
Review of **W1b**: "The work is recognizably illustrative, competently scored, successful in contrasts, and with moments of moving genuiness and soaring power. The style is a mixture of conservatism and modernity."

B170   Gilman, Lawrence. "A Lincoln Symphony." *NYH-T*, 11 October 1931, VIII:7.
Gilman's essay deals with both Bennett's career and with the *Abraham Lincoln* score itself, shortly before the premiere in Philadelphia [**W1a**].

B171   Laciar, Samuel L. "Audience Giggles, Stokowski Flees." *Philadelphia Public Ledger*, 25 October 1931, 1, 3.
Laciar reviews the premiere, **W1a**: "As a whole the symphony takes a reasonably high rank among contemporaneous American compositions in the larger form . . . . the work well held its own with the offerings of the European composers on the program." The headline makes reference to the audience's reception of a new work by Webern.

B172   Levant, Oscar. *The Memoirs Of An Amnesiac*. New York: G. P. Putnam's Sons, 1965; paperback ed., New York: Bantam, 1965, 81.
Levant amusingly recalls songwriter Irving Caesar's criticisms of *Abraham Lincoln*.

B173   "List of American Orchestral Works Recommended by WPA Music Project Conductors: July 1941." U.S. Works Projects Administration, Federal Works Agency, Washington, D.C. [1941?], 4.
Uncredited commentary about *Abraham Lincoln* author is someone connected with the Illinois (WPA) Symphony, likely conductor Izler Solomon [*See:* **W1e**]: "tells the story of the great emancipator. . . . It is a legitimate subject for an American composer, worked out, in this instance, with orchestral mastery and sincere feeling."

B174   Perkins, Francis D. "Evening of American Music." *NYH-T*, 20 March 1940.

Review of **W1f**: "the prevailing emotional atmosphere is often convincingly presented. . . . It did not seem, however, that composer had fully realized the expressive possibilities. . . .the interpretation suggested that the potential range of color and emotional content . . . had not been fully realized."

B175 S. "New York City Symphony Offers American Program." *Musical America* 60:7 (10 April 1940), 10.
A brief account of **W1f**.

B176 Sanborn, Pitts. "All-American On The Air." *Modern Music* 9:4 (May- June 1932), 176-178.
Review of **W1c**: "The third part . . . *His Humor* . . . suffered from too much clue. I believe I should have enjoyed it more as an anonymous symphonic scherzo without the attribution to the much debated Lincoln."

B177 _____. "City Orchestra Plays American Works." *NYW-T*, 20 March 1940, 21.
Sanborn's account of **W1f**; of Bennett's work, he remarks only that "The scherzo portion . . . went especially well, and for some listeners this scherzo, with its barn dance section, is the best part of the work, anyway."

B178 Smith, Cecil Michener. "What Chicago Needs." *Modern Music* 14:4 (May-June 1937), 224-225.
Recounting the Illinois Symphony Orchestra's recent programs, Smith describes a group of new works, including *Abraham Lincoln* [**W1e**], as "several interesting, though not invariably exciting pieces . . ."

B179 B. D. U. "Five American Works Performed by Rodzinski and Orchestra." *Musical Courier* 106:10 (11 March 1933), 7.
Review, by Bruno David Ussher, of **W1d**: "although coming at the close of a thought-absorbing repertoire, [it] proved the outstanding item from a viewpoint of public success as well as inherent worth." Other works on the program were by Piston, Harris, Shepherd, and John Powell.

B180 "Works of Six Native Composers in WPA Concert." *North Side News* [New York], 7 March 1940.
Bennett's work is included in an account of **W1f**.

ADAGIO EROICO [W2]

B181   Coddington, Margaret M. "N.F.M.C. Biennial Convention Draws
Throng to Philadelphia." *Musical Courier* 110:18 (4 May 1935), 5, 7.
Review of the Iturbi/Philadelphia Orchestra premiere, **W2a**: "It was a
sincere, well scored and excellently written work."

B182   Eaton, Frances, and Murphy, W. R. "Music Clubs Hold Impressive
Biennial." *Musical America* 55:9 (May 1935), 3-8, 17.
Review of **W2a**, at the National Federation of Music Clubs' 1935
Biennial Convention in Philadelphia.

B183   F.D.P. "Bennett Music Heard at Stadium." *NYH-T*, 27 July 1936, 6.
Perkins enthusiastically reviews **W2b**: [a] "dignified and eloquent
threnody, which is marked by the composer's notable mastery of the
use of orchestral hues and timbres."

B184   [photograph and announcement]. *NYT*, 14 July 1936, IX:5.
Publicity for **W2b**, first performance in New York: "[Bennett's] Adagio
Eroico will have its first New York performance [on 26 July]"; photo is
of Bennett.

ALLEMANDE [W91]

B185   H. I. B. "Louis Kaufman Plays New Violin Works." *Musical Courier*
137:8 (1 May 1948), 23.
Brief account of **W91a**.

B186   G. "Louis Kaufman, Violinist: Town Hall March 25." *Musical
America* 68:5 (April 1948), 31.
Reviewer's reaction to **W91a** is mixed: "The Bennett Allemande has
some sprightliness and dash, but gives an impression more of
painstaking polish than of genuine inspiration."

B187   C. H. "Kaufman, Violinist, Features New Music." *NYT*, 26 March
1948, 25.
Brief account of **W91a**.

ANTIQUE SUITE FOR CLARINET AND ORCHESTRA [W4]

B188   Mills, Charles. "Over The Air." *Modern Music* 18:4 (May-June 1941), 270-274.
Mills reviews broadcast **W4a**: "This was more simple and clean than most of Bennett's fat, juicy writing and it was beautifully played . . ."

ARMED FORCES SUITE [W5]

B189   Darrell, R. D. [record review] *High Fidelity*, October 1960, 106.
Darrell is enthusiastic about the work, its performance, and the quality of the RCA recording [D33] as well: "One of Bennett's most ambitious and powerful works . . ."

B190   J. T. [John Thornton] [record review] *HiFi/Stereo*, January 1961, 60.
Highly complimentary review of **D33**: "Fascinating tone history. . . . a recording of fascinating interest. . . . a crackerjack score, clever, witty, musical, and very well directed by the composer . . ."

AUTOBIOGRAPHY [W51]

B191   Sherman, Robert. "Make Way for the Goldman Band." *NYT*, 26 June 1977, 17, 24.
An account of recent Goldman Band programs in New York, including the **W51a** premiere.

CHARLESTON RHAPSODY [W6]

B192   F. "New York Sinfonietta" *Musical America* 51:5 (10 March 1931), 20.
A very positive review of **W6a**: "The outstanding feature was a performance of . . . Bennett's 'A Charleston Rhapsody', based on the dance which was so popular a few years ago, and frankly in jazz mood and idiom. The composer conducted and was recalled several times . . ."

B193   H. H. "Music: New Chamber Orchestra Heard." *NYT*, 18 May 1933, 17.
W6b is reviewed; reviewer may be Henry Hadley: "The virility of [its] formal lines, close-knit and clear, showed the practiced composer as

much in his admirably economic use of his material as in the extreme effectiveness of his instrumentation. . . . much of it is excellent."

B194   Mills, Charles. "Over The Air." *Modern Music* 19:3 (March-April 1942), 201-205.
Review of **W6d**, from Bennett's "Notebook" show: "somewhat derivative, with many charming moments a la Milhaud, it shows a kind of integrity that seeems convincing and sincere."

CHRISTMAS OVERTURE [W52]

B195   Hughes, Allen. "Band: Grainger and Bennett." *NYT*, 25 July 1982, 42.
Hughes dismisses the piece as "an uncharacteristically dreary arrangement of Christmas songs . . ."

CLASSIC SERENADE FOR STRINGS [W7]

B196   Charlesworth, Hector. "Notable Program At Proms As Mahler Leads." *Toronto Globe and Mail,* 3 August 1945, 11.
A review of **W7b**, Fritz Mahler/Toronto Philharmonic: "A most interesting episode. . . . A number of the composer's works have been heard here, and are unfailing [*sic*] interesting."

COMMEMORATION SYMPHONY [W8]

B197   Darrell, R. D. [record review] *High Fidelity*, November 1960, 80.
A review of **D12**, a recording by Steinberg/Pittsburgh Symphony, who premiered the work: "although . . . Bennett's elaboration on tunes (purportedly styled in the manner of the Troubador's contemporaries) may have effectively served to celebrate . . . Pittsburgh's bicentennial festivities, its interest for other listeners is likely to be limited to a momentary admiration for the orchestrator's ingenuities in tackling a tricky and basically impossible problem." The "problem" he refers to is Bennett's attempt to score the work as a composer/orchestrator might have a century earlier, in Foster's time.

B198   Howard, John Tasker. "Foster with counterpoint." *American Record Guide* 26:10 (June 1960), 810.
A full-page essay throughly describing the work and evaluating the merits of the both the score and the recorded [**D12**] performance:

"Bennett has [worked] with his customary mastery. . . . It is but a skillfully orchestrated succession of Foster melodies, treated with expertly devised counterpoint, and joined with appropriate episodes or bridges of Bennett's own composing."

CONCERTO, HARP/CELLO/ORCHESTRA [W10]

B199 "Composers." *Musical Courier* 162:2 (August 1960), 18.
A brief account of the premiere, **W10a**.

CONCERTO FOR VIOLIN [W12]

B200 "American Scores Heard." *Musical Courier* 129:5 (5 March 1944), 13.
Review of **W12d**: "Broadway stuff adeptly clothed in concert rainment. Such combinations are a Bennett specialty and he manages them altogether successfully. The Concerto pleased through its catchy themes and their transparent treatment."

B201 [Announcement, publicity photo, **W12c**]. *NYT*, 22 March 1942, VIII:3.

B202 Aprahamian, Felix. "Zeal Behind The Baton." *The Sunday Times* [London] 27 May 1956.
Review of **W12e** examines the Bennett *Concerto* briefly: "solidly, even dully, academic."

B203 J. B. "Louis Kaufman Plays Recital in Town Hall." *NY Post*, 26 March 1942.
Review of **W12c**: "Mr. Bennett . . . seemed ill at ease in the inflexible concerto mold and his contribution . . . was a bit labored."

B204 P. B. "Concerto For Foot-Tappers." *The Star* [London], 21 May 1956, 8.
Review of **W12e**: "His concerto was largely bits of tune like those tossed around by jazzmen. . . . This was as easy to accept as an ice cream sundae."

B205 "Barzin Presents Three New Works." *NYT*, 15 February 1944, 14.
Review of **W12d**: "Like most of Mr. Bennett's efforts, the concerto is pleasant, likeable music that is neither hard to understand nor dull to hear. . . . The thematic material is appropriate to the work . . ."

B206   Bennett, Grena. "American Artists Featured at Carnegie." *NYJ-A*, 15
       February 1944, 8.
       Review of **W12d**: "typical American idiom tinged with the elemental
       quality of a spiritual, the melodic content simple and of pleasing
       character, the four movements deftly designed and orchestrated."
       Grena Bennett—apparently no relation—was among those New York
       reviewers most consistently enthused about each of Bennett's new
       works.

B207   Berger, Arthur V. "Barzin Conducts American Music." *NY Sun*, 15
       February 1944.
       Mixed review of **W12d**: "customary fine perspective of Robert Russell
       Bennett's scoring. . . . [but] rarely rises above the most commonplace
       cinema music . . ."

B208   Biancolli, Louis. "Bennett Concerto Jazz-Tinged." *NYW-T*, 15
       February 1944, 6.
       Review of **W12d**; Biancolli's opening comment suggests a less-than-
       complete familiarity with Bennett's range as a composer: "Mr. Bennett
       can no more avoid syncopation than Bach could avoid fugues. But he
       knows how to dress it up for a Carnegie airing and bring it in classic
       line with fine grasp of technic."

B209   C. "Louis Kaufman, Violinist." *Musical America* 62:7 (10 April 1942),
       27.
       Review of **W12c**, a performance with a piano reduction of the
       orchestral score played by Bennett: "Of the newer works [on the
       program] the most stimulating proved to be the Bennett concerto. . . .
       [it is] harmonically idiomatic of the present day while indulging in no
       new harmonic experiments. . . . Given the prescribed orchestral
       background, the work would undoubtedly be heard to better effect."

B210   Freed, Richard [record review] *Stereo Review*, December 1976, 135.
       A review of the Kaufman/London Symphony recording, **D3**: "It is a
       tuneful, animated, eminently agreeable piece which could stand
       exposure on concert programs. . . . performance [is] definitive . . ."

B211   Fuller, Donald. "New York, Spring '42; Music of the Americas."
       Modern Music 19:4 (May-June 1942), 254-260.
       Fuller reviews **W12c**: "Though he manipulated the form . . . with
       dexterity and interest, the matter, refreshing as usual, missed filling the
       lines."

B212 Johnson, Harriet. "Night of All-American Music by National
Orchestral Association." *NY Post*, 15 February 1944.
Very positive review of **W12d**: "Mr. Bennett's composition has a
rhythmically intriguing main theme for the first movement. The
whole concerto has an arresting vitality."

B213 I. M. J. [Isabel Morse Jones] "Kaufman, Violinist, Plays Several 'Firsts'
At Ebell." *Los Angeles Times*, 2 March 1942, I:12.
Review of **W12b**: "Bennett's very interesting . . . Concerto. . . . has a
future on the concert stage . . ."

B214 Kolodin, Irving. "Kaufman Offers Work By Bennett." *NY Sun*, 26
March 1942.
Review of **W12c**: "The Bennett concerto has the air of musical breeding
native to his talent. . . . a score whose distinctions would undoubtedly
multiply, given the proper orchestral background [it was played with
piano accompaniment]."

B215 Mills, Charles. "Over The Air." *Modern Music* 19:2 (January-February
1942), 134-138.
Mills reviews **W12a**, the broadcast premiere on Bennett's "Notebook"
program. He calls it "A surprisingly nice work. . . . This is undoubtedly
his best piece. . . . The program needs more works of such calibre."

B216 "Mr. Bernard Herrman: American Conductor's London Concerts."
The Times [London], 21 May 1956.
A generally positive review of **W12e**: "the music made very few
concessions to popular taste. It was busy, brittle, brilliant music, quite
effective to listen to at the time, but not very memorable in thematic
invention."

B217 S. "Barzin Conduct American Works." *Musical America* 64:4 (10
March 1944), 20.
Review of **W12d**: "Mr. Bennett has followed the principles of certain
chefs of putting a little of everything into his concerto. . . . It is often
trivial . . . but unquestionably entertaining to the music public at large."

B218 N. S. "4 Premieres Given By Louis Kaufman." *NYT*, 26 March 1942, 27.
Noel Straus compares the *Concerto* to the other works receiving their
premieres on the recital [**W12c**]: "[it was] the most warmly welcomed
of the new compositions, and it contained as its slow movement a
'Meditation,' which was less artificial than the rest of the new music

scheduled. This division of the eclectic opus had mood and meaning . . ."

B219 Shupp, Enos E., Jr. [record review] *The New Records*, November 1976, 5-6.
Review of **D3**: "The performance is highly polished, tense, and most effective. The music offers nothing new or difficult, for it was planned to be conventional. Despite all of this it has an aura of originality, and it surely lacks nothing in technical expertise."

B220 Simon, Henry. "America Gets 'Recognized'." *PM* [NY], 15 February 1944.
A short but glowing review of **W12d**: "as always his music is set out with such a mastery of orchestral effect, that it made the hit of the evening."

B221 _____. "Themes and Variations." *PM* [NY], 19 March 1942, 23.
Louis Kaufman is interviewed concerning his upcoming Town Hall concert, on which the *Concerto* will receive its first New York concert performance [**W12c**].

B222 Simon, Robert A. "Musical Events: Almost All New." *The New Yorker* 20:2 (26 February 1944), 74-75.
Glowing review of **W12d**: "a rewarding vehicle for the soloist and good fun for the listeners. The wonted Bennett expertness in writing for orchestra was always in evidence."

B223 Thomson, Virgil. "Music: New Works for Orchestra." *NYH-T*, 15 February 1944.
Thomson tended to have mixed reactions to new Bennett works; in this review of **W12d**, he evaluates the piece as "a skillful composition, but quite without originality. . . . Mr. Bennett seems to think that the music called 'popular' is a style, a domain in itself like folklore, and hence material for art. He is wrong. It is the last stage of art music's natural decomposition."

B224 J. W. "'In A Popular Style' A Gay Violin Concerto." *Daily Telegraph And Morning Post* [London], 21 May 1956.
Brief mention of **W12e**.

B225 Weiler, A. H. "Odds and Ends." *NYT*, 20 February 1940, II:3.
A profile of violinist Louis Kaufman and his dual career as concert

soloist and Hollywood concertmaster. Includes a concise account of **W12d** as well.

CONCERTO, VIOLIN/PIANO/ORCHESTRA [W13]

B226 Kammerer, Rafael. "Rabinofs Discuss Premiere of Creston Work." *Musical America* 78:5 (April 1958), 28.
The majority of the article deals with the new violin concerto by Paul Creston, which is to receive its first performance by Benno Rabinof. Also mentioned are three Bennett works often programmed by the couple: *Hexapoda* [**W101**], *A Song Sonata* [**W110**], and *Five Tune Cartoons* [**W98**], as well as the "double concerto" being written by Bennett for the Rabinofs "at the present time [**W13**]."

B227 "Portland Hears New Work By Robert Russell Bennett." *NYT*, 20 March 1963, 5.
A brief account of the Portland, OR premiere [**W13a**], without commentary.

CONCERTO GROSSO, DANCE BAND/ORCHESTRA [W14]

B228 "Berlin Hails Hanson Offering Our Music." *NYT*, 9 January 1933, 22.
Without mentioning any pieces from the Howard Hanson/Berlin Philharmonic program of American works [**W14b**] specifically, it is noted that "The press comments [in Berlin] thus far have not been especially favorable to the various works performed."

B229 "Berlin Welcomes Hanson." *NYH-T*, 8 January 1933.
A brief account of the **W14b** program.

B230 Hooker, Adelaide. "Crusading for Americans at Rochester." *Modern Music* 10:4 (May-June 1933), 207-209.
Review of the premiere, **W14a**: "an unusual departure in a classical form. . . . Mr. Bennett's skill is unquestioned, his music is clever. It is a fine work if one's tastes run to symphonic jazz."

B231 "Native Program Given At Stadium." *NYT*, 5 July 1934, 20.
Short review of **W14c**: "The second movement . . . was skillfully wrought. . . . But other sections did not come off."

B232   "Native Works Delight On July 4." *Musical America* 54:12 (July 1934), 20.
       A concise account of the **W14c** program.

B233   "Our Music In Berlin." *NYT*, 22 January 1933, IX:7.
       The **W14b** concert is briefly described.

B234   Perkins, Francis D. "Stadium Hears Musical Satire Of Tin Pan Alley."
       NYH-T, 5 July 1934.
       A generally favorable review of **W14c**: "As a satire . . . its meaning is
       clear, and . . . clever and effective. . . . orchestration is deftly
       wrought. . . . The first movement is rater [*sic*] conglomerate . . . [but]
       the others make their point with able conciseness."

B235   "Rochester, N. Y. Hears All-American Program." *Musical Courier*
       105:26 (24 December 1932), 20.
       A brief account of the first [**W14a**] performance.

B236   "Rochester Orchestra All-American Program." *Musical Courier*
       106:1 (7 January 1933), 21.
       The work [**W14a**] is described briefly as a "witty concoction."

B237   Rodgers, Bernard. "Rochester Twenty Years After." *Modern Music* 22:4
       (May-June 1945), 262-3.
       Bennett's *Concerto Grosso* is included in a chronicle of pieces that
       were premiered on the Eastman School "All-American" programs of
       the 1920s and 1930s and played again at the 1945 Festival [**W14d**].

B238   Stuckenschmidt, H. H. "German Season Under The Crisis."
       Modern Music 10:3 (March-April 1933), 163-167.
       The prominent German musicologist-critic's review of **W14b**: "[the
       piece] does not achieve more than a witty, humorous Ravel-Stravinsky
       eclecticism . . ."

B239   Veinus, Abraham. *The Concerto*. New York: Doubleday, Doran and
       Co., 1945; reprint ed., New York: Dover Publications, 1963; 277, 289.
       Discussion of the *Concerto Grosso* as one of a limited number of
       20th-century examples of the form: "The undertaking is a provocative
       one, but the execution extremely routine. . . . There is no vital
       juxtaposition of choirs, no real playing off of one against the other."

B240   Will, Mary Ertz. "American Program Proves Attractive." *Musical America* 52:20 (25 December 1932), 12.
Enthusiastic review of **W14a**: "The concerto, humorous and original and orchestrated with skill, consists of five movements which seemed all too short."

B241   _____. "Eastman Festival Marks 20th Year." *Musical America* 65:8 (May 1945), 8.
Brief account of **W14d**.

B242   _____. "Premieres Given As Rochester Festival Is Concluded." *Musical America* 53:12 (25 May 1933), 16.
Brief account of **W14a**.

CONCERTO GROSSO, WIND QUINTET/WIND ORCHESTRA [W53]

B243   Steinfirst, Donald. "Wind Symphony Concert Again Feature at Point." *Pittsburgh Post-Gazette*, 7 July 1958, 9.
An account of the premiere, **W53a**.

CONCERT VARIATIONS ON A CROONER'S THEME [W15]

B244   [announcement and photograph]. *Musical America* 70:5 (April 1950), 42.
Bennett and violinist Aaron Rosand, who premiered the work, are pictured; caption gives details of upcoming premiere, **W15a**.

B245   H. I. B. "New York Concerts: Aaron Rosand, Feb. 9." *Musical Courier* 143:5 (1 March 1951), 22.
Review of **W15b**, a recital performance by Rosand with the piece retitled *Theme and Variations*: "[the piece is] marked by modern tonal effects and skillful scoring. . . . the audience appeared to approve of [Bennett's] complex contribution to the violin repertory."

B246   Berger, Arthur. "Concert And Recital." *NYH-T*, 10 February 1951, 6.
Berger's review of **W15b**: "What we heard last night was colored by Bennett's Broadway affiliations, and his use of the violin was in the virtuoso style of Wieniawski and somewhat less imaginative than we had anticipated it would be in view of the composer's skill with instrumentation. It is the kind of work violinists will, no doubt, be attracted to . . ."

B247   Brandeis, Fanny. "Notes on the Program." [Program for 30 November-
1 December 1949 premiere by the Louisville Orchestra, **W15a**].
Program essay for the *Concert Variations* is written by the composer.

B248   "Current Chronicle." *Musical Quarterly* 41:1 (January 1955), 76-85.
Part of the article is devoted to a list of all Louisville Orchestra-
commissioned works, including Bennett's *Concert Variations*.

B249   L. M. G. "New Work and Violinist Click." *Louisville Times*, 2
December 1949.
Review of the premiere, **W15a**: "an interesting and distinctive
contemporary expression. . . . wistful and appealing little theme, simply
presented. . . . [the] instrumentation is colorful and skillful as might be
expected . . ."

B250   Grace, Nancy. "Mr. Bennett is a 'Bop' Fan." *Louisville Courier-
Journal*, 1 December 1949, II:2.
Interview with Bennett, who was in Louisville for the premiere, **W15a**.
The article details Bennett's credits as both composer and arranger, and
mentions his enthusiasm for bebop in general and Dizzy Gillespie in
particular. This is noteworthy, as Bennett's comments about jazz
rarely appeared in print.

B251   A. H. "Aaron Rosand, Violinist: Town Hall, Feb. 9." *Musical America*
71:4 (March 1951), 16.
Review of **W15b**, in which the Bennett work is briefly evaluated: "the
composition is a pleasantly unpretentious one that should bear
repetition."

B252   Kupperheim, Dr. Hans F. "Martha Graham Dances in Louisville
Premiere." *Musical Courier* 141:4 (15 February 1950), 35.
Concise-but-enthusiastic review of **W15a**: "based upon an appealing
melody, the score is of the lighter type, gay and sentimental, and
delightfully orchestrated."

B253   "Whitney Conducts First Performance of Bennett Piece." *Musical
America* 69:16 (15 December 1949), 17.
Review of **W15a**: "As a whole, the composition is agreeably
lighthearted, containing some brilliant display passages for the solo
instrument . . ."

DANCE, FLUTE/PIANO [W95]

B254 "Give First Hearings Of Chamber Music." *NYT*, 10 February 1930.
Account of the first program of the third season of the Copland-
Sessions Concerts on which the *Dance*, as well as Bennett's *Nocturne*,
received their American premiere [W95b] at Steinway Hall. The
writer does not critique pieces individually, but concludes that "The
compositions heard last night justified the high aims of the organizers
of the concerts."

DANCE SCHERZO [W96]

B255 Jones, Isabel Morse. "Pro Musica Chapter Gives Concert, Federals
Present Young Artists." *Los Angeles Times*, 15 March 1938.
Positive review of **W96a**: "especially interesting. . . . more serious in its
intent and decided in its rhythm [than the Guentzel quintet also
performed]. . . . [Bennett] is one of the most gifted of the American-born
composers."

[B188, Mills]
Review of a *Dance Scherzo* performance on a "Notebook" broadcast,
W96b: "What more thinning out and concentration on line can do for
Bennett is clear from his *Dance Scherzo*. . . a fairly amusing and clever
work."

B256 R. D. S. "Pro-Musica American List." *Musical Courier* 117:7 (1 April
1938), 40.
Review, by Richard Drake Saunders, of **W96a**: "composed for the
occasion, [it] was filled with rhythmic vitality, amusing in its
exposition, and adroit in its part writing."

A DRY WEATHER LEGEND [W16]

B257 "Bennett Will Conduct Symphony in 'Legend'." *Knoxville* [TN]
News Sentinel, 2 February 1947.
Publicity for the **W16a** program; conductor/flutist Lamar Stringfield,
who conducted the Knoxville Symphony and was soloist for the
premiere, recalls his twenty-five years of association with Bennett.

B258   Evans, Dick. "Bennett To Conduct Symphony Orchestra." *Knoxville*
[TN] *News Sentinel*, 19 February 1947.
An interview with Bennett at the time of the **W16a** premiere; Bennett
tells the story behind the *Dry Weather Legend* and shares his thoughts
about American composers' use of folk music and folk themes.

B259   Miller, Malcolm. "Music and Drama." *Knoxville* [TN] *Journal*, 2
February 1947.
Publicity material, giving a complete program listing for the **W16a**
premiere.

B260   _____. "Music and Drama." *Knoxville* [TN] *Journal*, 19 February
1947.
Review of the **W16a** premiere: "The composition contributed eight
minutes of delectably descriptive music . . ."

B261   "Noted Composer Due Here Monday." *Knoxville* [TN] *News
Sentinel*, 16 February 1947.
Biographical sketch of Bennett, coming to Knoxville to conduct the
W16a concert.

B262   Rule, Gunby. "The Symphony." *Knoxville* [TN] *News Sentinel*, 19
February 1947.
An account of the **W16a** program, though no critical opinion is
expressed.

EARLY AMERICAN BALLADE [W17]

B263   "Radio Impressions Of A Week." *Musical Courier* 104:16 (16 April
1932), 21.
Announces Bennett's work as the first in a series of "five-minute . . .
compositions" to be heard on Nathaniel Shilkret's CBS radio program:
"Other composers represented in the series will be Percy Grainger,
Ferdie [*sic*] Grofé, Werner Janssen, John Alden Carpenter, Charles
Wakefield Cadman, John Powell, David Guion, Pietro Florida
(Shilkret's former teacher) and Ben Bonnell (his chief arranger).
Ottorino Respighi will also contribute [a composition]."

EIGHT ETUDES FOR ORCHESTRA [W18]

B264 Bennett, Grena. "Tchaikovsky Opus Played By Rubinstein." *NYJA*, 7 January 1942, 12.
In this review of **W12c**, the *Etudes* are described as "a diverting piece of writing, artfully orchestrated . . ."

B265 Biancolli, Louis. "Bach, Ormandy, and Bennett." *NYW-T*, 7 January 1942, 20.
Generally favorable review of **W18c**: "typically quippish and snappy in style, though only the distaff Etude came up to Mr. Bennett's inventive best."

B266 Cohn, Arthur. "Philadelphia Story." *Modern Music* 19:3 (March-April 1942), 187-189.
Highly complimentary review of **W18b**: "proved a delight. . . . Bennett manipulates the orchestra so as to make it a full-blooded seething mixture. There were concise contrasts, pithy contours to the melodic lines, and suavity to the humor. . . . This piece and the *Violin Concerto* convince me that Bennett at some time will be up front where he belongs."

B267 "Columbia Orchestra Plays Robert Bennett Sketches." *NYH-T*, 18 July 1938, 4.
Review of the broadcast premiere, **W18a**: "The diversity of subjects and moods made it less easy to gather an impression of the composer's creative musical individuality than it might have been in a work of more unified character. . . . skillfully wrought instrumental investiture . . . a work liberally supplied with melody."

B268 Fuller, Donald. "New York Mid-Season, 1942-'43." *Modern Music* 20:3 (March-April 1943), 112-117.
The **W18c** program is briefly noted.

B269 _____. "Winter To Spring, New York, 1942." *Modern Music* 19:3 (March-April 1942), 173-178.
Review of **W18c**: "the continuity is sometimes too easy-going. But as the intention is always clear, and what is offered direct, natural, and winning, everything comes off."

B270   K. "Rubinstein Is Soloist Under Ormandy." *Musical America* 62:2
       (25 January 1942), 10.
       Review of **W18c**: "The studies are eminently successful in
       accomplishing the composer's purpose. . . . They are well written, and
       expertly orchestrated. . . . Adroit craftsmanship is revealed in all the
       etudes, and that was all Mr. Bennett intended."

B271   Kochnitzky, Leon. "Musical Portraits." *Modern Music* 20: (November-
       December 1942), 23-32.
       The author evaluates the many *Portraits* by Virgil Thomson, the new
       Lincoln Portrait by Copland, and Bennett's *Eight Etudes*, noting that
       "The results are more than interesting. They promise to give us a new
       American vogue in composition."

B272   Lieberson, Goddard. "Over The Air." *Modern Music* 15:1 (November-
       December 1937), 53-55.
       Discusses American composers and the works resulting from the CBS
       (radio) Columbia Compositions Commission program, also recently-
       awarded commissions to Bennett [which resulted in the *Eight Etudes*]
       and others.

B273   _____. "Over The Air." *Modern Music* 16:1 (November-December
       1938), 65-69.
       Review of **W18a**: "has qualities—smooth impressionist harmonies,
       and a facile orchestration—which make for a good evening in the
       theatre. Intellectually, the music goes no deeper. . . . The content of
       these pieces range from satire to a kind of youthful adulation."

B274   "Looking the Town Over: 'Eight Etudes'." *Harrisburg* [PA] *News*, 27
       December 1941.
       Announcement of forthcoming performances of *Eight Etudes* in
       Harrisburg and elsewhere by the Philadelphia Orchestra as part of a
       regional tour.

B275   "Ormandy Conducts New Dances By Rachmaninoff . . . Bennett Etudes
       Given." *Musical America* 61:2 (25 January 1941), 3, 27.
       Glowing review of **W18b**: "artfully fabricated miniatures demanding
       great orchestral virtuosity. . . Brilliantly set forth, the work found
       hearty favor and there was prolonged applause . . ."

B276   Perkins, Francis D. "Philadelphians and Rubinstein in Carnegie Hall."
       NYH-T, 7 January 1942, 14.

Review of **W18c**: "the ideas were engaging and the range of moods and atmospheres were generous . . . memorable skill and effectiveness in the use of instrumental colors . . ."

B277 "Reiner Back on Podium for Concert." *Chicago Daily Tribune*, 14 November 1958, III:4.
Account, without commentary, of **W18f**.

B278 H. A. S. "Radio Highlights." *Musical Courier* 117:3 (1 August 1938), 23.
Review of **W18a**: "atmospheric to a large degree and skillfully instrumented. . . . If transoceanic influences were apparently present, also was liberal melody."

THE ENCHANTED KISS [W40]

B279 "Opera And Concert: Bennett Completing New One-Act Work—
Chicago Orchestra Finances." *NYT*, 23 October 1938, IX:7.
Article notes that Bennett "is at work on an opera drawn from one of this country's best spinners of tales. . . . O. Henry. It is not possible yet to reveal which story [of the author's will be used]. . . . Mr. Bennett is finishing it between Hollywood and Broadway chores."

B280 "Preparation for a Premiere." *NYT*, 30 December 1945, 5.
To publicize that evening's premiere [**W40a**] of the work over the Mutual Broadcasting System. Photographs are of Bennett, conductor Sylvan Levin, and the vocal soloists.

ENDIMION [W41]

B281 "American Music In Rochester." *NYT*, 10 March 1935, VIII:5.
An announcement of **W41a**.

B282 "Bennett's Opera-Ballet Given By Eastman School." *NYH-T*, 6 April 1935.
An account, without criticism, of **W41a**.

B283 "Eastman Festival In April." *NYT*, 3 February 1935, VIII:8.
An announcement of **W41a**.

B284   Gorton, Thomas. "Rochester Has Fifth American Festival." *Musical Courier* 110:16 (20 April 1935), 5, 10.
Review of **W41a**: "The Bennett score fluently suggests a definite pagan atmosphere, yet is not entirely consistent in the realization of the story's dramatic possibilities."

B285   Hooker, Adelaide V. "Tenth Rochester Celebration." *Modern Music* 12:4 (May-June 1935), 201-3.
Review of **W41a**: "[the work is] lacking the red-blooded quality that we today expect from Bennett. The music is rhythmically well adapted to the dance. . . . However, the score has the French mannerisms of ten years ago." The ballet was composed in Paris while studying with Boulanger.

B286   Will, Mary Ertz. "American Music Festival Ends In Rochester." *Musical America* 55:8 (25 April 1935), 61.
Review of **W41a**: "The music gives one the feeling of old far-off things, rather in the style of wandering shepherds and their flutes."

FIVE IMPROVISATIONS ON EXOTIC SCALES [W97]

B287   L. H. "Festival Concert." *NYH-T*, 15 February 1947, 9.
Review of **W97a**; the *Improvisations* are described as "vaguely concealed waltzes, jazz and popular mannerisms seen through exotic orientation. They resemble 'white man's burden' styles in their handling of Balinese, Ancient Chinese, Ancient Greek, and the Negro Blues idiom."

FIVE TUNE CARTOONS [W98]

B288   A. V. B. "Marc Brown." *NYH-T*, 28 February 1949, 11.
Arthur Berger's review of **W98a**: "Bennett's Tune Cartoons . . . did not have enough fun in them to justify their length."

B289   H. W. L. "Marc Brown, Violinist, In Bennett Premiere." *Musical Courier* 139:6 (15 March 1949), 17.
An account of **W98a**, with no specific comments about the *Cartoons*.

B290   C. S. "Marc Brown, Violinist: Carnegie Hall, Feb. 27, 5:30." *Musical America* 69:4 (March 1949), 24.

A short review of **W98a**; reviewer states that "The music is cleverly contrived . . ."

B291 N. S. "Brown Returns in Violin Recital." *NYT*, 28 February 1949, 16.
Noel Straus describes them as "light-weight creations, which hardly belonged on a serious program" in this review of **W98a**.

FOUR DANCES FOR PIANO TRIO [W100]

B292 "Composers Corner." *Musical America* 74:5 (March 1954), 37.
Announces the completion of **W100**, written for the Columbia Concert Trio.

B293 "In Concert Premiere." *Musical America* 74:13 (1 November 1954), 29.
Photograph of the Columbia Concert Trio and details of the work's premiere [**W100a**] in Scranton, PA.

THE FOUR FREEDOMS (Symphony) [W19]

B294 "Announcing The Four Freedoms Symphony." *Saturday Evening Post* 216:25 (18 December 1943), 102-103.
Two-page announcement of the work's completion, with photographs of Bennett, Frank Black, the NBC Symphony, and of the four Norman Rockwell paintings originally commissioned by the *Post*. Also includes details of forthcoming performances by the NBC Symphony [**W19a**], Philadelphia Orchestra [**W19b**], and Los Angeles Philharmonic [**W19c**].

B295 "Authoritative Music Critics Have This To Say About Robert Russell Bennett's The Four Freedoms Symphony." [advertisement by music publisher G. Schirmer] *Music Publishers Journal* 2:2 (March-April 1944), 12.
Advertisement provides lengthy reprints (undated) of concert reviews. Florence Lawrence (*Los Angeles Examiner*) comments [**W19c**]: "Musically intriguing. . . . the symphonic movements all are interesting." Olin Downes (*NYH-T*) reviews **W19b**: "His method is symphonic in a full four movements; his style that of the cultivated and accomplished craftsman that he is, and a musician who seeks the path of straight developments and genuine evolution of themes and not merely that of superficial effect . . ."

B296 J. D. B. "Philadelphia Orchestra in American Program." *NYH-T*, 15
December 1943, 20.
A negative review of **W19b**: "It is essentially a Tin Pan Alley version of
a subject which should never have been chosen for musical setting in
the first place." Reviewer is Jerome D. Bohm.

B297 Bennett, Grena. "Levant Plays With Philly Orchestra." *NYJ-A*, 15
December 1943, 11.
A brief review of **W19b**; *Four Freedoms* is described as "an eloquent
musical illustration . . ."

B298 Biancolli, Louis. "Oscar Levant Plays Own Concerto." *NYW-T*, 15
December 1943, 32.
Enthusiastic review of **W19b**: "I think it is Bennett's finest score yet. . . .
the score translates brave words into American idiom, stemming in
part from popular usage like syncopation and rollicking folk ways, but
basically sound and symphonic in best concert tradition."

B299 E. "Levant Soloist With Philadelphians." *Musical America* 63:17
(25 December 1943), 33.
Mixed review of **W19b**: "The talky, boisterous first movement and the
jazzily rhythmic and gay third movement display some interesting
invention; but the other two are flat, unprofitable and platitudinous."

B300 "Four Freedoms Heard in Music Broadcast." *NYT*, 27 September
1943, 23.
This account of **W19a** includes a reprint of a telegram sent to Bennett
by Norman Rockwell (this lengthy telegram is reprinted in **B295** as
well); also, Bennett's comment about his approach to the composition:
"I tried to follow the pictures as a motion-picture score follows the idea
of a film . . ."

B301 Jones, Isabel Morse. "New Suite Appraised." *Los Angeles Times*, 18
December 1943, 9.
Review of **W19c**: "He takes his native land rather lightly, kidding the
country he loves. 'Freedom of Worship' is pure New England,
descriptive, religious and quite the best writing of the four."

B302 Liebling, Viva. "News and Previews of Radio, Stage & Screen."
Musical Courier 128:5 (20 October 1943), 7.
Review of the radio premiere, **W19a**: "brilliantly orchestrated, filled

with clever if not completely developed ideas. Its title seems to be arbitrary and another might have fitted it just as well."

B303   Mills, Charles. "Over The Air." *Modern Music* 21:1 (November-December 1943), 57-60.
Mills briefly evaluates the premiere, **W19a**: "I found none [of its four movements] good, all of them stale and pretentious."

B304   Morton, Lawrence. "American Conductor and Works for L. A."
Modern Music 21:1 (November-December 1943), 37-39.
Brief account of the **W19c** performance in Los Angeles.

B305   _____. "American Symphonists in Los Angeles." *Modern Music* 21:2 (January-February 1944), 100-102.
A more detailed and thorough discussion of the work by Morton than **B304** above; referring to **W19c**, a concert which included new works by Paul Creston and William Schuman, he notes that the work "sounded much better in the concert-hall than it did on the air. I am not at all tempted to dispose of it with the usual reference to slick orchestration, especially after observing the clumsiness of some of Creston's scoring and the naivete of much of Schuman's."

B306   Persichetti, Vincent. "Philadelphia Takes A Flier." *Modern Music* 21:2 (January-February 1944), 104-106.
The **W19b** performance is reviewed briefly; his evaluation parallels that of Charles Mills [**B303**] to a curious degree: "the pretentious Bennett four-movement affair is obvious and stale."

B307   [press release, *The Saturday Evening Post*, n.d.]
This untitled release begins: "The Four Freedoms Symphony—from the pen of Robert Russell Bennett, distinguished American composer . . ." One page in length, it dates from Spring, 1944. The release chronicles performances to date, **W19a-b-c**, and gives a biographical sketch of Bennett. It also notes that "Piano scores of The Four Freedoms Symphony will be distributed by The Saturday Evening Post to the music departments of colleges and high schools and conservatories of music." This was not mentioned by the *Post* in **B294**, and there is no indication that this wide distribution of free copies of the piano reduction ever took place.

B308   Quinn, Alfred Price. "Music." *B'nai B'rith Messenger* [Los Angeles], 17 December 1943, 9.

Lengthy article includes a substantial biographical sketch of Bennett. Previews *Four Freedoms* performance by L. A. Philharmonic [W19c].

B309   Smith, George H. Lovett. "Americana, New And Old." *Modern Music* 21:3 (March-April 1944), 177-179.
A terse, negative review of **W19d**: "[the piece] has received such cordial panning in these pages that I need not add further commentary on its tastless pomposities . . . . Mr. Bennett's creative ability has not yet caught up with his great skill as an orchestrator and arranger."

B310   "Youngsters Dance Four Freedoms Ballet." *NYW-T*, 15 May 1944.
Short account of **W19e**, the New York Teen-Age Ballet performance of *The Four Freedoms* as arranged for two pianos and percussion by Bennett.

B311   Zuck, Barbara A. *A History of Musical Americanism* (Studies in Musicology, no. 19). Ann Arbor: UMI Research Press , 1980, 190-191.
In her chapter, "Musical Americanism and World Ward II," Zuck discusses the work and its background (Roosevelt, Norman Rockwell, etc.). Included are two excerpts from the published piano reduction by Helmy Kresa.

FOUR PRELUDES FOR BAND [W59]

B312   Davis, Peter G. "Goldman Band Opens With Typical Potpourri." *NYT*, 26 June 1978, III:14.
Davis, reviewing **W59a**, describes the *Preludes* as "cleverly devised."

FOUR SONGS (Teasdale) [W140]

B313   F. "League of Composers." *Musical America* 51:5 (10 March 1931), 43.
A short account of the **W140a** program.

B314   "Six Americans Are Represented On League's List." *NYH-T*, 22 February 1931.
Publicity for 1 March 1931 League of Composers concert [**W140a**] at which the work was premiered.

B315   "Yaddo Festival For Contemporary American Music Held At Saratoga Springs, N. Y." *Musical Courier* 104:19 (7 May 1932), 32.

An account of the entire Festival, with no criticism of Bennett's
Songs specifically.

THE FUN AND FAITH OF WILLIAM BILLINGS, AMERICAN [W86]

B316   Hume, Paul. "Patriotic Singing Forth." *Washington Post*, 30 April
1975, B1, 5.
Hume, reviewing the premiere [W86a], notes that a good portion of the
choral music is undisturbed by Bennett, being left as originally scored
by Billings. He then comments: "[Bennett's] own writing sounds an
appropriate note in the introduction, and in some of the brief
interludes that lead from one tune to the next."

B317   "National Symphony Orders 12 Works for the Bicentenary." *NYT*,
24 April 1974, 49.
Lists Bennett and 11 other composers commissioned to write works
to be premiered by the National Symphony in its 1975-76 and 1976-77
seasons; *The Fun and Faith* [W86] was the result of Bennett' s
commission, and the first of the twelve to be performed.

HAMLET (Incidental music) [W47]

B318   Corbin, John. "The Play." *NYT*, 17 November 1922, 14.

B319   Lewisohn, Ludwig. "Drama: Hamlet Himself." *The Nation* 115:2996
(6 December 1922), 646, 648.
This review of W47a mentions Bennett's score only briefly: "The
music is the music of the inevitable sadness of things."

HEXAPODA [W101]

B320   L. B. "Kaufman Recital." *NYW-T*, 21 March 1940, 17.
Louis Biancolli's commentary after hearing the first peformance
[W101a] is positive but brief: "Other violinists take note."

B321   C. "Benno Rabinof, Violinist." *Musical America* 65:16 (10 December
1945), 28.
An account, without commentary, of W101c.

B322   Chislett, W. A. "Nights At The Round Table." *The Gramophone*,
August 1955, 107. [record review of **D9**]
The reviewer is entirely unfamiliar with Bennett's compositions and
misspells his name as "Bennet" throughout. He writes: "They are
slickly clever and some are diabolically difficult, but as to their
suitability for the violin, except perhaps as an exercise, there is room
for two opinions."

B323   Downes, Olin. "Jascha Heifetz Heard in Recital." *NYT*, 30 October 1940,
28.
Review of **W101b**: "The pieces, highly modern in texture and
resourceful in device, are very amusing and make an uncommonly
piquant effect."

B324   Fuller, Donald. "New York, 1940—The Season Opens." *Modern Music*
18:1 (November-December 1940), 37-41.
Review of **W101b,** Heifetz's Carnegie Hall program: "These short
pieces were polished, charming, and sophisticated. Their cosmopolitan
measures were beautifully scored. . . The jazz influence was pretty
remote for a good part of the time and, when present, seemed of a
definite early vintage and somewhat too refined. I liked best the slower
numbers with their charming feeling of nostalgia."

B325   Haggin, B. H. "Records." *The Nation* 152:9 (1 March 1941), 247, 249.
[record review of **D4**]: "[the pieces are] a mildly diverting parodistic use
of jazz idioms."

B326   King, William G. "Heifetz Begins Another Season—." *NY Sun*, 26
October 1940.
Interview with Heifetz regarding his upcoming [29 October] recital,
W101b: " 'I hope Mr. Bennett will write many other things for the
violin [Heifetz said]; I think he's one of the most interesting of our
composers'."

B327   "Louis Kaufman in Novelties." *Musical Courier* 121:8 (15 April
1940), 10.
Review of **W101a**: "a most amusing set of descriptive pieces . . . with a
jazz basis and ingenious, lively scoring."

B328   Miller, Phillip L., and Shank, William. "Recorded Music." *Library
Journal* 80:17 (1 October 1955), 2076-2079. [review of **D9**].

B329   "National Symphony Auditors Choose 3 American Scores."
       Musical Courier 121:8 (15 April 1941), 35.
       Review of an undated Heifetz recital in Washington, D.C., c. 1 April
       1941: "Hexapoda . . . by Bennett created a stir . . ."

B330   S. "Louis Kaufman Offers Unusual Program." *Musical America*
       60:7 (10 April 1940), 14.
       The reviewer [W101a] comments briefly upon *Hexapoda:* "It is
       genuinely witty and well-fashioned."

[B219, Shupp]
       Review of D3: "The two works for violin and piano [*Hexapoda* and *A
       Song Sonata*] are equally fresh [as the *Concerto for Violin*] in
       inspiration and completely violinistic in writing . . ."

B331   Simon, Robert A. "Musical Events." *The New Yorker* 16:22 (9
       November 1940), 68-69.
       Review of W101b: "[*Hexapoda* is a] brilliant and entertaining
       [composition] . . . . [it] managed to capsize the audience successfully."

B332   _____. "Musical Events: American Music Everywhere." *The New
       Yorker* 16:7 (30 March 1940), 58.
       Review of W101a: "The composer, in a program note, hoped that his
       suite was 'both good music and good sport.' It was all of that. . . . You'll
       be hearing more of 'Hexapoda' at other concerts."

B333   Taubman, Howard. "Records: Verdi Requiem." *NYT*, 9 February 1941,
       IX:6.
       Review of D4: "It is witty, skilfully written music that employs the
       idiom of swing."

B334   Thomson, Virgil. "Music: Silk-Underwear Music." *NYH-T*, 31 October
       1940, 18.
       In this review of W101b, notorious for Thomson's chastising of
       Heifetz for what he feels is an emphasis upon polish and virtuosity
       above all else, he comments upon *Hexapoda:* "Bennett's musical
       sketches . . . are pretty music. They manage with skill and integrity to
       use swing formulae as a decor for the musical depiction of those nerve
       reflexes and soul states that swing lovers commonly manifest when
       exposed to swing music. They are, in addition, magnificently written
       for the violin."

B335 _____. *The Musical Scene*. New York: Alfred A Knopf, 1947, 218-219.
Thomson's "Silk-Underwear Music" review [B334] of Heifetz's
performance of *Hexapoda* [W101b] is reprinted.

B336 _____. *Music Reviewed: 1940-1954*. New York: Vintage Books, 1967,
10-11.
Another reprint of B334, Thomson's review of W101b.

B337 "Violin-And-Piano 'Hexapoda' Are Studies In 'Jitteroptera.' " *Musical
America* 61:3 (10 February 1941), 223.
Announcement of the work's publication by Chappell; reviewer notes
that "all the writing is that of an experienced and resourceful craftsman
in modernistic idioms." A not-published-elsewhere photograph of the
composer accompanies the review.

B338 Yoell, John H. "In Conversation With Louis Kaufman." *Fanfare*,
March-April 1986, 78-87.
Kaufman discusses *Hexapoda*—written for Kaufman—and other
Bennett concert works, many of which are unfamiliar to the reviewer.

HOLD YOUR HORSES (musical comedy) [W42]

B339 Atkinson, Brooks. "The Play: Joe Cook and His Mountebanks in a
Musical Merry-Go-Round Entitled 'Hold Your Horses.' " *NYT*, 26
September 1933, 26.
Review of W42a comments briefly upon the music: "Russell Bennett
and a whole blacksmith shop of composers and bards have written . . .
jingles . . . of buoyancy."

B340 Brown, John Mason. "The Play." *NY Evening Post*, 26 September 1933.
Generally favorable account of the production, with no specific
comments about the score.

B341 Caldwell, Cy. "To See Or Not To See." *New Outlook* 162:5 (November
1933), 43.
A positive review, though the songs are not discussed.

B342 Gabriel, Gilbert. "Hold Your Horses: With All Due Deference to the
Return of Joe Cook." *NY American*, 26 September 1933.
A mixed review; the music is not evaluated by Gabriel.

B343 Garland, Robert. [review]. *NYW-T*, 26 September 1933.

B344 Hammond, Percy. "The Theaters." *NYH-T*, 26 September 1933.

B345 "Joe Cook Makes Hit In New Show." *NYT*, 31 August 1933, 20.
In one of the few reviews bothering to consider the music specifically,
he makes mention of the "many excellent tunes by Russell Bennett,
notably the title song . . ."

B346 Kolodin, Irving. "Music In Musical Comedy." *Theatre Arts Monthly*
17:12 (December 1933), 965-970.
A thorough critique of the music for three contemporary shows:
Gershwin's *Let ' em Eat Cake*, Berlin's *As Thousands Cheer*, and
Bennett's *Hold Your Horses*. About the latter, he comments:
"Russell Bennett's orchestrations [are] the only musical interest in the
score. The actual tunes are so much routine."

B347 Lockridge, Richard. "Hold Your Horses." *NY Sun*, 26 September 1933.

B348 Pollock, Arthur. "The Theaters." *Brooklyn Daily Eagle*, 26 September
1933.

B349 Stagg, Jerry. *The Brothers Shubert*. New York: Random House, 1968,
306-310.
Included in this very fine study of theatrical promoters Lee and J. J.
Shubert is considerable information on the writing and staging of
Hold Your Horses in 1933, much of which is elsewhere unavailable.

B350 [review]. *Catholic World* 138 (November 1933), 218.

B351 [review]. *Commonweal* 18 (20 October 1933), 592.

B352 [review]. *Stage* 10 (December 1933), 9, 11.

HOLLYWOOD [W20]

B353 Bauer, Marion, and Reis, Claire R. "Twenty-Five Years With The
League Of Composers." *Musical Quarterly* 34:1 (January, 1948), 1-14.
Contains a list of all League-commissioned works, including
Bennett's *Hollywood*.

B354 "Behind the Scenes: Composer Invited to Write New Music For Radio, Including 29-minute Opera." *NYT*, 24 October 1937, XI:14.

B355 Berger, Arthur. "Once Again, The One-Man Show." *Modern Music* 20:3 (March-April 1943), 175-182.
A review of **W20b**: "[*Hollywood*] began with a grandiose, dull introduction, continued with brilliant fast passages superbly orchestrated, and collapsed later in crude burlesque."

B356 Biancolli, Louis. "Hollywood Tone-Poem At Carnegie." *NYW-T*, 16 February 1943, 13.
A review of **W20b**: "Mr. Bennett evidently took Film Town seriously. . . . In fact, solemnity rises to churchly pomp in spots. Then come breezy stretches of sauciness, and the composer begins to sound like Robert Russell Bennett . . ."

B357 Bohm, Jerome D. "Barzin Leads Orchestra in Carnegie Hall." *NYHT*, 16 February 1943, 15.
An account of the **W20b** concert by the National Orchestral Association.

B358 Norman, Gertrude, and Shrifte, Miriam Lubell, eds. *Letters of Composers: an anthology, 1903-1945*. New York: Knopf, 1946; 368.
Included is a letter from Bennett to the National Orchestral Association dated 21 January 1943; it includes biographical material and program notes for *Hollywood*, and is obviously connected with the **W20b** performance shortly thereafter by the Association.

B359 Reis, Claire R. *Composers, Conductors, and Critics*. New York: Oxford University Press, 1955; reprint ed., Detroit: Detroit Reprints In Music, 1974.
Includes some details about the League of Composers' commissioning of *Hollywood*.

KANSAS CITY ALBUM [W21]

B360 "KC will hear the colorful, exciting saga of its 100 yrs." *Kansas City Star*, 20 September 1949.
Announcement/preview of the work, commissioned by Bennett' s home town to celebrate its centennial.

MACBETH (Incidental music) [W49]

B361 Hornblow, Arthur. "Mr. Hornblow Goes to the Play." *Theatre Magazine* 33:15 (April 1921), 261, 262, 264, 298, 304.
Hornblow's review of the production is mixed, but he extends his compliments to the composer: "The incidental music, by Robert Russell Bennett, it seemed to me, was the nearest note to truth in the whole production."

B362 Lewisohn, Ludwig. "Drama: 'Macbeth' in the Void." *The Nation* 112:2904 (2 March 1921), 349-350.

B363 Wollcott, Alexander. "The Play." *NYT*, 18 February 1921, 16.

MADEMOISELLE [W63]

B364 J. B. "Goldman Starts 35th Band Season." *NYT*, 19 June 1952, 33.
Concise review of **W63a**, the premiere: "It is an urbane, witty and delightful piece. The second movement, a marche militaire . . . sounds rather like genial Shostakovich."

B365 Bagar, Robert. "Music: 20,000 Enjoy Opening of Concerts in Mall." *NYH-T*, 19 June 1952, 14.
Positive but brief evaluation of **W63a**: "entertainment over and above the ordinary. . . . by [a composer] experienced in the craft . . ."

B366 A. H. "Goldman Band Opens 35th Season." *Musical America* 72:9 (July 1952), 18.
Enthusiastic review of **W63a**: the writer considers the piece to be "by far the most interesting of all [of the new works on the program]. An urbane, witty, and wholly delightful work, it is the product of a master craftsman guided by imagination rather than the dreary conventions of band writing and scoring. Particularly notable was his avoidance of clarinets as violin substitutes."

B367 "Radio Notebook." *Musical Courier* 146:1 (July 1952), 10.
Review of broadcast of **W63a**; *Mademoiselle* is described as "a tuneful work."

MARCH FOR TWO PIANOS AND ORCHESTRA [W24]

B368   Downes, Olin. "A Program of Native Works." *NYT*, 9 August 1931, 6.
Includes a short biographical sketch, publicity for the New York
premiere, **W24b**, and a lengthy description of the piece written by
Bennett.

B369   Levant, Oscar. *The Unimportance of Being Oscar.* New York: G. P.
Putnam's Sons, 1968, 143.
Levant discusses his performing, with Bennett, the *March for Two
Pianos and Orchestra* in Los Angeles in 1930 **[W24a]**.

B370   "New York Stadium Audience Enjoys All-American Program."
Musical Courier 103:8 (22 August 1931), 5, 9.
In this review of **W24b**, the writer describes the *March* as having
"a distinct personality if not always a flowing inspiration."

MARIA MALIBRAN [W44]

B371   Bauer, Marion. "Native Opera—Metropolitan and Juilliard." *Modern
Music* 12:4 (May-June 1935), 194-196.
Composer Bauer evaluates *Malibran* and other American operas
being premiered in New York, noting that "The work is neither
musical comedy nor grand opera, although it borrows from both, with
definite experiments in declamation, orchestration, and stage
setting. . . . In place of time honored recitative or spoken dialog without
music, he uses an uninterrupted flow of music depicting the action and
accompanying the voice. . . . [this] was disturbing, but it had elements of
surprise and novelty."

B372   "Bennett, composer, sails—will complete opera in Europe." *NYT*, 12
May 1932, 23.
Announces Bennett's departure; he stayed in Europe (mostly Berlin)
for several months, though the work was still incomplete when
he returned to the U. S. late in 1932.

B373   "Bennett Sailing for Europe to Finish Opera." *NYH-T*, 12 May 1932.
Outlines of the plot of *Malibran*, then in progress, and gives profiles of
Bennett and Simon. The reviewer, having interviewed both of them,
notes that "Mr. Bennett and Mr. Simon [the librettist] said they had

both become interested in the idea of writing an American opera that would feature neither Negroes nor Indians."

B374 "Chautauqua Closes Successful Season." *Musical America* 55:14 (September 1935), 26.
Brief account of **W44b**.

B375 Gilman, Lawrence. "An American Opera About A Singer." *NYH-T*, 6 February 1935.
Writing in advance of the premiere, Gilman outlines the plot and gives biographical details of Malibran's life; comments from Simon and Bennett are included.

B376 _____. "Music: A New American Opera About A Famous Singer Produced by the Juilliard." *NYH-T*, 9 April 1935, 13.
Gilman's review of **W44a** is, overall, quite positive. He terms Bennett's contribution "a score of unusual quality. For this is not only music of rare delicacy and subtlety of facture, beautifully, knowingly, and reticently orchestrated, but it is the music of a composer who has worked out for himself a very personal sort of poetic comedy—deft, sly, subtly textured."

B377 Howard, John Tasker. *Our Contemporary Composers: American Music In The Twentieth Century*. New York: Thomas Y. Crowell Company, 1941, 311.
An extended discussion of the plot and music of *Malibran*.

B378 Johnson, H. Earle. *Operas on American Subjects*. New York: Coleman-Ross Co., Inc., 1964, 32.
General details about the opera are given.

B379 Kiesler, Frederick. "Design For Act II of Malibran." *Modern Music* 12:4 (May-June 1935), 179.
A monochrome illustration of designer Kiesler's backdrop and set pieces for the second act of *Malibran's* Juilliard premiere [**W44a**].

B380 Knerr, R. M. "Maria Malibran, Native Opera, Premiered by Juilliard School." *Musical Courier* 110:16 (20 April 1935), 5, 23.
An extended discussion of the plot, followed by Knerr's critique of the first performance[**W44a**]: "In general [Bennett] is most successful when underscoring a mood . . . . In general, it can not be said that Mr. Bennett has always set his vocal lines as expressively as he might have . . . ."

B381   Loewenberg, Alfred, comp. *Annals of Opera, 1597-1940*. 2nd ed.
        Geneva: Societas Bibliographica, 1955.
        General details about the work are given.

B382   "Malibran at Chataqua." *NYH-T*, 18 August 1935.
        Publicity for the second production [**W44b**], including names of
        performers in principal roles, some of which were in the Juilliard
        premiere as well.

B383   Moore, Lillian. "Malibran in America." *Musical Courier* 110:19 (11
        May 1935), 6; continued in 110:20 (18 May 1935), 6, 26.
        A detailed study of Malibran's years in the U. S.: "The recent New York
        production [**W44a**] of . . . Bennett's opera, Maria Malibran . . . makes
        this period of her life . . . of particular interest at this time."

B384   "New American Opera at Juilliard." *Musical Leader* 67:9 (April
        1935), 8.
        Short announcement of **W44a**; Malibran's career and the plot of the
        opera are briefly described.

B385   "New American Opera Staged At Juilliard School." *Musician* 40:4
        (April 1935), 7.
        Half-page synopsis of the story, with some commentary on the music
        by Bennett. A photograph, of the production's second act, includes
        Risë Stevens.

B386   "Opera Season Near Close at Chautauqua." *NYH-T*, 11 August 1935.
        Publicity for **W44b**, opening that evening.

B387   Rosenfeld, Paul. "Maria Malibran and Mona." *New Republic* 83
        (19 June 1935), 167.
        Half of Rosenfeld's one-page review of **W44a** is devoted to *Maria
        Malibran*. Rosenfeld states his case bluntly: "the piece is flat; and the
        fault is the composer's." He is not without praise for Bennett's score,
        opining that "[it] does reveal anew the minor virtuosity of the
        composer of the 'Lincoln' symphony. The orchestration is expertly
        brilliant. The harmony is unhackneyed, very modern, and in places
        subtly managed." Still, he concludes that "in most cases, the germinal
        ideas fail to develop or expand, and the numbers hang fire, leaving the
        drama to its own devices."

B388 "Scenes From Maria Malibran." *Musical Courier* 110:16 (20 April 1935), 2.
Photographs of three of the principals, in costume, from the Juilliard production, **W44a**..

B389 Simon, Robert A. "Musical Events." *The New Yorker* 11:10 (20 April 1935), 94.
Simon, who wrote the libretto, notes that he considered recruiting a "guest reviewer" to critique the premiere for *The New Yorker*, then goes on to explain why he dropped the idea. He extends his thanks to the "Juilliard organization" and to Bennett for his "sensitive, inventive, and charming score."

B390 " 'Sorry,' Says Bennett To Opera, Begging Him To Write It Down." *NY Evening Post*, 31 December 1932.
Lengthy interview with Bennett about the commercial obbligations forcing postponement of work on *Malibran*: " 'What we want very much to produce,' [Bennett] said, 'is an opera which the well-informed musically will praise, and which will be at the same time a great popular success.' "

B391 H. T. [Howard Taubman] "Maria Malibran Sung in Premiere." *NYT*, 9 April 1935, 24.
A lengthy discussion both of the opera itself and of the first night's performance: "There are movement, dramatic contrast and vitality in his score. His orchestral writing is shrewd and resourceful. . . . But the writing for the voices is not always grateful . . ."

B392 Thompson, Oscar. "Maria Malibran Has Premiere At Juilliard." *Musical America* 55:8 (25 April 1935), 16, 53.
A detailed examination of the new work and its initial production, **W44a**: "The music, also, is expert. If it is somewhat less successful than the book, this is not due to a lack of technical resource."

B393 Thomson, Virgil. "In The Theatre." *Modern Music* 14:3 (March-April 1937), 170-173.
Thomson discusses *Malibran* and other contemporary American operas premiered at the Juilliard School in the mid-1930s.

B394 "To Stage Native Opera." *NYT*, 3 February 1935, II:4.
Announcement of upcoming **W44a** production.

MUSIC BOX OPERA #1 [W158]

B395   Mills, Charles. "Over The Air." *Modern Music* 18:2 (January-
        February 1941), 131-133.
        Discusses Bennett's new "Notebook" radio program; reviewing the
        Music Box Opera #1 specifically: "amusing. . . . This slight and
        unpretentious work . . . managed to sustain its charming fun for
        thirty . . . minutes."

MUSIC BOX OPERA #2 [W159]

[B188, Mills]
        Article includes a brief review of **W159a**: "[it] consists of an overture,
        prologue, two scenes and epilogue, all of which make for some very
        obvious fun."

MUSIC BOX OPERA #5 [W162]

B396   Mills, Charles. "Over The Air." *Modern Music* 19:1 (November-
        December 1941), 59-62.
        Review of **W162a**: "a hybrid of blues, barbershop, and Broadway. . . .
        The vocal lines are curiously mechanical . . . . The most natural bits
        [in Bennett's *Music Box Operas*] are the pure, unadulterated jazz
        songs, the tin-pan pieces that don't try to forget their native alley."

NIETZSCHE VARIATIONS [W87]

B397   "Women's University Singers To Give Scandanavian Program."
        NYH-T, 4 May 1930.
        An announcement of the **W87b** program; Bennett's *Nietzsche
        Variations* are mistakenly presumed to be "an instrumental
        interlude."

NOCTURNE AND APPASSIONATA [W25]

B398   "Beecham Leads Philadelphians; Rose Cavalier Sung in English."
        Musical Courier 124:9 (15 December 1941), 24.

Review of **W25b**: "It is modern through much of the two movements, lightly orchestrated in the first, and much more heavily scored in the last."

B399   Smith, William E. "Beecham Conducts Thomson Symphony; Haydn And Mozart Works Also Figure—New Bennett Opus Played By Orchestra." *Musical America* 61:19 (10 December 1941), 13.
Review of **W25b**; "Bennett's creation furnished more than casual interest in material and writing . . . [with] the audience signifying approbation."

ORCHESTRAL FRAGMENTS FROM "MARIA MALIBRAN" [W26]

B400   De Reus, Miguel. "American Opera Introduced by Wallenstein." *Illustrated Daily News* [Los Angeles], 8 February 1935.
Review of **W26a**: "Bennett's music is content to endow some old dance forms with the glittering garments of modern orchestration and with the knowing leer of advanced harmonic idioms. It is clever music, witty music, with just enough cunning dissonance to appear contemporaneous."

B401   "L.A. Hears Malibran Excerpts." *Musical America* 55:4 (25 February 1935), 34.
An account of the **W26a** performance of the *Orchestral Fragments.*

B402   "Wallenstein Flys [*sic*] to Introduce 'Maria Malibran'." *Newsweek* 5:24 (16 February 1935), 24.
An account of the premiere, **W26a**: "radio listeners [and] the local audience . . . liked Mr. Bennett's melodious use of such old dance forms as the gigue and gavotte. Mr. [conductor Alfred] Wallenstein crowed: 'it is delightful; no pretense, purely good music.' "

B403   "Wallenstein in Dual Duty." *Los Angeles Times*, 8 February 1935, I:13.
A short review of **W26a**: "Bennett's music . . . proved of unusual interest."

OVERTURE TO AN IMAGINARY DRAMA [W27]

B404   A. B. "Bennett Overture Given First Performance." *Musical America* 69:16 (15 December 1949), 10.

A review of the **W27f**, the first performance in New York: "a brief adventure into vague emotional realms, reminiscent of the music that accompanies the credits of many a Hollywood film. . . . [with] rich and skillful orchestration . . ."

B405 "Bennett Overture Presented." *NYT*, 28 November 1949, 22.
A brief account of **W27f**.

B406 Fairley, Lee. "Program Notes." *The Symphony Magazine*, National Symphony Orchestra, concert of 23 February 1947 [**W27c**], 25.
A descriptive essay by Bennett is included.

B407 J. S. H. "Bennett's Overture." *NYH-T*, 28 November 1949.
Jay S. Harrison, reviewing **W27f**, finds the piece to be "thin expressively, totally lacking in theater contrasts . . ."

B408 Sabiston, Colin. "Mahler Directs Tuneful Program At Second Prom." *Toronto Globe & Mail*, 15 May 1946, 10.
Review of **W27a**: "this is in the up-to-the-minute-mode. . . . many, like this reviewer, would like to hear it again."

B409 Walz, Audrey. "National Gallery Begins Festival." *Musical America* 67:3 (25 March 1947), 47.
Includes a brief account of **W27c**.

OVERTURE TO THE MISSISSIPPI [W28]

B410 Durgin, Cyrus. "Boston Symphony Introduces Three Preludes by Pfitzner." *Musical America* 70:4 (15 March 1950), 12.
The reviewer [of **W28a**] describes the *Overture* as "slick."

PAYSAGE [W29]

B411 "American Composers' Concert Given By Rochester Orchestra." *Musical Courier* 108:1 (6 January 1934), 7.
This perceptive review of **W29a** describes *Paysage* as "a piece descriptive of a cowboy tale. It is derivative music, French in feeling and style, and represents in an interesting way an early period of Bennett's creative life."

B412 Croughton, Amy H. "The Concert." *Rochester [NY] Times-Union,* 16 December 1933, 4.
An account of **W29a**; no evaluation of *Paysage.*

B413 T. G. "Dr. Hanson Schedules American Symphonic Music For Rochester." *Musical Courier* 107:24 (9 December 1933), 8.
Announces the 15 December program at the Eastman School, given entirely to works produced by American Guggenheim fellows. The program [**W29a**] included also works by Roy Harris, Quincy Porter, George Antheil, and others.

PIANO CONCERTO IN B MINOR [W30]

B414 "Composers Corner." *Musical America* 77:12 (October 1952), 33.
An account of the **W30a** performance by pianist Andor Foldes.

PRINCESS CHARMING [W45]

B415 [review]. *The Outlook* 58:1500 (30 October 1926), 409.

QUINTETTE, ACCORDION/STRING QUARTET [W104]

B416 Kelli, Sandor. "New Accordion Role." *Kansas City Times,* 22 April 1963, 11.
An account of the **W104a** performance in Kansas City, Missouri.

ROMEO AND JULIET (Incidental music) [W50]

B417 Corbin, John. "The Play: Muted Juliet." *NYT,* 28 December 1922, 20.

B418 Lewisohn, Ludwig. "Drama: Minuet." *The Nation* 116:3002 (17 January 1923), 77.

RONDO CAPRICCIOSO [W106]

B419 "The Flute in American Music." program for New York Flute Club concert of 21 March 1976 [**W106c**], CAMI Hall, New York. Includes descriptive program notes by Bennett.

[B194, Mills]

Article includes a review of **W106b**: "[the piece] shows definite French influence . . . it is a beautiful little piece for radio. . . . it is florid, inventive and extremely well scored."

ROSE VARIATIONS [W68]

[B13, Cohn]

In this review of **D14**, Arthur Cohn describes the *Rose Variations* as" 'Pops'-type music with good opportunities for the trumpeter . . ."

SIGHTS AND SOUNDS [W31]

B420   "Bennett Item For Novelty At Symphony." *Christian Science Monitor*, 23 January 1943.
The bulk of this lengthy review of **W31b** is given *Sights and Sounds* and a discussion of Koussevitzky's encouragement of Bennett and other American composers. The reviewer comments: "nothing more could be demanded in the way of mastery of means of expression, but does the piece tell much of anything?"

B421   "Burgin and Szell Lead Boston Men." *Musical America* 63:3 (10 February 1943), 230.
Brief account of **W31b**.

B422   C. W. D. "Music: Symphony Hall." *Boston Globe*, 23 January, 1943.
Review of **W31b**: "To put it briefly . . . [it] is trivial and dated stuff. Time has weathered it drastically."

B423   Devries, René. "Illinois Symphony Orchestra Concerts." *Musical Courier* 119:1 (1 January 1939), 24.
Devries reviews **W31a**, a premiere taking place almost a decade after the work was completed. He terms it "[a work that is] well deserving hearing . . ."

B424   Elie, Rudolph, Jr. "Music: Symphony Concert." *Boston Herald*, 23 January 1943.
Review of **W31b**: "it is an enormously clever piece requiring a prodigious executant technique, and some of its effects, purely as

sound, are astonishing. . . . it reveals Mr. Bennett as one of the country's most gifted technicians, and certainly earns for him the right to be heard here in his more serious moments."

B425 Smith, Warren Storey. "Much Variety In Symphony." *Boston Post*, 23 January 1943.
Review of **W31b**: "Possibly Mr. Bennett's effects . . . were striking in 1928, but today they fall rather flat."

B426 Thompson, Randall. "The Contemporary Scene In American Music." *Musical Quarterly* 18:1 (January 1932), 9-11.
Thompson's review suggests that he is quite familiar with the piece, published in 1931, though there is no evidence of a performance of the work prior to 1937. He comments: "by sticking to the spirit rather than the letter of jazz, Russell Bennett in *Sights and Sounds* has spoken, at length, in a strong and unmistakably American accent."

SIX VARIATIONS . . . ON A THEME OF JEROME KERN [W32]

B427 H. H. "Orchestra Debut Is Vital Concert." *NYT*, 4 December 1933.
A very encouraging review of **W32a**, perhaps by Henry Hadley. The reviewer describes the *Variations* as "what may turn out to be the best American piece of the year . . . sparkling, witty, and deft . . . a tour de force in instrumentation, and an apotheosis of parody at its most subtle and delicious . . . [it] abounds in originality and invention."

B428 "New York Concerts." *Musical Courier* 117:24 (9 December 1933), 13, 22.
Review of **W32a**: "an amusing parodistic composition . . . his technical equipment is a superb one, though it is regrettable to find him wasting it on negligible material."

B429 R. A. S. "Musical Events." *The New Yorker* 9:44 (16 December 1933), 55.
Robert A. Simon notes that, at the **W32a** premiere, "the tumult and the shouting [following the performance] were a long time a-dying. Our maestri might as well make note . . ."

SOAP BOX DERBY (March) [W69]

B430 Endres, Fred. "Soap Box Derby Champ Failed to Qualify in his 1965 Outing." *Cleveland Plain Dealer*, 7 August 1966, 13A.
Includes an account of Bennett's visit to Akron to guest conduct the first performance of the *March* the previous day [W69a].

SIX PARAGRAPHS . . . SODOM BY THE SEA [W165]

B431 Stewart, R. A. "One Thing And Another." *NYT*, 20 July 1941, IX:10.
The writer provides background information about the piece—impressions of scenes at New York's Coney Island—shortly before the composition's airing [W165a].

SECOND SONATINA [W134]

B432 P. B. "Milton Kaye Is Heard In Debut at Town Hall; Pianist Plays New Sonatina by Robert Russell Bennett." *NYH-T*, 2 October 1945, 17.
A curious, somewhat negative review of W134c: "Its most irritating characteristic was its harmonic irresponsibility. The politest thing one might say of it is that it was in the best of taste."

B433 Bennett, Grena. "Orchestral's Concert Held." *NYJ-A*, 2 October 1945, 8.
Included is a brief account of W134c.

B434 Fuller, Donald. "Prokofiev And Milhaud In The Winter Season." *Modern Music* 22:2 (January-February 1945), 103-107.
Fuller reviews W134b briefly: "There were new ideas every few measures, none treated to development and none really worthy of it."

B435 R. L. "Gimpel at Town Hall." *NYT*, 14 December 1944, 29.
A short account of W134b.

B436 "Milton Kaye at Town Hall." *NYW-T*, 2 October 1945, 12.
Anonymous review of W134c; he mentions "a Second Sonatina by R. Russell Bennett, who wraps up some of today's brightest gags in nifty keyboard parcels." This comment is curious, as the *Sonatina* is somewhat austere and serious in tone.

B437 P. "Jakob Gimpel, Pianist." *Musical America* 64:17 (25 December 1944), 26, 31.
Brief account, without comment, of **W134b**.

B438 P. "Milton Kaye, Pianist." *Musical America* 65:13 (October 1945), 8.
The *Second Sonatina* is dismissed quickly in this review of **W134c**: "[the piece] sounds like a shapeless and empty improvisation . . ."

B439 Saunders, Richard Drake. "Los Angeles: Philharmonic Orchestra Triumphs At Inaugural." *Musical Courier* 130:8 (1 December 1944), 24.
In this synopsis of fall 1944 concerts in Los Angeles, Saunders briefly mentions Gimpel's concert, **W134a**, and "the short but enjoyable Second Sonata [*sic*] by . . . Bennett . . ."

SONATINE, SOPRANO/HARP [W146]

B440 A. B. "NAACC Concert: Times Hall, Dec. 20." *Musical America* 71:2 (15 January 1951), 18.
Review of **W146b**, making reference to "Bennett's delightful, impressionistic Sonatina . . ."

B441 Berger, Arthur V. "Jean Love's Debut." *NYH-T*, 2 October 1947, 20.
Berger, reviewing **W146a**, notes that "Though it is directly out of impressionist tradition . . . [it] is a suavely made piece, with striking sophistications that indicate a knowledge of the more recent French composers such as Sauguet and Poulenc, and the Francophile Stravinsky."

B442 M. C. "Jean Love's Song Program." *Musical Courier* 136:5 (15 October 1947), 26.
Review of **W146a**: "this proved an interesting work, fluent and expressive with contrapuntal play of tonal nuance between voice and instrument."

B443 H. "Jean Love, Soprano (Debut)." *Musical America* 67:13 (October 1947), 23.
The reviewer of **W146a** briefly describes the work as one that "proved original in form and agreeable melodically."

B444 Kastendieck, Miles. "Jean Love Captivating." *NYJ-A*, 2 October 1947, 18.

A review of **W146a** that terms the *Sonatine* "a pretentious piece by Robert Russell Bennett . . ."

B445   R. P. "Jean Love Makes Debut." *NYT*, 2 October 1947, 32.
An account of the **W146a** premiere.

A SONG SONATA [W110]

B446   J. B. [record review] *Fanfare*, November-December 1982, 106.
Review of **D27**: "I rather prefer Louis Kaufman's brisker reading of the [*Song Sonata*] . . . . It strikes me as a rather insipid work, so the choice isn't all that important."

[B13, Cohn]
Arthur Cohn, in his review of **D30**, comments: "while the three movements . . . of the *Song Sonata* are not jazz per se, there is such matter in their sonorous overtones . . . in a seamlessly suave style."

B447   G. "Benno Rabinof, Violinist." *Musical America* 67:16 (15 December 1947), 8.
In this review of **W110a**, the writer notes: "The work has an appealing melodic line sustained through the five movements or, more properly, moods; it is lucidly constructed and lends itself well to the intimate delicately textured performance given it on this occasion."

B448   Harrison, Jay S. "Heifetz, at Carnegie Hall, Plays Brahms, Vieuxtemps." *NYH-T*, 16 February 1955.
A review of **W110b**; Harrison has much to say about Heifetz's playing, but no opinions regarding the *Song Sonata*.

B449   M. D. L. "Jascha Heifetz, Violinist: Carnegie Hall, Feb. 15." *Musical America* 75:5 (March 1955), 25.
Review of **W110b**: "a pleasant, idiomatic piece full of rhythmic bumps and grinds."

B450   Moore, David W. [record review] *American Record Guide* 46:3 (February 1983), 7-8.
He compares the Malan-Sutherland recording [**D26**], with that by Louis and Annette Kaufman [**D3/D23**]: "This is a substantial five-movement work which, though attractive, lacks character unless imbued with the disarming schmaltz of the Kaufmanns [*sic*]."

B451 F. D. P. [Francis D. Perkins] "Rabinof's Recital." *NYH-T*, 25 November 1947, 26.
Review of **W110a**: "it gave the impression of conservatism, occasional reminiscence, pleasing lyricism and considerable expressive color, if not expressive profundity."

B452 R. P. "Rabinof Is Heard In Local Recital." *NYT*, 25 November 1947, 38.
Review of **W110a**: "It had some nice melodies, but little originality or importance."

B453 T. P. "Rabinof Program Includes Novelties." *Musical Courier* 136:9 (15 December 1947), 15.
The review of **W110a** terms the piece "a sensitive study."

[**B219**, Shupp]
Review of **D3**: "The two works for violin and piano [*A Song Sonata* and *Hexapoda*] are equally fresh [as the *Concerto for Violin*] in inspiration and completely violinistic in writing . . ."

B454 Taubman, Howard. "Heifetz Recital: Violinist in Program at Carnegie Hall." *NYT*, 16 February 1955.
Taubman, reviewing **W110b**, finds the *Song Sonata* to be "full of rhythmic vitality and sensuous colors. This music is made to order idiomatically for the violin, especially for a virtuoso like Heifetz . . ."

STRING QUARTET [W111]

B455 "Composers Corner." *Musical America* 77:1 (1 January 1957), 47.
A brief account of the *String Quartet's* premiere [**W111a**].

B456 M. D. L. "NAACC: Bennett Quartet." *Musical America* 78:2 (15 January 1958), 26.
Review of **W111b**: "Robert Russell Bennett's String Quartet seemed sleek and well-scored while the musical invention seemed dull."

A STUDY IN ORCHESRATION [W167]

[**B188**, Mills]
Charles Mills reviews several performances of Bennett's works heard on the "Notebook" radio program, with this to say about **W167a**: "The

build-up was interesting enough; the rub came in the revelation of the long awaited orchestration which turned out to be simple Broadway corn played by pretty instruments."

SUE ANN [W147]

[B131, Wind]
Bennett discusses this popular song, his only independently-written one to date. According to Bennett, it came to him in a dream one night. Bennett remarks: " 'It was just an obvious little tune . . . . Max Dreyfus, at Chappell, published it more as a gag than anything else. It entirely fulfilled our expectations. I think it sold fifty copies.' "

SUITE OF OLD AMERICAN DANCES (band) [W70]

B457 Fennell, Frederick. "Basic Band Repertory: Suite of Old American Dances." *The Instrumentalist* 34:2 (1979), 28.
The most extensive published essay on any single Bennett composition. Aimed at conductors, it includes a brief history of the work's creation—an account not published elsewhere—as well as an extremely detailed discussion of musical and technical problems. A list of errata in the published parts is also included. Conductor Fennell has championed Bennett's work; in his writing he clearly communicates his respect for both Bennett and his music.

B458 A. H. "Bennett Conducts Goldman Band." *NYH-T*, 3 August 1957, 5.
A review of W70d: "This set of pieces was not made for a show, of course, but it made for easy listening all the same."

B459 Hamburger, Philip. "Musical Events: The Best Things in Life." *The New Yorker* 225:19 (2 July 1949), 54.
The writer, reviewing W70a, makes reference only to the work's "jolly, sprightly" character.

B460 Johnson, Charles E. *Common Musical Idioms in Selected Contemporary Wind Band Music* (Ed. D. dissertation, Florida State University, 1969), 191-248.
Eight original compositions for band are examined, including the *Suite of Old American Dances*. Though Johnson evaluates briefly the formal organization of each movement, the emphasis in his study

is on motivic, melodic and harmonic analysis. He dissects vertical sonorities in an extremely thorough manner, but mentions only in passing the tonal centers of individual movements. There is no discussion of harmonic *relationships*; he uses no roman numerals, and does not seek to determine how tonal centers are established.

B461   H. F. P. "Goldman Band Opens Park Series." *Musical America* 69:9 (July 1949), 12.
A detailed account of the **W70a** premiere; the reviewer, however, does not critique Bennett's *Suite.*

B462   Perkins, Francis D. "Goldman Opens Season in Central Park." *NYH-T,* 18 June 1949, 6.
A brief account of the **W70a** concert.

B463   Shupp, Jr., Enos E. *The New Records,* July 1971, 14.
A review of **D6**, a recording by the Cornell University Wind Ensemble: "Bennett's *Suite* . . . enjoys his superior scoring skill . . . it's a dashing work and perfectly wind oriented; the best thing for bands since Sousa and Goldman."

B464   "Speaking of Music: The Crowd Is Back On The Mall." *International Musician* 18:1 (July 1949), 15.
An account of the **W70a** program; the Bennett *Suite* is not evaluated.

B465   Straus, Noel. "Goldman Starts Annual Concerts." *NYT,* 18 June 1949, 10.
A review of **W70a**: "These dances, treating 'some of the composer's dance moods of his early youth', in modern manner, were cleverly devised and made especially effective by knowing play of color and infectious rhythms."

B466   Wolter, Richard Arthur. *A Description and Analysis of Selected Music Written for the Concert Band Performable by American High School Bands.* A.M. Thesis, Washington University, 1959.
The *Suite of Old American Dances* is among works analyzed and discussed.

SYMPHONIC SONGS FOR BAND [W71]

B467   Clark, John W. [review of **D19**] *Musical America,* August 1961, 49.

[B13, Cohn]

Arthur Cohn has this to say about the *Symphonic Songs* in his review of **D19**: "Publishers of rich and penetrating junk for bands would do well to give a listen to this light and lucid, gay and gingerly music."

B468   "Convention Feature: Nat'l Talent to play S. L. Concert Tonight." *Salt Lake Tribune*, 24 August 1957, 7.
An announcement of the **W71a** premiere in Salt Lake City; no special detail is provided relative to the *Songs*.

B469   Erickson, Raymond. "Music: Goldman Time." *NYT*, 22 June 1979, III:20.
W71d is briefly reviewed; Erickson calls it "one of the most effective pieces" on the program.

B470   Fennell, Frederick. Manuscript in preparation; to be published in *B. D. Guide* [Traverse City, MI], 1990 or 1991.
This essay is a companion to his "Basic Band Repertory" study [B457] of Bennett's *Suite of Old American Dances*. Fennell, conducting his Eastman Wind Ensemble, made the first recording of the *Symphonic Songs* [D19], and he has frequently been the source of advice for other conductors concerning the musical and technical problems involved in rehearsing and performing the composition.

B471   A. H. "Goldman Band Led By Bennett." *NYH-T*, 28 July 1958, 13.
A review of **W71b**: "[the Symphonic Songs] demonstrated that Mr. Bennett's skill in the handling of band sonorities is as admirable as it ever was and that his wit is undiminished. There is absolutely nothing lumpy or square about his band writing; it flows, sings, and dances buoyantly, and with grace. The "Symphonic Songs" are rather more complex structurally than [the new "Gigi" medley of Bennett's, also on the program] . . . but they tell of Mr. Bennett's association with Broadway nevertheless. Sometimes, indedd [*sic*], it seemed that banal syncopations and tired harmonic clinches [*sic*] were about to get the better of the composer's worthy ideas, and one wondered if he were relying too little on the strength of his own inventive powers."

B472   Hall, David. [record review] *HiFi/Stereo Review*, August 1961, 59-60.
Review of **D19**, the Fennell/Eastman Wind Ensemble recording: "Bennett's *Symphonic Songs* are entertaining period pieces in the manner of his earlier and deservedly successful band piece, *Suite of Old American Dances* . . . but they don't quite match the earlier work."

B473 Hastings, Baird. [record review] *American Record Guide* 41:5 (March 1978), 46-47.
Review of **D24**, the recording by Paynter/Northwestern University Wind Ensemble: "[the] composers represented here have each contributed greatly to the development of the genre. . . . Bennett begins his *Symphonic Songs* with a witty serenade, neo-classic American, while not neglecting recent developments in popular rhythms and "minor" sonorities (which he helped establish). The second movement [is] a sophisticated and nostalgic spiritual. . . . In his peppy finale . . . [he] lets out all the stops, and sends us home happy."

B474 J. [record review] *The New Records*, June 1961, 13.
Review of **D19**: "another in this composer's long line of original compositions—a must for his many fans . . ."

B475 Miller, Phillip L. "Recorded Music." *Library Journal* 86:14 (August 1961), 2640-2641.
Under the heading "Band Music: Recommended," Miller lists Mercury MG 50220 [**D19**] in his review and calls it "a superb disc of original works for band, although none sounds more modern than Ravel."

B476 "Sixth Biennial National Intercollegiate Band." *The Podium* [published by Kappa Kappa Psi and Tau Beta Sigma], November 1957, 4-5.
Lengthy article about the 1957 meeting of the National Intercollegiate Band in Salt Lake City and the **W71a** concert, premiering the Bennett *Symphonic Songs*. The work was commissioned by these two fraternal organizations.

SYMPHONY (#1—"UKE") [W34]

B477 "Bloch's Rhapsody Wins Award." *Musical America* 48:8 (9 June 1928).
Details Bloch's winning of the $3000 award in *Musical America'*s 1927-1928 composition contest. Bennett's *Symphony* and works of the others receiving "honorable mentions" are included.

B478 "Congratulations!" *Musical America* 48:8 (9 June 1928), 10.
Account of Bloch's winning the magazine's symphony contest. The writer notes that "All of the prominent and outstanding scores

of this competition with one exception were written by well known American composers. The one exception proved to be a new symphony **[W34]** by Robert Russell Bennett of New York City."

B479   "Ernest Bloch Wins $3,000 Music Prize." *NYT*, 8 June 1928, 29.
Announces of Bloch as winner of the *Musical America* composition contest of 1927 for his symphony, *America*, and gives a short profile of Bloch. Also included are names and compositions of the four receiving an "honorable mention," including Bennett—his symphony **[W34]** here titled simply *Uke*—and the names of the judges for the competition.

SYMPHONY (#7, 1962) [W36]

B480   [concert program notes]. Chicago Symphony Orchestra, 50th season. Program for 11-12 April 1963 **[W36a]**, Symphony Hall, Chicago. Includes an extended essay by the composer, describing each movement in the *Symphony*, as well as some autobiographical material in Bennett's characteristically unassuming tone.

B481   Cassidy, Claudia. "On The Aisle." *Chicago Daily Tribune*, 12 April 1963, II:11.

B482   "Reiner Conducts Twice This Week." *Chicago Daily Tribune*, 7 April 1963, V:10.

SYMPHONY IN D FOR THE DODGERS (#3) [W37]

B483   Bennett, Grena. "Dodgers Get Musical Lift At Stadium Concert." *NYJ-A*, 4 August 1941, 8.
A review of the first public performance, **W37b**, at New York's Lewisohn Stadium: "It was by all means popular 'stuff,' with 'basses' and 'runs' stressed in the score."

B484   Biancolli, Louis. "Dodgers Win In Symphony Tra-la-la." *NYW-T*, 4 August 1941, 9.
Review of **W37b**: "Mr. Bennett's pert and peppery music scores brilliantly on its own."

B485   F. Q. E. "Eminent Artists Attract Many to Stadium." *Musical America* 61:13 (August 1941), 10-11, 33.

Review of **W37b**: "As music goes, the score was amusing in a half-hearted way. . . . He writes simply and often ingratiatingly, but there was no profile to this work, and his talents could be put to better effect."

B486   Lawrence, Robert. "Dodgers' Symphony At Stadium; Total, No Runs, No Hits, No Errors." *NYH-T*, 4 August 1941.
Review of **W37b**: "Mr. Bennett's music, crisp and simple, often recalled the "Classical Symphony" of Prokofieff. . . . Much of this new work seemed ingratiating and deftly scored, but it bore no clear-cut style."

B487   Mooney, George A. "Radio Notes And Comment." *NYT*, 11 May 1941, X:10.
Publicity for the **W37a** premiere, to be aired 16 May.

B488   "Our Dodgers, Words And Music." *PM* [NY], 16 May 1941, 22.
Article includes a short profile of Bennett and some details concerning his "Notebook" show. The *Symphony in D*, to be aired that evening [**W37a**] is described as "the timeliest and most unexpected of the Bennett ingenuities . . ."

B489   "Our Musical Dodgers." *PM* [NY], 30 July 1941, 22.
Announcement of **W37b** concert.

B490   Stewart, R. W. "One Thing And Another." *NYT*, 27 July 1941, IX:10.
Gives background on Bennett's career and the work itself. The [concert] premiere date is announced as 30 July; the performance was delayed until 3 August [**W37a**].

B491   Straus, Noel. "Stadium Premiere For Baseball Epic." *NYT*, 4 August 1941, 10.
Extended discussion of **W37b**. Straus's review, surprisingly, critcizes Bennett's efforts at restraint and tasteful writing: "The conventional, eclectic treatment of all four movements could have been condoned more easily had Mr. Bennett been less repressed and restrained in his reproach and keener in his humor." This stands in contrast with the innumerable instances when Bennett's original works were criticized for their wittiness by Straus and other critics.

B492   "Symphony For The Dodgers." *Time* 37:21 (26 May 1941), 57.
A quarter-page account and review of **W37b**; the reviewer comments that the work "had much of the Dodgers' elusive, faunlike charm, and

rated a place with such sporting music as Constant Lambert's *Prize-Fight*, Arthur Honegger's *Rugby* and *Skating Rink*, the ballets *Card Game* (Igor Stravinsky), *Checkmate* (Arthur Bliss)."

TEMA SPORCA CON VARIAZONI [W114]

B493   Perkins, Francis D. "Two-Piano Recital." *NYH-T*, 18 October 1946, 18.
Review of **W114a**: "[the composer] showed a praiseworthy ability to utilize this medium to best advantage, and to avoid its liabilities. . . . The theme itself, if not unusually memorable, has a well-defined profile . . ."

B494   S. "Appleton and Field, Duo-Pianists." *Musical America* 66:16 (10 November 1946), 24.
Review of **W114a**: "Mr. Bennett's music, whose jazz character explains its delicious title, is clever and rhythmically piquant."

B495   N. S. [Noel Straus] "Duo-Pianists Give Original Program." *NYT*, 18 October 1946, 28.
Review of **W114a**: "[the piece,] though superficial, demanded brilliance and received it . . ."

B496   Simon, Robert A. "Musical Events: Hopeful Signs." *The New Yorker* 22:37 (26 October 1946), 63-64.
Simon, reviewing **W114a**, writes that the *Tema Sporca* "touched off an effective and entertaining display of piano dexterity, including some pleasant kidding on the keys."

THEME AND VARIATIONS . . . ABOUT A LORELEI [W88]

B497   Blitzstein, Marc. "New York Chronicle of New Music." *Modern Music* 8:2 (January-February 1931), 39-42.
A review of the Women's University Glee Club performance, W88b: "Randall Thompson's *Rosemary*, and the three Chaucer poems by Robert Russell Bennett were the best things of the December 18th [1932] program. . . . Bennett's Chaucer songs have a certain melancholy, a wild and remote sadness, not unlike the Hebridean folk tunes, though more definitely *moyen age* in content. I preferred them to his *Lorelei*, a small burlesque cantata. The intention in this work was to be funny, and the music was certainly not very funny."

THEME AND VARIATIONS (MY LOST YOUTH) [W170]

[B188, Mills]

Charles Mills reviews several Bennett works premiered on the "Notebook" program. He writes of **W170a**: "[it is] far too long and too weak in interest to be successful as radio music. The device of reading the poem between the variations wears thin . . ."

THREE CHAUCER POEMS [W148]

[B497, Blitzstein].

A review of **W148c**: "The intention in this work was to be funny, and the music was certainly not very funny. The work is too pretentious to be low-down, and too low-down to be serious."

B498 Meyer, Alfred H. "Yaddo—A May Festival." *Modern Music* 9:4 (May-June 1932), 172-176.
A review of **W148b**: "Fine songs. . . . Low-toned, downcast moods dominated the first two, great exuberence the last."

B499 "Yaddo Festival for Contemporary American Music Held at Saratoga Springs, N. Y." *Musical Courier* 109:19 (7 May 1932), 32.
An account of the Yaddo Festival, including the **W148b** concert. Does not critique the *Songs* specifically. Names Bennett and others who are to remain for three additional days at the Festival's end to make plans for future festivals.

A TNT COCKTAIL [W73]

B500 Downes, Olin. "Music Today For The 'World of Tomorrow'." *Musical Digest* 23:9 (April 1939), 33.
A review the **W73a** premiere; the date is not given. Downes calls it "a perfect masterpiece of technique and imagination which [Bennett] humorously but logically called 'TNT Cocktail' . . ."

TONE POEMS FOR BAND [W74]

B501 Carter, Elliot. "O Fair World of Music." *Modern Music* 16:4 (May-June 1939), 238-243.

Carter's review of the "George Washington" segment: "Bennett has very wisely used a concert band. . . . I only deplore the conscious writing down to popular taste which has led him in his *George Washington* piece . . . to do up all the national anthems . . . in Wagnerian style, as if the World of Tomorrow were the Dusk of the Gods."

B502   Downes, Olin. "Launching the Fair's Program." *NYT*, 30 April 1939, X:7.
Briefly describes Bennett's compositions, to be synchronized with the fountain displays, and notes that one of the segments, "The Spirit of George Washington," will be premiered at the Fair's opening that evening [W74a].

B503   _____. "Music at the Fair: Concerning Russell Bennett's score for fountains in Lagoon of Nations." *NYT*, 27 August 1939, X:5.
Downes writes: "the very exceptional character of the scores . . .brilliant inventiveness, suppleness and modernity of . . . workmanship and instrumentation. . . . [make this a] significant creative effort."

B504   King, William. "Music and Musicians: Fountain Music—Robert Russell Bennett's Scores for the Fair's Water-spectacles." *NY Sun*, 6 May 1939.
King writes: "[Bennett's scores are,] To these eyes and ears, the most beautiful and unusual offerings of the World's Fair to date . . . a medium of expression of potentially high aesthetic value . . ."

B505   Kolodin, Irving. "Surprise at the World's Fair." *NYT*, 7 May 1939, X:7.
Details a variety of musical events at opening of New York World's Fair. Kolodin comments: "The highly effective and individual scoring of music by Russell Bennett for the fountain in the Lagoon of Nations is a new idiom of a highly individual character."

B506   "Light, Spray Blend in 'Flower' Cycle." *NYT*, 7 May 1939, 20.
A lengthy description of the music, fountain display, and lighting at the first performance of the "Story of Three Flowers" segment at the New York World's Fair.

B507   R. S. "Guggenheim Memorial Concerts Inaugurate 34th Season." *Musical America* 71:9 (July 1951), 18.
An account of the **W74b** concert by the Goldman Band.

B508 Simon, Robert A. "Musical Events." *The New Yorker* 15:4 (20 May 1939), 68-69.
Simon, writing shortly after the opening of the 1939 World's Fair, describes the *Tone Poems* as "brilliant and imaginative scores."

B509 "World's Fair Abandons Music Festival." *Musical America* 119:9 (25 May 1939), 3, 30.
The 1939 New York World's Fair, shortly after its 30 April opening, scaled down its festival of opera and concert music. Olin Downes, who headed the music department for the Fair, lists the department's responsibilities and achievements, noting that Bennett "has already completed eight of these scores [for the Lagoon of Nations], and more are coming."

B510 "World's Fair Music Festival." *Musical America* 119:8 (10 May 1939), 12-13.
Bennett's scores, conducted by Littau, are mentioned; also included are photographs of Bennett and of the fountain displays at the Lagoon.

B511 "World's Fair Programs Assailed As 'Overlooking Native Music.' " *Musical Courier* 119:7 (1 April 1939), 5.
Overview of musical fare, including Bennett's *Tone Poems*, to be heard in the early weeks of the Fair.

TOY SYMPHONY [W116]

B512 Murphy, W. R. "Wagner Operas And Modern Works Prominent in Quaker City Fare." *Musical America* 51:2 (25 January 1931), 77.
Reviewing **W116a**, Murphy mentions the work briefly, stating that "each movement is inspired by a certain type of doll"; no critical comment is given.

A TRIBUTE TO JAMES WHITCOMB RILEY [W175]

B513 Biltcliffe, Edwin. "Sevitzky Leads Musical Tribute to Hoosier Writer." *Musical America* 69:16 (15 December 1949), 21.
An account and short review of **W175a**. Bennett's contribution is not reviewed individually; Biltcliffe singles out "Mr. Carmichael and Mr. Sevitzky, whose works conveyed some of Riley's character."

TRIO, FLUTE/CELLO/PIANO [W117]

B514 R. S. "American Music Festival, Town Hall, Feb. 12." *Musical America*
71:4 (March 1951), 18.
A review of **W117a**; the writer states that the work "begins in an
impressionistic style and ends . . . without ever establishing an
individual form or texture. The introduction, marked Moderato
Misterioso in 12 Tone Style does not resemble any twelve tone music I
have ever heard before."

VICTORY AT SEA [W174]

B515 Adams, Val. "Naval History: 'Victory At Sea'." *NYT*, 26 October 1952,
II:11.
Includes commentary from both Richard Rodgers and Bennett; Adams
notes: "Airplanes fly in F Sharp Minor, according to the arranger, and
this was taken into account in orchestrating the score."

B516 DeVoto, Bernard. "The Easy Chair: Victory at Sea." *Harper's
Magazine* 208:1249 (June 1945), 8-11, 13.
The Rodgers-Bennett score is briefly discussed in this generous
essay; the writer comments that "Their contribution here was beyond
price but their availability was a stroke of great good fortune . . ."

[B457, Fennell]
Remarking upon Bennett's contributions as a theater orchestrator,
Fennell adds this footnote: "Richard Rodgers's music for 'Victory at
Sea,' the great World War II documentary, was another of Bennett's
remarkable enhancements of minimum materials supplied by a
colleague."

B517 Hamburger, Philip. "Television: Far-Off Places." *The New Yorker*
29:7 (4 April 1953), 77-79.
An enthusiastic review of the production. Hamburger's notion of
the Rodgers-Bennett alliance is typical of the contemporary press:
"Rodgers went to work and came up with a memorable and
tremendously moving marathon score, thirteen hours long [!], which
was brilliantly orchestrated by Robert Russell Bennett. . . . an
extraordinary achievement."

B518   Mr. Harper [pseud.]. "After Hours: V for Video." *Harper's Magazine* 205:1229 (October 1952), 99-100.
The score is mentioned only briefly: "technically speaking . . . the longest symphony ever written."

B519   "Man Behind the Tune." *Newsweek*, 20 July 1953, 86.
A profile of Bennett, along with details of his work on both the television and theatrical productions of *Victory at Sea*.

VU ("SEEN IN PARIS") [W138]

B520   J. D. B. "Amparo Navarro Gives Recital at Town Hall." *NYH-T*, 21 January 1942, 14.
Jerome D. Bohm's account of **W138d**.

B521   R. B. "Amparo Navarro's Debut." *NYW-T*, 21 January 1942, 17.
An account of **W138d**.

B522   Bennett, Grena. "Amparo Navarro Gives Recital." *NYJ-A*, 21 January 1942, 10.
An account of **W138d**.

B523   M. M. C. "Close of Club Biennial Marked by Outstanding Philadelphia Programs." *Musical Courier* 110:17 (11 May 1935), 10.
Jose Iturbi's **W138b** performance at the National Federation of Music Clubs' biennial meeting is briefly noted; reviewer is Margaret M. Coddington.

B524   M. L. H. "Iturbi's Versatile Gifts Shown on Rochester Podium and Piano Bench." *Musical Courier* 117:7 (April 1938), 28.
A brief account of **W138c**.

B525   "Jose Iturbi: November 30." *Musical Courier* 105:24 (10 December 1932), 10.
Review of **W138a**: "The études really are miniature tone paintings and cleverly descriptive of their titles . . . . The auditors applauded the excellent music with such insistence, that Mr. Bennett . . . had to rise and bow his thanks."

[B70, "Orchestrator . . ."]
Includes an account of **W138a**, with this to say about the *"Vu"* etudes

premiered by Iturbi a few weeks earlier: "They were so vivid and neatly wrought that listeners could fairly see the children . . . playing behind Notre-Dame . . . Montmartre's tinseled night life, the noisy Place d'Italie . . . the tomb of the Unknown Soldier which through Bennett's eyes seemed more futile than impressive."

B526 Simon, Robert A. "Musical Events." *The New Yorker* 8:44 (17 December 1932), 72.
Simon reviews **W138a**: "Iturbi . . . introduced a bracket of short works by . . . Bennett, to the obvious delight of an audience which almost rose up and shook hands with this sensitive, imaginative music. . . . an American musician doesn't have to be born in Europe to write with absolute mastery of his idiom."

WATER MUSIC [W120]

B527 Carter, Elliott. "Scores For Graham; Festival at Columbia." *Modern Music* 23:1 (Winter 1946), 53-55.
A concise review of **W120b**, noting that "Bennett's cutely clever *Water Music* [was] performed . . ."

B528 R. S. "Columbia University Offers First Festival of American Music." *Musical America* 65:9 (June 1945), 12.
Review of **W120b**: "Mr. Bennett's ingenious little variations on the 'Sailor's Hornpipe' were tossed off, according to the composer's account, one day when he 'stayed home from a ball game.' They sounded that way."

WOR ANNIVERSARY OVERTURE [W173]

B529 "Anniversary." *NYT*, 16 February 1947, II:11.
Publicizes the upcoming 25th anniversary program at WOR radio, on which the premiere [**W173a**] is to take place.

[B258, Evans]
This 19 February 1947 article, publicizing the *Dry Weather Legend* [**W16a**] premiere, also mentions the "Anniversary Overture" for WOR, completed "two days ago."

ZIMMER's AMERICAN GREETING [W78]

B530 Anderson, George. "Robert Russell Bennett: Music Man." *Pittsburgh Post-Gazette*, 27 May 1974, 16.

B531 Crown, Robert. "New Season Opened By Wind Symphony." *Pittsburgh Post-Gazette*, 27 May 1974, 17.

Appendix A:
Theater Orchestrations

This is a chronological list of Bennett-orchestrated musical plays, nearly all of them originally staged in New York or London. Bennett is reputed to have worked, alone or as a collaborator, on approximately 300 productions in the U. S. and Europe; as orchestrators were not always credited on theatre programs, this list is necessarily incomplete, especially for the 1920s.

This list is based primarily on program credits for individual shows. When additional information is known—not in the "official" credits—this is included. Bennett and his colleagues sometimes worked uncredited (and unpaid) on each others' shows, often simply to help a friend meet a deadline. The only certain way to establish absolutely the orchestrators working on a show in question would be to examine the manuscript scores.

Initials for other theater orchestrators listed below are as follows:

R B	(Roy Bargy)	EP	(Edward Powell)
B B	(Bill Brohn)	DR	(David Raksin)
CLC	(Charles L. Cooke)	T R	(Ted Royal)
MC	(Murray Cutter)	FS	(Frank Saddler)
W D	(William Daly)	CS	(Conrad Salinger)
MBDeP	(Maurice B.DePackh)	MS	(Menotti Salta)
AD	(Adolph Deutsch)	A S	(Arthur Schutt)
GG	(George Gershwin)	HS	(Hans Spialek)
JG	(Joe Glover)	BS	(Bill Stegmeyer)
CNG	(Charles N. Grant)	MS	(Max Steiner)
LH	(Luther Henderson)	FT	(Frank Tours)
EJ	(Elliot Jacoby)	JTy	(Jim Tyler)
SOJ	(Stephen O. Jones)	JTu	(Jonathan Tunick)

HK	(Hershey Kay)	NVanC	(Nathan Lang VanCleve)
FHK	(F. Henri Klickmann)	JVerP	(J. "Billy" VerPlanck)
PJL	(Phillip J. Lang)	DW	(Don Walker)
PL	(Paul Lannin)	PW	(Phil Walsh)
BN	(Bob Noelmeter)	RW	(Roy Webb)
JN	(Joseph Nussbaum)	CFW	(Carl F. Williams)
WP	(Walter Paul)	RW	(Russell Wording)

1918-1925

HITCHY-KOO OF 1920 (Kern; 19 October 1920; probably FS and Bennett)

DAFFY DILL (Kern; 22 August 1922)

WILDFLOWER (Youmans, Herbert Stothart; 7 February 1923)

GREENWICH VILLAGE FOLLIES (Louis M. Hirsch and Con Conrad;
   20 September 1923)

ZIEGFELD FOLLIES OF 1923 (20 October 1923)

STEPPING STONES (Kern; 6 November 1923)

MARY JANE McKANE (Youmans, Stothart; 25 December 1923)

SITTING PRETTY (Kern; 8 April 1924)

ZIEGFELD FOLLIES OF 1924 (24 June 1924)

GEORGE WHITE'S SCANDALS OF 1924 (Gershwin; 30 June 1924)

ROSE MARIE (Friml; 2 August 1924)

DEAR SIR (Kern; orig. title was *Vanity Fair*; 23 September 1924;
   O: Bennett and FS);

THE MAGNOLIA LADY (M. Harold Levey; 25 November 1924)

LADY BE GOOD (Gershwin; 1 December 1924; O: Bennett, CNG, PL, SOJ,MS,
   WD)

LOLLIPOP (Youmans; 24 January 1925)

TELL ME MORE (Gershwin; 13 April 1925)

SUNNY (Kern; 22 August 1925)

NO NO NANETTE (Youmans; 16 September 1925)

THE CITY CHAP (Kern; 26 October 1925; O: Bennett and FS, who scored a
   few early songs before his death in 1921)

SONG OF THE FLAME (Gershwin and Herbert Stothart; 30 December 1925)

1926-1930

QUEEN HIGH (Lewis E. Gensler; 8 September 1926)

CRISS CROSS (Kern; 12 October 1926; O: Bennett and MBdeP)

PRINCESS CHARMING (Albert Sirmay, Harry Ruby, Jack Waller, Russell
   Bennett; 21 October 1926; London)

LUCKY (Kern, 22 March 1927; O: Bennett, CNG, HS)

ONE DAM THING AFTER ANOTHER (Rodgers; 20 May 1927, London;
　　O: Bennett and others)

THE GIRL FROM COOK'S (1 November 1927, London; O: FT and Bennett)

A CONNECTICUT YANKEE (Rodgers; 3 November 1927; O: Bennett and
　　RW)

FUNNY FACE (Gershwin, 22 November 1927; O: Bennett and GG)

SHOW BOAT (Kern; 27 December 1927)

SHE'S MY BABY (Rodgers; 3 January 1928; O: HS, Bennett, RW, SOJ,CFW,
　　FHK, CNG, CM)

BLUE EYES (Kern; 27 April 1928; London)

THAT'S A GOOD GIRL (Phil Charig and Joseph Meyer; 5 June 1928,
　　London)

SWEET ADELINE (Kern; 3 August 1929; O: Bennett, MS, FHK, HS)

HEADS UP (Rodgers; 11 November 1929; O: Bennett and CM)

FIFTY MILLION FRENCHMEN (Porter; 27 November 1929; O: HS, FHK,
　　Bennett, MBDeP, CM)

GIRL CRAZY (Gershwin; 14 October 1930)

EVER GREEN (Rodgers; 3 December 1930; London)

1931-1935

AMERICA'S SWEETHEART (Rodgers; 10 February 1931)

THE BAND WAGON (Arthur Schwartz; 3 June 1931)

SINGIN' THE BLUES (Jimmy McHugh; 16 September 1931)

THE CAT AND THE FIDDLE (Kern; 15 October 1931)

THE LAUGH PARADE (Harry Warren; 2 November 1931; O: Bennett
　　and HS)

OF THEE I SING (Gershwin; 26 December 1931; O: Bennett, WD, GG)

FACE THE MUSIC (Berlin; 17 February 1932; O: Bennett, FT, MBDeP)

HOT-CHA! (Ray Henderson; 8 March 1932)

FLYING COLORS (Arthur Schwartz; 15 September 1932; O: Bennett, EP, AS,
　　HS)

MUSIC IN THE AIR (Kern; 8 November 1932)

TAKE A CHANCE (Nacio Herb Brown and Richard Whiting; 26 November
　　1932; O: Bennett, WD, SOJ, EP)

GAY DIVORCE (Porter; 29 November 1932; O: HS, Bennett)

WALK A LITTLE FASTER (Vernon Duke; 7 December 1932; O: Bennett and
　　CS)

PARDON MY ENGLISH (Gershwin; 20 January 1933; O: WD, Bennett, AD)

HOLD YOUR HORSES [music by Bennett] (25 September 1933)

ROBERTA (Kern; 18 November 1933)

ALL THE KING'S HORSES (Edward A. Horan; 20 January 1934; O: Bennett
and HS)
THREE SISTERS (Kern; 9 April 1934; London)
SAY WHEN (R. Henderson; 8 November 1934)
ANYTHING GOES (Porter; 21 November 1934; O: HS, Bennett, MS)
REVENGE WITH MUSIC (Arthur Schwartz; 28 November 1934)
FOOLS RUSH IN (Will Irwin, others; 25 December 1934; O: Bennett,
CS, HS)
GEORGE WHITE'S SCANDALS OF 1935 (R. Henderson; 25 December 1935)
PARADE (Jerome Moross, others; 20 May 1935; O: Moross, Bennett, DR, CS)
AT HOME ABROAD (Arthur Schwartz; 19 September 1935; O: Bennett, DR,
HS, DW, PW, RW)
JUBILEE (Porter; 12 October 1935)
JUMBO (Rodgers; 16 November 1935; O: AD, MC, JN, HS, Bennett, CS, RB)
MAY WINE (Romberg; 5 December 1935; O: Bennett and DW)

1936-1940

ZIEGFELD FOLLIES OF 1936 (Vernon Duke and Gershwin; 30 January 1936;
O: HS, CS, DW, Bennett)
RED, HOT AND BLUE (Porter; 29 October 1936)
THE SHOW IS ON (Vernon Duke, others; 25 December 1936)
GENTLEMAN UNAFRAID (Kern; 3 June 1938, St. Louis)
VERY WARM FOR MAY (Kern; 17 November 1939)
DUBARRY WAS A LADY (Porter; 6 December 1939; O: HS; add'l orchs. by
Bennett, TR, WP)
LOUISIANA PURCHASE (Berlin; 28 May 1940; O: Bennett; add'l orchs. by
NVanC)
WALK WITH MUSIC (Hoagy Charmichael; 4 June 1940)
BOYS AND GIRLS TOGETHER (Sammy Fain; 1 October 1940;
O: Bennett, HS, DW)
PANAMA HATTIE (Porter; 30 October 1940; O: Bennett, HS, DW)

1941-1945

COUNT ME IN (Ann Ronell; 8 October 1942; O: Bennett, HS, DW)
SOMETHING FOR THE BOYS (Porter; 7 January 1943; O: Bennett, HS, DW,
TR, WP)
OKLAHOMA! (Rodgers; 31 March 1943)
CARMEN JONES (Bennett adaptation of Bizet's score; 2 December 1943)
JACKPOT (Vernon Duke; 13 January 1944; O: Bennett, Duke, TR, HS)
MEXICAN HAYRIDE (Porter; 28 January 1944; O: Bennett and TR)

DREAM WITH MUSIC (Clay Warnick; 18 May 1944; O: Bennett, HS, TR, Warnick)

BLOOMER GIRL (Arlen; 5 October 1944)

RHAPSODY (Kreisler; 22 November 1944)

SEVEN LIVELY ARTS (Porter, Stravinsky, others; 7 December 1944; O: Bennett, TR, HS)

1946-1950

THREE TO MAKE READY (Morgan Lewis; 7 March 1946; O: Bennett, CLC, EJ, TR, HS, WP)

ANNIE GET YOUR GUN (Berlin; 16 May 1946)

AROUND THE WORLD IN EIGHTY DAYS (Porter; 31 May 1946; O: Bennett and TR)

HAPPY BIRTHDAY (one song by Rodgers; "incidental music by Robert Russell Bennett"; 31 October 1946)

IF THE SHOE FITS (David Raksin; 5 December 1946; O: Bennett, JG, WP, TR, HS)

IN GAY NEW ORLEANS (25 December 1946, Boston—did not open in New York)

SHOW BOAT (Kern; re-orchestrated for 27 December 1946 revival)

FINIAN'S RAINBOW (Burton Lane; 10 January 1947; O: Bennett and DW)

SWEETHEARTS (V. Herbert; re-orchestrated for 21 January 1947 revival)

LOUISIANA LADY (Alma Sanders; 2 June 1947; O: HS and Bennett)

ALLEGRO (Rodgers; 10 October 1947)

MAKE MINE MANHATTAN (Richard Lewine; 15 January 1948)

LOOK MA, I' M DANCING (Hugh Martin; 29 January 1948; O: Bennett and probably DW)

INSIDE U.S.A. (Arthur Schwartz; 30 April 1948)

SALLY (Kern; re-orchestrated for 6 May 1948 revival)

HEAVEN ON EARTH (Jay Gorney; 16 September 1948; O: Bennett and DW)

THAT'S THE TICKET (Harold Rome; 24 September 1948, Philadelphia; never opened in New York)

KISS ME KATE (Porter; 30 December 1948)

ALL FOR LOVE (22 January 1949; O: TR, DW, Bennett, HS)

SOUTH PACIFIC (Rodgers; 7 April 1949)

TEXAS LI' L DARLIN' (Robert Emmett Dolan; 25 November 1949)

DANCE ME A SONG (James Shelton, Herman Hupfeld, Albert Hague, Maurice Valency, Bud Gregg; 20 January 1950; O: Bennett and TR)

GREAT TO BE ALIVE (Abraham Ellstein; 23 March 1950; O: Bennett and DW)

OUT OF THIS WORLD (Porter; 21 December 1950)

1951-1955

THE KING AND I (Rodgers; 29 March 1951)
A TREE GROWS IN BROOKLYN (Arthur Schwartz; 19 April 1951;
     O: JG and Bennett)
MUSIC IN THE AIR (Kern; re-orchestrated for 8 October 1951 revival)
PARIS '90 (Kay Swift; 4 March 1952)
THREE WISHES FOR JAMIE (Ralph Blaine; 21 March 1952)
BY THE BEAUTIFUL SEA (Arthur Schwartz; 8 April 1954)
PIPE DREAM (Rodgers; 30 November 1955)

1956-1960

MY FAIR LADY (Loewe; 15 March 1956; O: Bennett and PL)
BELLS ARE RINGING (Jule Styne; 29 November 1956)
ZIEGFELD FOLLIES OF 1957 (various composers; 1 March 1957; O: Bennett,
     BS, JG, BN)
NEW GIRL IN TOWN (Bob Merrill; 14 May 1957; O: Bennett and PL)
CINDERELLA (Rodgers; 31 March 1957, television, then adapted for stage)
FLOWER DRUM SONG (Rodgers; 1 December 1958)
REDHEAD (Albert Hauge; 5 February 1959; O: PL and Bennett)
JUNO (Blitzstein; 9 March 1959; O: Bennett, Blitzstein, HK)
THE SOUND OF MUSIC (Rodgers; 16 November 1959)
CAMELOT (Loewe; 3 December 1960; O: Bennett and PL)

1961-1966

THE HAPPIEST GIRL IN THE WORLD (adapted from Offenbach; 3 April
     1961; O: Bennett and HK)
THIRTEEN DAUGHTERS (Eaton Magoon, Jr.; 2 March 1961; O: JG; addl.
     orchs. by Bennett)
WE TAKE THE TOWN (Harold Karr; 19 February, New Haven; 17 March
         1962, Philadelphia—did not open in New York; O: Bennett and HK)
JENNIE (Arthur Schwartz; 17 October 1963; O: PL and Bennett)
THE GIRL WHO CAME TO SUPPER (Noel Coward; 8 December 1963)
ON A CLEAR DAY YOU CAN SEE FOREVER (Burton Lane; 17 October
     1965)

1966-1971

SHOW BOAT (Kern; re-orchestrated for summer 1966 revival)
ANNIE GET YOUR GUN (Berlin; re-orchestrated for 1966 revival)
MATA HARI (Edward Thomas; 18 November 1967, Washington, D.C.—did
    not open in New York)
THE GRASS HARP (Claibe Richardson; 2 November 1971; O: JVerP, JT,
    Bennett)

1972-1975

RODGERS AND HART (1975; O: LH, JT, BB, Bennett)

Appendix B:
Film and Television
Scores/Orchestrations

This is a list of theatrical films with which Bennett was associated as Orchestrator (O); Bennett is credited as sole orchestrator unless otherwise noted. Additional credits, if known, are given; both Music Director (MD) and "Music by" (M) credits indicate work as composer and/or conductor. Consistent with most of his commercial work in the 1930s, film credits were at that time usually given to "Russell Bennett."

MEN OF THE SKY (First National/Warner Brothers, 1931); MD: Erno Rapee; Jerome Kern was contracted to write songs for the film, but they were later cut.

I DREAM TOO MUCH (RKO, 1935) (MD); Songs by Kern, with the score credited to Max Steiner. MD: Bennett.

SHOW BOAT (Universal, 1936); M: Kern. Bennett had done the orchestrations for the original (1927) stage version.

SWING TIME (RKO, 1936); M: Kern; MD: Nathaniel Shilkret.

ALI BABA GOES TO TOWN (20th Century-Fox, 1937); MD: Louis Silvers; O: Bennett, Gene Rose, Walter Scharfe, David Buttolph; Cyril Mockridge; Herbert Spencer; Charles Maxwell.

A DAMSEL IN DISTRESS (RKO, 1937); M: George Gershwin; MD: Victor Baravelle; O: Bennett; Additional Orchestrations: Ray Noble and George Bassman.

HIGH, WIDE AND HANDSOME (RKO, 1937); M: Kern; MD: Boris Morros.

HITTING A NEW HIGH (RKO, 1937); O: Bennett and George Bassman.

SHALL WE DANCE (RKO, 1937); M: Gershwin; MD: Nathaniel Shilkret; O: Bennett and Joseph A. Livingston.

THIN ICE (20th Century-Fox, 1937); MD: Louis Silvers; O: Bennett, Cyril Mockridge, Walter Scharfe, Herbert Spencer, Charles Maxwell, Paul VanLoan, Gene Rose.

ANNABEL TAKES A TOUR (RKO, 1938); MD: Bennett.

FUGITIVES FOR A NIGHT (RKO, 1938); M: Bennett.

JOY OF LIVING (RKO, 1938); M: Kern.

CAREER (RKO, 1939); M: Bennett.

FIFTH AVENUE GIRL (RKO, 1939); M: Bennett.

GUNGA DIN (RKO, 1939); M: Alfred Newman; O: Bennett.

THE HUNCHBACK OF NOTRE DAME (RKO, 1939); M: Alfred Newman; Bennett was one of several uncredited orchestrators.

THE STORY OF VERNON AND IRENE CASTLE (RKO, 1939); MD: Victor Baravelle; O: Bennett, Roy Webb.

PACIFIC LINER (RKO, 1939); MD: Bennett.

VIVACIOUS LADY (RKO, 1939); M: Roy Webb.

STANLEY AND LIVINGSTONE (RKO, 1939); M: Bennett.

REBECCA (Selznick/United Artists, 1940); M: Franz Waxman.

BRIGHAM YOUNG, FRONTIERSMAN (Twentieth-Century-Fox, 1940); M: Alfred Newman.

LADY IN THE DARK (Paramount, 1944); M: Kurt Weill; MD: Robert Emmett Dolan; O: Robert Russell Bennett.

CARNEGIE HALL (Federal/United Artists, 1947); MD: Robert Russell Bennett.

HELEN KELLER IN HER STORY (produced by Nancy Hamilton, 1955; the title was previously *The Unconquered*); M: Robert Russell Bennett. A study starring Helen Keller, it received a 1955 Academy Award for Best Documentary—Feature.

OKLAHOMA (Rodgers & Hammerstein Pictures/Magna, 1955); M: Richard Rodgers. O: Bennett, who had orchestrated the 1949 Broadway production. MD: Jay Blackton (who conducted the original production); musical "adaptations" by Adolph Deutsch. Bennett was awarded an Academy of Motion Picture Arts and Sciences "Oscar" for Best Scoring of a Musical Picture.

SOUTH PACIFIC (Magna, 1958); M: Rodgers; MD: Alfred Newman. Though Bennett's name appears with the other credited orchestrators, he did not work on the film. Because his original Broadway orchestrations played an important part in the shaping of Rodgers's material, Newman insisted that Bennett be given screen credit.

VICTORY AT SEA (NBC/United Artists, 1954); Bennett again reworked the material he had developed from Rodgers's sketches for the 1952-3 television series, and conducted additional recording sessions.

NBC TELEVISION "PROJECT 20" PRODUCTIONS

Bennett began composing, arranging, and conducting for network television in the mid-1940s. His association with NBC's "Project 20" series of films produced for television included those programs listed below. Bennett conducted recording sessions for all of these, composed original music, and, for a few productions, arranged others' music. Bennett was involved with a great many other television broadcasts as arranger, music director, etc; this list is limited solely to the NBC "Project 20" productions. The date of the first network airing is given.

VICTORY AT SEA (26 half-hour episodes, aired October 1952-April 1953); "Music by Richard Rodgers"; *See:* **W174**.

Appendix C:
Alphabetical Works List

mbers following each title, e.g. **W1**, refer to the **Works and Performances**
tion of this volume.

raham Lincoln: A Likeness In Symphony Form [**W1**]
lagio Eroico (To The Memory Of A Soldier) [**W2**]
Adventure In High Fidelity [**W3**]
lemande [**W91**]
ong The Navajo Trail (Double Concerto For Bass Clarinet And Temple
  Blocks) [**W149**]
tique Suite For Clarinet And Orchestra [**W4**]
abesque [**W92**]
med Forces Suite [**W5**]
Sundown: Romance For Violin And Piano [**W93**]
utobiography [**W51**]
ux Quatre Coins [**W79**]

Belasco Sonata [**W121**]
tty Wave [**W150**]

nzonetta For Strings [**W151**]
rol Cantatas I-II-III-IV [**W80**]
lebration Festive [**W122**]
arleston Rhapsody [**W6**]
ester [**W81**]
ristmas Overture [**W52**]
arinet Quartet [**W94**]
assic Serenade For Strings [**W7**]
lumbine [**W38**]

NIGHTMARE IN RED (27 December 1955)
THE TWISTED CROSS (14 March 1956)
THE GREAT WAR (16 October 1956)
THE JAZZ AGE (6 December 1956)
CALL TO FREEDOM (7 January 1957)
THE INNOCENT YEARS (21 November 1957)
MEET MR. LINCOLN (11 February 1959)
LIFE IN THE THIRTIES (16 October 1959)
MARK TWAIN'S AMERICA (22 April 1960)
VICTORY AT SEA (29 December 1960; 1-1/2 hour condensation o
THE COMING OF CHRIST (21 December 1960)
THE STORY OF WILL RODGERS (28 March 1961)
THE REAL WEST (29 March 1961)
MUSIC OF THE THIRTIES (5 November 1961)
COPS AND ROBBERS (18 March 1962)
HE IS RISEN (15 April 1962); Bennett received an "Emmy" awar
    "outstanding achievement in composing original music for
THE TALL AMERICAN . . . GARY COOPER (26 March 1963)
THAT WAR IN KOREA (20 November 1963)
THE RED, WHITE AND BLUE (9 June 1964)
THE ISLAND CALLED ELLIS (13 January 1967)
THE END OF THE TRAIL (16 March 1967)
THE LAW AND THE PROPHETS (23 April 1967)
DOWN TO THE SEA IN SHIPS (13 December 1968)
MEET GEORGE WASHINGTON (24 April 1969)
THE FABULOUS COUNTRY (20 October 1972)
STRANGE AND TERRIBLE TIMES (27 April 1973)

A Commemoration Symphony: Stephen Collins Foster [W8]
Concerto For Harmonica And Orchestra [W9]
Concerto For Harp, Violoncello, And Orchestra [W10]
Concerto For Viola, Harp, And Orchestra [W11]
Concerto For Violin In A Major (In The Popular Style) [W12]
Concerto For Violin, Piano And Orchestra [W13]
Concerto Grosso For Dance Band And Orchestra (Sketches From An
    American Theatre) [W14]
Concerto Grosso For Wind Quintet And Wind Orchestra [W53]
Concert Variations On A Crooner's Theme For Violin And Orchestra [W18]
Cowboy Overture [W152]
Crazy Cantata #1 [W82]
Crazy Cantata #2 ("I Took A Spanish Lesson") [W83]
Crystal [W39]

Dance [W95]
Dance Scherzo [W96]
Dartmouth Overture [W54]
Douglas MacArthur (March) [W55]
Down To The Sea In Ships [W56]
A Dry Weather Legend [W16]

An Early American Ballade On Melodies Of Stephen Foster [W17]
The Easter Story [W84]
Echoes Of Palermo [W123]
Eight Etudes For Symphony Orchestra [W18]
The Enchanted Kiss [W40]
Endimion [W41]
Epithalamium [W85?]

The Fabulous Country [W56]
Fanfare For The American Wind Symphony [W57]
The Firebrand [W46]
Five Dances For The Camp Fire Girls [W153]
Five Improvisations On Exotic Scales [W97]
Five Tune Cartoons [W98]
A Fleeting Fancy [W124]
A Flute At Dusk [W99]
Fountain Lake Fanfare (March) [W58]
Four Dances For Piano Trio [W100]
"The Four Freedoms": A Symphony After Four Paintings By Norman
    Rockwell [W19]

Four Nocturnes [W125]
Four Preludes For Band [W59]
Four Songs (Teasdale) [W140]
The Fun And Faith Of William Billings, American [W86]

General Douglas MacArthur (March, Band) [W60]
Give Me Liberty [W154]
The Grey Flute Song (Based On A Hopi Indian Song) [W155]

Hamlet [W47]
Happy Birthday [W48]
Hexapoda [W101]
Hold Your Horses [W42]
Hollywood (Introduction And Scherzo) [W20]
An Hour Of Delusion [W43]

Jazz? [W61]
June Twilight [W126]

Kansas City Album (Seven Songs For Orchestra) [W21]
Kentucky (From Life) [W62]
Kisselberry Pie [W141]
Kreutzer Duo [W156]

Macbeth [W49]
Mademoiselle (Ballet For Band) [W63]
March For America [W22]
March For General MacArthur [W23]
The March For Might [W64]
March For Two Pianos And Orchestra [W24]
Maria Malibran [W44]
Melody [W127]
Mill Potatoes [W157]
Music Box Opera #1 (Clementine) [W158]
Music Box Opera #2 (The Man On The Flying Trapeeze) [W159]
Music Box Opera #3 (The Band Played On) [W160]
Music Box Opera #4 (Kefoozelum, Methuselum) [W161]
Music Box Opera #5 (My Old Kentucky Home) [W162]
My Garden [W142]
My Star [W143]

Nietschze Variations [W187]
Nocturne [W102]
Nocturne And Appassionata, For Piano And Orchestra [W25]
Nocturne In A Flat [W128]

The Oaksmere Spirit [W129]
Ohio River Suite [W65]
Orchestral Fragments From The American Opera "Maria Malibran" [W26]
Overture To An Imaginary Drama [W27]
Overture To The Mississippi [W28]
Overture To Ty, Tris, And Willie [W66]

Paysage (Landscape) [W29]
Piano Concerto In B Minor [W30]
Piano Trio In F (Op. 1) [W103]
"Pickle" Overture [W67]
Prayer For Fritz Kreisler [W163]
Princess Charming [W45]

Quintette ("Psychiatry") [W104]

Railroad Cantata [W164]
Rhythm Serenade [W105]
Romance [W144]
Romeo And Juliet [W50]
Rondo Capriccioso [W106]
Rose Variations [W68]

Second Sonatina [W134]
Seven Fox Trots In Concert Form [W130]
Seven Love Songs [W145]
Seven Postcards To Old Friends [W107]
Sights And Sounds (An Orchestral Entertainment) [W31]
Six Paragraphs On Sodom By The Sea [W165]
Six Souvenirs [W108]
Six Variations In Fox-Trot Time On A Theme By Jerome Kern [W32]
A Smattering Of Ignorance [W166]
Soap Box Derby March [W69]
Sonata For Violin And Piano [W109]
Sonata In G For Organ [W131]
Sonata (Ragtime) [W132]
[First] Sonatina [W133]

Sonatine Pour Sopran Et Harpe [W146]
A Song Sonata [W110]
Spirit Of The Dance [W135]
Spring Spirits [W136]
String Quartet [W111]
A Study In Orchestration [W167]
Sue Ann [W147]
Suite [W112]
Suite For Flute And B Flat Clarinet [W114]
Suite Of Old American Dances (Orchestra [W34] And Band [W70] Versions)
Symphonic Songs For Band [W71]
Symphony [First] [W34]
Symphony [Sixth, 1946] [W35]
Symphony [Seventh, 1963] [W36]
Symphony In D For The Dodgers [W37]
Symphony On College Tunes [Fourth] [W168]

Tema Sporca Con Variazoni [W114]
Theme And Variations [W115]—See Concert Variations...[W15]
Theme And Variations In The Form Of A Ballade About A Lorelei [W88]
Theme And Variations ("Father, Dear Father") [W169]
Theme And Variations ("My Lost Youth") [W170]
Three Chaucer Poems [W148]
Three Humoresques [W72]
A TNT Cocktail [W73]
Tone Poems For Band (For The Lagoon Of Nations) [W74]
Toy Symphony [W116]
Track Meet [W75]
Travel Sketches [W137]
A Tribute To James Whitcomb Riley [W175]
Trio [Flute-Cello-Piano] [W117]
Trio For Harp, Cello And Flute [W118]
Twain And The River [W76]

United Nations All Faith Prayer For Peace [W89]

A Valentine [W119]
Verses 1, 2, 3 [W90?]
Victory At Sea [W174]
Vocal Variations On "The Young Oysterman" [W171]
Vu ("Seen In Paris"): 20 Etudes In Miniature, From The 20 Arrondissements
    (Precincts) Of Paris [W138

Water Music [W120]
The Wedding Sextet [W172]
West Virginia Epic [W77]
Wildwood ("Scherzo For Piano") [W139]
WOR Anniversary Overture [W173]

Zimmer's American Greeting [W78]

Appendix D:
Chronological Works List

Individual works are listed below under year of completion. Numbers following each title, e.g. **W126**, refer to the **Works and Performances** section in this volume.

1911-19   Nocturne in A Flat (1911), **W128**
Melody (c. 1911-1915), **W127**
June Twilight (1912 or 1913), **W126**
At Sundown (1913), **W93**
Echoes of Palermo (1913), **W123**
A Fleeting Fancy (c. 1914), **W124**
Spirit of the Dance (1914), **W135**
Spring Spirits (c. 1914-1915), **W136**
Wildwood (c. 1914-1915), **W139**
Celebration Festive (c. 1915), **W122**
Piano Trio in F (1915), **W103**
My Garden (c. 1916), **W142**
Columbine (1916), **W38**
Rondo Capriccioso (1916), **W106**
Travel Sketches (1916), **W137**
My Star (c. 1917), **W143**
Romance (1917), **W1434**
A Belasco Sonata (1917), **W121**
The Oaksmere Spirit (c. 1917-1919), **W129**

1921   Macbeth (incidental music), **W49**

| 1922 | Hamlet (incidental music), **W47** |
| | Romeo and Juliet (incidental music), **W50** |

| 1924 | The Firebrand (incidental music), **W46** |

1926	Symphony (#1), **W35**
	Charleston Rhapsody, **W6**
	Princess Charming, **W45**

1927	Sonata (violin/piano), **W109**
	Endimion, **W41**
	Three Chaucer Poems, **W148**

1928	Four Songs (Teasdale), **W140**
	Toy Symphony, **W116**
	Seven Fox-Trots in Concert Form, **W130**
	Paysage, **W29**
	Dance (flute/piano), **W95**
	Nocturne (flute/piano), **W102**
	An Hour of Delusion, **W43**
	Aux Quatre Coins, **W79**

1929	Sights and Sounds, **W31**
	Nietschze Variations, **W87**
	Theme and Variations . . . Ballade About a Lorelei, **W88**
	Abraham Lincoln: A Likeness in Symphonic Form, **W1**
	Sonata in G for Organ, **W131**
	"Vu" ("Seen in Paris"): 20 Etudes in miniature, **W138**
	Seven Love Songs, **W145**

| 1930 | March for Two Pianos and Orchestra, **W24** |
| | Four Songs (Teasdale), **W140** |

1932	Adagio Eroico (c. 1932), **W2**
	Concerto Grosso for Dance Band and Orchestra, **W14**
	An Early American Ballade . . . Stephen Foster, **W17**

| 1933 | Six Variations . . . on a Theme by Jerome Kern, **W32** |
| | Hold Your Horses, **W42** |

| 1934 | Orchestral Fragments from "Maria Malibran", **W26** |
| | Maria Malibran, **W44** |

1936   Hollywood, **W20**

1937   Water Music, **W120**
                      Dance Scherzo (1937 or 1938), **W96**

1938   Eight Etudes for Symphony Orchestra, **W18**

1939   Tone Poems for Band, **W74**
                      Fountain Lake Fanfare, **W58**
                      A TNT Cocktail, **W73**

1940   The Grey Flute Song, **W155**
                      Hexapoda, **W101**
                      A Smattering of Ignorance, **W166**
                      Music Box Opera #1, **W158**

1941   Music Box Opera #2, **W159**
                      Music Box Opera #3, **W160**
                      Music Box Opera #4, **W161**
                      Music Box Opera #5, **W162**
                      Mill Potatoes, **W157**
                      Clarinet Quartet, **W94**
                      Antique Suite for Clarinet and Orchestra, **W4**
                      Nocturne and Appassionata, **W25**
                      Classic Serenade for Strings, **W7**
                      Concerto for Violin in A Major, **W12**
                      [First] Sonatina (1941?), **W133**
                      Kreutzer Duo, **W156**
                      Prayer for Fritz Kreisler, **W163**
                      Railroad Cantata, **W164**
                      Six Paragraphs on Sodom by the Sea, **W165**
                      A Study in Orchestration, **W167**
                      Symphony in D for the Dodgers, **W37**
                      Symphony on College Tunes, **W168**
                      Theme and Variations, "Father Dear Father", **W169**
                      Theme and Variations, "My Lost Youth", **W170**
                      A Valentine, **W119**
                      Concerto for Viola, Harp and Orchestra, **W11**
                      The Wedding Sextet (1941 or 1942), **W172**

1942   Canzonetta for Strings (c. 1942), **W151**
                      Five Dances for the Camp Fire Girls, **W153**

Give Me Liberty, **W154**
March for America, **W22**
March for General MacArthur, **W23**
Sue Ann, **W147**

1943	The Four Freedoms (Symphony), **W19**

1944   Betty Wave, **W150**
Second Sonatina, **W134**
The Enchanted Kiss (1944 or 1945), **W40**

1945   Along the Navajo Trail, **W149**
Suite (violin/piano), **W112**
Chester, **W81**
Cowboy Overture, **W152**
Crazy Cantata #1, **W82**
Vocal Variations on "The Young Oysterman", **W171**

1946   Tema Sporca con Variazoni, **W114**
Symphony (#6), **W35**
Happy Birthday (incidental music), **W48**
A Dry Weather Legend, **W16**
Overture to an Imaginary Drama, **W27**

1947   Crazy Cantata #2 (c. 1947), **W83**
A Song Sonata, **W110**
WOR Anniversary Overture, **W173**
Five Improvisations on Exotic Scales, **W97**
Sonatine pour Sopran et Harpe, **W146**
Piano Concerto in B minor, **W30**

1948   Allemande, **W91**
Six Souvenirs, **W108**

1949   Suite of Old American Dances (band), **W70**
Concert Variations on a Crooner's Theme, **W18**
Five Tune Cartoons, **W98**
A Tribute to James Whitcomb Riley, **W175**

1950   Kansas City Album, **W21**
Overture to the Mississippi, **W28**
Suite of Old American Dances (orchestra), **W33**

1950 (continued)   Trio (flute/cello/piano) (1950 or 1951), **W117**

1952   Mademoiselle (Ballet for Band), **W63**
A Flute at Dusk, **W99**
Victory at Sea (television score, 1952-1953), **W174**

1953   United Nations All Faith Prayer for Peace, **W89**
Four Dances for Piano Trio (1953 or 1954), **W100**

1954   An Adventure in High Fidelity, **W3**

1955   The March for Might, **W64**
Rose Variations (trumpet/cornet and band), **W68**

1956   Kisselberry Pie, **W141**
String Quartet, **W111**

1957   Symphonic Songs for Band, **W71**

1958   Concerto Grosso,Wind Quintet and Wind Orchestra, **W53**
Concerto for Violin, Piano and Orchestra (1958 or
1959), **W13**

1959   A Commemoration Symphony: Stephen Collins
Foster, **W8**
Ohio River Suite, **W65**
Four Nocturnes (accordion), **W125**

1960   Concerto for Harp, Cello and Orchestra (1959 or 1960 rev.
of the Concerto for Harp, Viola and Orchestra of 1941),
W10
Trio for Harp, Cello and Flute (c. 1960), **W118**
Armed Forces Suite, **W5**
Overture to Ty, Tris and Willie, **W66**
West Virginia Epic, **W77**
Track Meet (1960 or 1961), **W75**

1961   Kentucky (1961?), **W62**
Three Humoresques, **W72**

1962   Symphony (#7), **W36**
Quintette ("Psychiatry") (1962 or 1963), **W10**

1964	General Douglas MacArthur (March), **W60**

1966   Soap Box Derby March, **W69**
Seven Postcards to Old Friends, **W107**

1968   Down to the Sea in Ships, **W55**
Rhythm Serenade (solo percussion), **W105**
Twain and the River, **W76**

1969   Jazz?, **W61**

1971   Concerto for Harmonica and Orchestra (1971 or
1972), **W9**

1972   Crystal (opera), **W39**

1973   Suite for Flute and B flat Clarinet, **W113**
Sonata (Ragtime) (early 1970s?), **W132**
Dartmouth Overture, **W54**

1974   Four Preludes for Band, **W59**
Zimmer's American Greeting, **W78**

1975   The Fabulous Country, **W56**
The Fun and Faith of William Billings, American, **W86**

1977   Carol Cantatas I-IV, **W80**
Twain and the River, **W76**
Autobiography, **W51**

1978   Arabesque, **W92**
The Easter Story, **W84**

1980   Christmas Overture, **W52**

1981   Fanfare, **W57**

Index

About the Author

GEORGE J. FERENCZ is Associate Professor of Music at Idaho State University.

**Recent Titles in
Bio-Bibliographies in Music**

William Walton: A Bio-Bibliography
Carolyn J. Smith

Albert Roussel: A Bio-Bibliography
Robert Follett

Anthony Milner: A Bio-Bibliography
James Siddons

Edward Burlingame Hill: A Bio-Bibliography
Linda L. Tyler

Alexander Tcherepnin: A Bio-Bibliography
Enrique Alberto Arias

Ernst Krenek: A Bio-Bibliography
Garrett H. Bowles, compiler

Ned Rorem: A Bio-Bibliography
Arlys L. McDonald

Richard Rodney Bennett: A Bio-Bibliography
Stewart R. Craggs, compiler

Radie Britain: A Bio-Bibliography
Walter B. Bailey and Nancy Gisbrecht Bailey

Frank Martin: A Bio-Bibliography
Charles W. King, compiler

Peggy Glanville-Hicks: A Bio-Bibliography
Deborah Hayes

Francis Poulenc: A Bio-Bibliography
George R. Keck, compiler